The Complete
$\mathcal{J}$NCENSE
Book

The Complete
INCENSE
Book

Susanne Fischer-Rizzi

Illustrations by
Peter Ebenhoch

Sterling Publishing Co., Inc.
New York

The advice and recipes contained in this book have been checked carefully and tested by the author. Nevertheless, the author and publisher cannot be held responsible for any adverse reactions that develop as a result of following the instructions in this book. All recipes contained herein are protected by copyright by the author and may not be used for commercial purposes.

Library of Congress Cataloging-in-Publication Data

Fischer-Rizzi, Susanne.
    [Botschaft an den Himmel.   English]
    The complete incense handbook   /   Susanne Fischer-Rizzi.
       p.   cm.
    Includes index.
    ISBN 0-8069-9987-X
    1. Incense.   I. Title.
  TP983.F4913   1998
  668′.542—dc21   98-2573
                                                  CIP

10 9 8 7 6 5 4 3 2 1

Published by Sterling Publishing Company, Inc.
387 Park Avenue South, New York, N.Y. 10016
Originally published in Germany by Irisiana
under the title *Botschaft an den Himmel:*
Anwendung, Wirkung und Geschichten
von deftendem Räucherwerk
© 1996 by Heinrich Hugendubel Verlag, Munich
English translation © 1998 by Sterling Publishing Co., Inc.
Distributed in Canada by Sterling Publishing
c/o Canadian Manda Group, One Atlantic Avenue, Suite 105
Toronto, Ontario, Canada M6K 3E7
Distributed in Great Britain and Europe by Cassell PLC
Wellington House, 125 Strand, London WC2R 0BB, England
Distributed in Australia by Capricorn Link (Australia) Pty Ltd.
P.O. Box 6651, Baulkham Hills, Business Centre, NSW 2153, Australia
Manufactured in the United States of America
All rights reserved

Sterling ISBN 0-8069-9987-X

CONTENTS

FOREWORD

From the Stone Age to the Modern Age

What is essential is never lost; it lies dormant, only to reappear when the time is right, often presented as something "brand new." This is what has occurred with the practice of incense burning. For thousands of years, it was a very important part of human life. At times, people spent fortunes for incense and for anything that had to do with incense burning. People established trade routes with incense in mind, and during almost all of history, burning incense was as ordinary an activity as brushing teeth. Not until this century did people ignore incense burning. However, other cultures, particularly those in Asia, continued to use incense burning and the ceremonies connected with it. For millions of people, burning incense is an essential part of everyday life.

We can trace the origin of burning incense—that is, using aromatic substances in burning ceremonies—to the earliest days of human history, probably before or during the Stone Age. But what does all this have to do with the practice today?

I learned about the use and practice of burning incense many years ago from Native Americans. For the medicine men and women who educated me about the use of medicinal plants, burning incense is part of a very attentive way of approaching and experiencing the heavens and the earth. I also noticed this philosophy throughout my travels in the East. For a long time now, incense burning has been very helpful to me. It never occurred to me that a time would come a time when so many people would be interested in this subject.

I finally realized that the time was right for this ancient wisdom, with its power and healing ability, to surface again. As it turned out, I was at a management seminar teaching the participants how to use aromatherapy, massage, meditation, and breathing exercises to reduce stress. By coincidence, part of my luggage also contained the utensils I use for incense burning. One of the attendees asked me what these utensils were. I gave a few details, and she talked me into burning

some incense for the whole group. I was skeptical. Why on earth would I do that during a management seminar? But I didn't want to be a spoilsport and so I unpacked some of my very best incense. At the end of the ceremony, I could see for myself why this was important during a management seminar. The faces of the participants seemed relaxed, and the atmosphere in the rather uncomfortable and impersonal seminar room was one of openness and warmth. It was almost meditative.

That was it! Here was something people under severe performance pressure could use to relax quickly! Over the course of the weekend, we repeated this little ceremony a few more times, and at the end of the seminar I gave what was left of my frankincense to the participants who wanted it. From then on, I've always made sure to have all the utensils for incense burning with me whenever I participate in conferences, lectures, and seminars. I came away from that management seminar with a profound sense that in our hectic and stressful life we needed the age-old wisdom to support us and to encourage us to slow down and catch our breath.

This also awakened my interest in the history of incense burning. Unfortunately, little of the old knowledge has survived. What did people in the past know? These questions led me on a journey through time. I began by searching for the origins of incense burning, the different practices in different cultures. I searched for references in libraries and prepared questions to ask the healers and medicine women and men. I began to collect plants that I could use for incense burning, and I reconstructed old recipes.

I hope that this book contributes to the reintroduction of the valuable wisdom of burning incense. It all started during the Stone Age, only to reappear at this moment in time. . . .

Susanne Fischer-Rizzi
Sulzberg, Germany, 1996

INTRODUCTION

Incense Burning

What Is It?

Incense burning is the process of letting aromatic substances, particularly those from the plant world, burn slowly over a heat source, such as a charcoal cone or a candle. The resulting smoke drifts in the air, carrying the scent throughout the room. The smoke contains psychoactive, physical, and emotionally effective substances. Every ancient culture practiced incense burning, producing rich and unique knowledge.

Incense burning stimulates the senses in many different ways: the nose perceives the scent, and the eyes follow the delicate smoke as it moves in the air, creating endlessly different shapes

Aquillaria wood

and spirals. We experience the warmth of the fire when we light the candle and observe how the black color of the charcoal slowly begins to glow. Sand, pottery containers, and various other vessels connected with incense burning appeal to our tactile senses.

Incense burning provides us with a direct and immediate experience. It is the foundation of today's aromatherapy as well as that of the perfume industry. The word "perfume" comes from the Latin word *per fumum*, which means "through smoke." For our ancestors in every culture, life without incense burning was inconceivable. Its sacred purpose was to convey messages to the heavens, to carry prayers to their destination. And to this day, it deepens and supports prayer and meditation in all major religions.

Our ancestors also used incense burning to disinfect living spaces, sick beds, and animal stalls. They believed it healed the sick. They used it to make clothing and other objects smell good, to influence dreaming, to create visions, to improve the acoustics in churches, and for many other purposes. Today, only a few people have detailed information about incense burning. For some, the subject evokes unpleasant memories from their childhood. For instance, frankincense reminds many of us of a time when our parents forced us to go to church.

Only a few people are aware of

the fact that different substances used for incense burning create different effects. Unfortunately, the ancient art of incense burning was almost lost.

In Our Time

In times past, burning incense was a way of sending sacred messages to the heavens. Pleasant smoke drifted in a column towards the sky. In the process, the mortals present were pleasantly entertained and began to feel better. If we continue this story into the present, and we ask ourselves what kind of fragrances we send towards the sky, we would have to admit that our noses, as well as those of the gods, are sorely tried and stressed. Chimneys, cars, and industrial plants are throwing rather unpleasant scents into the air. In ancient times, people would have considered this a crime against the gods. And although we have little scientific proof, it is most certainly true that the presence of such industrial smoke does not make us feel better. More likely than not, we become sick from it.

Even indoors, we are exposed to tainted aromas, usually in the form of artificial fragrances. Instinctively, we keep searching for natural fragrances with which to surround ourselves. During the last 10 years, the interest in aromatherapy has been constantly growing. Today, essential oils, the liquid and volatile substances of plants, are enjoying great popularity. Our long neglected sense of smell, mistreated for so long with foul smells from industry, is awakening again. Science is dis-

covering how very important the sense of smell is in human life. And many people who have been dealing with essential oils

Rockrose

during the last couple of years are also becoming aware of the practice of incense burning. They are interested in discovering the fundamentals involved in aromatherapy.

The resurgence of interest in spiritual wisdom and renewed search for religious significance have also awakened an interest in incense burning. In ancient cultures, people used incense burning to support intellectual and emotional activities and experiences. Today, when the emphasis in Western culture is so heavily oriented toward the external, our desire is growing for things that can connect us to the inner spiritual values that reach beyond our harried daily living.

We are searching for a new connection to nature. Our short-term thinking, which is geared to the exploitation of nature, is going to destroy our living space. In ancient cultures, incense burning was a way of joining with the energy that surrounded us, in order to receive messages and understand connections. During incense burning, a plant reveals to us its power, its essence, and its wisdom. In the past, people understood this instinctively. If we pay careful attention when we burn incense, we can get in touch with nature, with the secrets of the plants, and with the mysteries of the energy of plants. In return, we will receive emotional enrichment. The original ritual purpose of incense burning was to unlock the ancient wisdom of the connection between man and plant.

The Muse of Fragrances

In our busy world, we are all yearning to make time for ourselves, to escape the hectic pace of everyday life, to let our souls "hang out," and to take time to contemplate and experience exquisite pleasures. All of us yearn for these pleasures in our performance-directed society. Many of us find it almost impossible to enjoy leisure time in today's relentless hustle and bustle. Maybe that's the reason we've rediscovered incense burning. Burning incense takes time. If we give it time, it will strengthen us.

Using an aroma vaporizer does not require us to interrupt our activities; all we need to do is add some essential oil to the water and we can go on doing what we were doing. Not so with incense burning. Here, we light a candle or cone, add the incense, fan it until the charcoal glows, remain seated, and then immerse ourselves in the immediate experience of fragrance and smoke. Before we know it, we've escaped the rush and are on a

A priestess of Bacchus burning incense on the altar of Jupiter

journey to the source of our inner strength. As we watch the incense burn and the smoke ascend, we recognize the experience as a symbol of how temporary material things are. At the same time, incense smoke gives a sense of timelessness. In the past, when people watched the smoke rise to the sky, they considered it a spiritual experience, a way of dissolving the boundaries of space and time. They saw incense burning as an inspiration for an inward journey and a discovery of one's own being. The Latin word *inspirare* also means "to breathe in" and points to the delicate way that fragrances influence and inspire us through the process of breathing. Burn-

ing incense gives a gift of time to our soul.

Sense of Smell and Incense Burning

From a developmental point of view, perceiving scents is the first and oldest of human senses. The so-called thinking brain, the cerebrum, developed from this fundamental olfactory center. Incense burning frees fragrant molecules embedded in plant tissue and releases them into space through smoke. When we breathe, these molecules come in contact with the mucous membrane at the base of the nose. And from the nose, this stimulation moves directly to the center of our brain, where fragrances begin to influence our emotions, the regulation of hormones, and the nervous system. Incense burning directly influences our perception. This explains the profound effect that fragrant smoke has on emotions, mood, and well-being and why it resonates so intensely in our psyche.

The When and Why of Incense Burning

From the many different ways available to burn incense, here are some of the most important.

Burning incense to cleanse the atmosphere

Burning incense has a very powerful effect on surroundings. It is as if the fragrant smoke creates its very own vibration, creating a new morphogenetic field in a room. I am sure that you are familiar with the phenomenon of negative energy in a room. Moods, thoughts, and actions influence the energy in a room; they seem to hang in the air. You enter a room and can almost immediately sense that the air is thick. The smell of fear, of arguments, of grief, and so forth, seems to linger in space, but so do the vibrations of these emotions. Nothing neutralizes and changes these vibrations better

than burning incense. People have practiced the ritual of incense burning throughout history to cleanse, neutralize, or positively change the atmosphere where many people gather together. That's why so many religious services include incense burning, particularly in temples in holy places and in churches.

We can clean the objects we use during healing ceremonies— for instance, healing crystals and icons—by suspending them in the smoke of burning incense. Sometimes burdensome and negative energies surround old pieces of jewelry or antiques. We can neutralize these energies through incense burning. The power of incense that cleanses the atmosphere can be effective in the following instances:

- Places in which there is a lot of argument or much grief
- Houses or apartments before you move in
- Places in schools where students take tests
- Every type of public space
- Sick rooms and rooms where people are dying or have died

This is how it's done:

To cleanse the atmosphere in a room or a space, keep the windows closed. Walk through the space or from room to room and fan the rising smoke in all directions. Then, leave the room and close the door. If this is done in the evening, leave the container used for burning the incense in the room and air out the space the next morning. Otherwise, leave the windows and doors closed and don't go into the space for at least three hours. Then, make sure that you air out the space.

Incense specially for cleansing the atmosphere indoors
Frankincense, sage, juniper, desert mugwort, pine

Names of recipes
Cleansing, Oraibi, Twelve Holy Nights, Patron Saints, Lawudo

Burning incense to calm and reduce anxiety, stress, and fear

Fragrances influence our emotional and mental moods. They can stimulate, calm, and harmonize. For the situations mentioned above, we use incense that has a direct and relaxing influence on the psyche. The incense burning may take place in the evening, possibly supported by relaxing background music and candlelight. Allow all your

tensions and troubles to dissipate along with the fragrant smoke. Of course, you may also burn incense just for the sheer pleasure of it.

Special incense for relaxation
Cinnamon, benzoin, sandalwood, golden copal, sandarac, storax, anise, costus, saffron, amber pine, galbanum, and propolis.

Names of recipes
Gulistan, Breath of the Soul, Blue Dragonfly on a Lotus Leaf, Afternoon of a Fawn, Harmony, Lugal Banda, Busamé, Kyphi, Greek Temple Incense, Island of the Blessed

Burning incense for revitalization, stimulation, and energy renewal

Some types of incense have stimulating as well as revitalizing effects. These may be helpful in strengthening our potential and energy when we feel weak, discouraged, or exhausted. The herbs used by Native Americans work particularly well here, as do those of the element fire.

While the incense is burning, and as the smoke ascends, we might want to envision our inner strength increasing.

Strengthening incense
Desert mugwort, pine, Himalayan rhododendron, cedar, juniper, ginger lily, galangal, dragon's blood, calmus, clove, camphor, Scotch pine

Names of recipes
Lawudo, Kailash, Ayla, Maneton, Energy, Oraibi, Gilgamesh, Frankincense of the Gods, Avalon, Ishtar, Shiva

Burning incense to help insomnia

Some plants provide substances that have balancing and calming effects and that might be helpful in dealing with insomnia. These substances are relaxing in an emotional as well as a physical sense. Burn the incense in the evening, before retiring, and try to get a sense of how the smoke from the incense is relaxing your body and calming your mind.

Burning incense from plants for a good night's sleep
Sandalwood, amber pine, asafetida, cinnamon, saffron, spikenard, aloe, galbanum, dream herb, avar wood, marsh forest

Names of recipes
Kyphi, Busamé, Island of the Blessed, Midnight Leaves, Jaguar of the Night

Incense for dreams

For centuries, people have used incense to encourage dreaming and even to create dreams that came true. Today, burning incense can help support therapeutic dreamwork because it increases the ability to remember dreams. As scientific dream labs have recently discovered, fragrances and aromas have a strong effect on dream activity. More about this later.

Dream incense herbs
Dream herb, true sage, laurel, mastic, hops, mistletoe, mugwort, elemi, ledum, white copal, elderberry, and iron herb

Names of recipes
Dream Colibri, Phyta, Nature's Spirit, Blue Bird, Play of the Elves, Goddess of the Moon

Burning incense for prayer, meditation, and contemplation

From early in human history people have recognized that the specific fragrances released when incense burns have the power to strengthen spiritual energies. Incense burning can open us up to the subtle planes that lie beyond our everyday world. It connects the human spirit with the energy of the cosmos. Prayers often are more effective when accompanied by incense-burning ceremonies. Burning incense is a profound symbol for change, for the process of transformation. It is inspiring to contemplate the transformation of the earthly to the heavenly. Fragrant smoke creates an atmosphere of worship, dignity, and reflection that can support prayer or meditation. The ascending smoke is a symbol for the soul seeking a connection to the godly. Thus, religious activities are almost always connected with incense

Burning incense during a ritual

burning. When you burn incense at the beginning of a meditation, the fragrant smoke accompanies your prayers, inspiring contemplation. During the ceremony, imagine how your thoughts and prayers connect to the sacred energies of the divine.

Incense for prayer and meditation
Frankincense, balsam, mastic, sandarac, dammar, common myrrh, cedar elemi, camphor

Names of recipes
Guardian Angel, Kingdom of the Angels, Oraibi, Energy, Isis and Osiris, Kailash, Shangri-La, Morning Meditation, Rosa Mystica, Flight of the Soul, Greek Temple Incense, Fleeing from Ignorance, Incense of the Gods, First Snowflake in the Pine Forest

Burning incense to celebrate the season

The seasons of the year are the moods of nature. Consciously becoming aware of them and getting in tune with them greatly contributes to our well-being and, in that sense, enriches our lives. Celebrations and incense burning can bring us into harmony with the seasons of the year and strengthen our experiences and awareness. People have always celebrated the rhythm of the moon with rituals and incense burning. In the past, the rituals during the full moon and the new moon were the most famous. They made it possible to consciously become aware of the impulses of these important periods. Try to celebrate a seasonal feast, such as Christmas, Easter, or the solstice, by including the appropriate incense-burning ceremony.

Recipes for the seasons of the year
Twelve Holy Nights, Avalon, Duir, Druid, Lugal Banda, Rosa Mystica, Ishtar, Frankincense

Full Moon: Elemi, camphor, mastic, myrtle, costus, common myrrh

New Moon: Ledum, agar wood, spikenard, myrrh, black copal

Burning incense at a campfire

Burning incense for love

As scientific research has shown, the fragrances of some of the classic incense-burning substances are very similar to human pheromones. These fragrances send messages that have a strong influence on human sexuality. Throughout history, people have known that burning incense stimulates their capacity for love and eroticism. Allow yourself to be seduced by a fragrant incense and enjoy the pleasure of incense burning with your partner.

Sensually stimulating incense
Sandalwood, vetiver, benzoin, agar wood, ledum, patchouli, rose

Names of recipes
King David's Temptation, Lugal Banda, Secret Garden, Shakti, Afternoon of a Fawn

Burning incense for creativity

Many artists have used fragrances for inspirations. They found that the fragrant smoke of incense burning supported their imagination and helped their creativity. Let the fragrances inspire you when you are involved in music, painting, writing, or any creative work. Start your day in the studio with incense burning. Use incense burning to heighten your enjoyment of a concert.

Incense that stimulates creativity
Cinnamon blossoms, frankincense, benzoin, balsam of tolu, tonka bean, Japanese anise, ledum, dream herb, hops

Names of recipes
Breath of the Soul, Blue Dragonfly on a Lotus Leave, Gulistan, Egypitium Pleasure of the Heart, Shakti

Burning incense for healing

Burning incense for therapeutic purposes originated in ancient times. Through the Middle Ages, people considered incense burning part of taking care of their bodies and their homes. As recently as the 1970s, a compilation of common remedies included several incense substances in powdered form used primarily for asthmatic conditions. Because the process of burning frees fragrant substances and has a pharmacological effect, incense burning was often used to treat respiratory illnesses, muscle tension, rheumatism, insomnia, and pain. People have also used it during childbirth and as a disinfectant. Today, incense burning is very helpful when used in conjunction with other thera-

Burning incense indoors

pies, such as Reiki, massage, color therapy, and psychotherapy.

Incense and rituals

Since the beginning of time, incense burning and rituals have belonged together. Rituals strengthen incense burning and journey, such as birth, initiation, marriage, and death. These rites give it a much greater dimension. A ritual is like a magnifying glass, concentrating and increasing energy. They serve religious as well as social purposes. Today, many people no longer feel the necessity for rituals. But, most of us do practice them every day of our lives. Unfortunately, consumerism and advertising have exploited our deep and buried need for rituals. However, rituals are a timeless way of supporting our inner development and of experiencing it consciously. They are powerful forces, enabling us to master our lives and overcome crises. They help us gain wisdom and expand emotionally. Incense can support our mental experiences and increase our spiritual growth. We should find our way back to rituals again and experience rituals alone or in groups. Incense can be a great help in this endeavor.

Most importantly, we need rituals when we want to experience significant events in our life's of passage help us enter safely and consciously into new phases of our life. They support us as we peacefully let go of something old. They also allow us to turn to something new with a positive attitude. Rituals aid us in finding conscious closure to something old. In addition, rituals can accompany us during painful situations and during crises. They also serve as a connection to the energy of the earth, to angels, and to other supernatural beings. Using incense can be helpful when we pose questions to the I Ching, Tarot, and similar cards. In addition, very specific incense burning can enrich Native American rituals, such as the medicine wheel, vision search, and sweat lodge.

Be attentive when you burn incense as a ritual. Determine beforehand what purpose the incense is to serve and specifically how you want to achieve this.

A small altar, a beautiful cloth, candles, statues, and pictures can increase the effects. Bring total concentration to your actions and to what you want to achieve.

Following are a few examples of how to make use of incense burning during simple rituals in everyday life.

Problem solving

Sit in front of an incense bowl and concentrate on what is creating the problem. Imagine that as the fragrant incense drifts upwards, it carries your problem into the sphere of the spirit. As you watch the smoke rising, feel the problem solving itself. The problem is connected to the solution above and will return to you in a neutralized form. Be open. During the next few days or during a dream, expect that the possibilities of a solution will find their way to you. The following types of incense are particularly helpful in this instance: frankincense, mastic, sandarac, desert mugwort, and white sage.

New Year's ritual

The old year is behind us. Sitting around the incense bowl, we are reliving the events of the past year. Some things we would love to let go of, such as characteristics that we don't want to hinder us in the new year. Write these down individually on small pieces of paper, roll them into paper balls, and place them on the glowing charcoal in the bowl. As the paper burns, imagine these negative characteristics dissolving in reality and that with the rising smoke they are changing into something positive.

Meditation on the planet Venus

For a certain number of evenings (three, nine, or 12), as soon as Venus appears, start burning incense. You may choose to sit in a meditation position in front of a small altar, or, if that is not possible, you may sit comfortably in a chair. Every night, burn a different incense, creating different emotions with distinct fragrances. Close your eyes and open yourself to the wisdom offered by each specific fragrance. Enrich and open your soul. End this ritual by expressing your gratitude. Think about the experience and make notes about what you have experienced.

Incense Burning and Its Practical Application

What You Need in Order to Burn Incense

You need the following items to burn incense:

- a container
- incense substances
- charcoal and charcoal tablets
- a candle for the charcoal dish
- a feather or a piece of stiff cardboard or paper for fanning
- matches or a cigarette lighter
- sand
- a pair of tweezers
- mortar and pestle

Incense-burning vessel

In the beginning, use a simple container or bowl for burning incense. Such containers are commonly available where you buy incense substances. The dish or vessel is usually stoneware, often supported by thick legs. These legs prevent the heat from damaging the surface of the table. The traditional vessel for incense burning has three legs, symbolizing the number three and the trinity of body, mind, and soul. The diameter of the container should be 4 in. (10 cm) or larger. For groups, or when burning incense during a seminar, a larger bowl works better than a smaller one. I have a reproduction of a three-legged Minoan incense-burning bowl with a 14 in. (35 cm) diameter. During seminars, many people are able to gather around this bowl to enjoy the in-

cense burning together.

You may of course also use a porcelain or metal bowl, but be sure to place these containers on a fireproof surface. Containers for incense burning come in a wide range of prices and in many different designs. In Arab countries, we found metal bowls and vessels with delicate engraving. In Japan, we discovered bowls exquisitely decorated with beautiful *raku* borders; in Somalia, we saw vessels carved of meerschaum. The Native American style is to use a large abalone shell for burning incense.

Maybe you would enjoy mak-

Minoan incense-burning bowl

ing your own incense-burning vessel or have a potter make one according to your design. You may also fill these containers with sand or wood ash and use them for incense sticks, which you light at the upper end and insert into the sand.

If you do not want to use charcoal, you may also use a small stove designed specifically for incense burning. The difference between a stove and charcoal is

that with a stove, the incense substance burns much more slowly, creates less smoke, and takes longer to distribute the fragrance. This is particularly worthwhile when the substance is very expensive.

Stoves have either a metal or a stoneware base. They should be large enough to accommodate a small lighted candle. The design is similar to that used to keep tea warm. The upper portion of the stove is copper, which conducts heat particularly well. The stove should be approximately 4 in. (10 cm) tall. Place the incense substances in the bowl and heat them from below with the small candle. You can clean the bowl with alcohol.

Another type of stove uses a very fine metal mesh to cover an opening above the candle. You place the incense substances on the top of this sieve to burn slowly. If you use substances that are damp or that contain wax, you must cover the metal mesh with aluminum foil or these substances will clog up the sieve.

When you want to conduct incense-burning rituals outside, you'll have the best results if you

Incense-burning stove

Children love to burn incense

sprinkle the incense substances on top of a flat hot stone that has been in a campfire. If you throw the substances directly into the flame, they will burn quickly, and the fragrance will disappear just as quickly.

If you want to burn incense in the fireplace in your house, you might want to place a hot rock or flat stone close to or directly in the fire and burn your incense that way.

Maybe you don't have a container, or you don't have charcoal at hand, but you are still in the mood for burning incense. For such a spontaneous ceremony, a simple metal tea sieve works just fine, as long as it is large enough for the incense substances. Simply hold the tea sieve above a candle. You can also use aluminum foil. Fold a large piece of aluminum foil three times; shape a bowl on one end to accommodate the incense; shape a smaller bowl that will hold the candle.

Charcoal

You can buy charcoal in tablet form. The tablets come in rolls of 10 each. The size of these tablets varies, with a diameter anywhere from 1¼ to 2 in. (3 to 5 cm). Choose the smaller size when you want to burn only a small amount of incense. These tablets are easy to light and get hot very quickly. However, they do give off a slight odor.

Charcoal needs to be wrapped very tightly in aluminum foil and then placed in an airtight container for storage. If a piece of charcoal does not light easily, it might be damp. If so, dry it in the stove or on top of a radiator. Japanese charcoal has no odor and is much more elegant than regular charcoal. You can purchase it in specialty shops; however it is more expensive.

Always place the charcoal on a bed of sand. It will keep its amberlike glow much longer that way. In addition, the sand reduces the risk of the container cracking due to the extensive heat created in the process. The layer of sand underneath the charcoal should be at least ¾–1¼ in. (2–3 cm) thick.

Feather

Traditionally, you use a feather to fan the lighted charcoal. Fanning assures that the charcoal will burn uniformly. Any kind of large feather will do. You might be able to find one when hiking in the woods or walking around

Eagle feather

a lake that is frequented by swans or geese. Of course, you can also use a rigid piece of paper, such as a postcard, instead of a feather. Fanning lighted charcoal provides oxygen to the fire, allowing the charcoal to create an amberlike glow very quickly.

Sand

When you burn incense in a bowl, you need to place sand in the bowl. Small incense-burning stoves do not need to be filled with sand. For a normal-size bowl, you need about a cup of sand. You can purchase small amounts of sand at many pet stores, plant nurseries, and hardware stores. Obviously, buying sand in larger quantities, for instance from a construction site, is much less expensive. And you may simply use sand from a sandbox or bring some home from a vacation at the beach.

Instead of sand, you may also use finely sifted ash, as is the custom in Japan. This type of ash turns charcoal into an amber glow much more uniformly. However, when you fan the charcoal or blow on it, you stir up the ash and distribute it into the air. Finely sifted rice-straw ashes are available at Japanese stores that carry ingredients for incense burning. Incense-burning stoves from Japan are made of porcelain and are equipped with a small fire stone. You don't use sand or ashes with these stoves.

Fire plays an important role in the process of burning incense. For that reason, you should not use electric stoves. They deprive you of the experience of watching real flames and fire.

Tweezers

Use tweezers to suspend the charcoal over the candle flame long enough for it to begin to glow. Then place the charcoal in the vessel or bowl. Use a pair of tweezers that has a long handle. You can find these in stores that sell laboratory equipment or similar utensils. To burn incense in the Japanese tradition, you can buy a kit that includes metal sticks and pliers for holding the

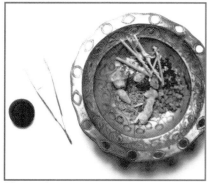
Charcoal, tweezers, and incense

charcoal. After concluding the incense-burning ceremony, use the tweezers to dip the charcoal in water.

Mortar and pestle

Like coffee, incense substances are best when fresh. Finely ground powder loses its fragrance and aroma quickly. Buy resins, wood, and seeds in chunks and crush them yourself in a mortar and pestle. That way you will experience their true and priceless aroma. In addition, you'll know that the incense powder is pure, not diluted with other substances. Porcelain mortar and pestle sets are often used in pharmacies. They are available in many different sizes. A mortar and pestle made from

Marble mortar and pestle

granite or stone is even better, because you can grind wooden pieces, resins, and seeds to powder without creating problems.

Incense substances

Once you are ready to start your journey of discovery into the world of incense burning and to progress from reading about it to actually experiencing it, start with substances that create compatible fragrances and that are easy to mix. Dry all the ingredients well.

Incense-burning ingredients . . . a pleasure even for the eye

Ingredients for the beginner

Frankincense resin
Myrrh resin
Sandalwood
Cinnamon
Cedar tips (Indian juniper tips)
Mastic resin
White sage

Some of the ingredients are solid, such as resins, seeds, and needles; others are waxy, gum-like, or thick (viscous). Prepared mixtures often come in fine or coarse powders. Incense substances also come in pea-size pellet form with a waxlike consistency. You burn these individually.

If you like incense cones, which are often used during the Christmas season, you might want to use the recipes provided in this book to create your own. Ready-made cones, available in stores, usually have synthetic substances added to give them color or even synthetic aroma. If you are going to make your own, use a mortar and pestle to crush all the ingredients to a fine powder according to the instructions provided. Dissolve gum arabic in water (1 part powder to 2 parts water) and let it soak for about three hours. Mix the resulting viscous liquid with the incense powder until you can shape it into small cones. Allow the cones to dry in a warm place. Place the cones, one at a time, in the burner and enjoy experiencing the wonderful aroma.

Only then ought you to think of adding other ingredients to

your mixture and start to experiment. Choose one of the recipes given in this book. Use the recipes as a foundation for your own incense mixtures. Over time, you will become curious and experiment with new combinations. Before you know it, you will become an expert in the art of incense burning, even starting a collection of different ingredients. The experience will be like a library where you can reach for a book with valuable information, looking and reading simply for the enjoyment of browsing through a whole different world.

Valuable Information about Buying Incense Ingredients

The ingredients needed for incense burning are available in several types of stores: those that deal with fragrances, sometimes in drugstores, in health food stores and herbal stores, and in stores that carry devotional subject matter. Catalogs carrying specialty items are another good source. The beginning of each chapter lists and categorizes incense ingredients according to appearance, their consistency, as well as their fragrance. This allows you to check out the quality of a specific ingredient.

If you make your own mixture you have the assurance that all ingredients are pure. If you choose to buy ready-made mixtures, pay special attention to quality. Some mixtures contain extraneous material that might be detrimental to your health when burned. I have discovered pieces of glass, cardboard, and even plastic in mixtures I have bought.

Incense-burning mixtures often have fragrances added to them, such as essential oils or synthetic oils that intensify the fragrance of the mixture. However, this diminishes the quality of the mixture. A mixture contains substances that unfold

This Is How It's Done

1. Prepare your utensils.

2. Hold charcoal over a flame with a pair of tweezers.

3. Fan the air above the lighted charcoal; place incense substances on the charcoal.

7.

their own fragrance. Burning synthetic fragrance substances can cause headaches, inflammation of the eyes, and coughing.

How to Burn Incense

Set aside enough time so you can enjoy the experience of incense burning as a small ritual. Gather your container, candle, feather, incense, charcoal, and matches ahead of time. You might also consider appropriate music in the background. First, light one end of the charcoal with a candle or a cigarette lighter. That end of the charcoal will start to crackle and glow. Next, place the charcoal on top of the sand with a pair of tweezers or metal pliers and gently blow or fan the air above the charcoal with a feather. Only after all the charcoal is aglow and stops crackling do you place the incense substance into the indentation of the charcoal tablet. Usually, a small amount is sufficient. Use the tip of a knife to place the substance, repeating as needed. Too much incense may extinguish the fire.

When burning incense, make sure that no easily combustible objects, such as curtains, cloth, or newspaper, are nearby. Fanning and blowing on the charcoal may send sparks into the air. Consider placing the incense container on a metal tray. Children have a great deal of fun with incense burning. However, take special care to reduce the risk of fire. Charcoal may glow for up to two hours, so do not throw it into a wastepaper basket or into the garbage. Do not leave the incense-burning vessel alone until the charcoal has burned out. Then, lift the charcoal out of the container with tweezers and submerse it in cold water. Don't put water on charcoal in a ceramic bowl. The bowl might crack.

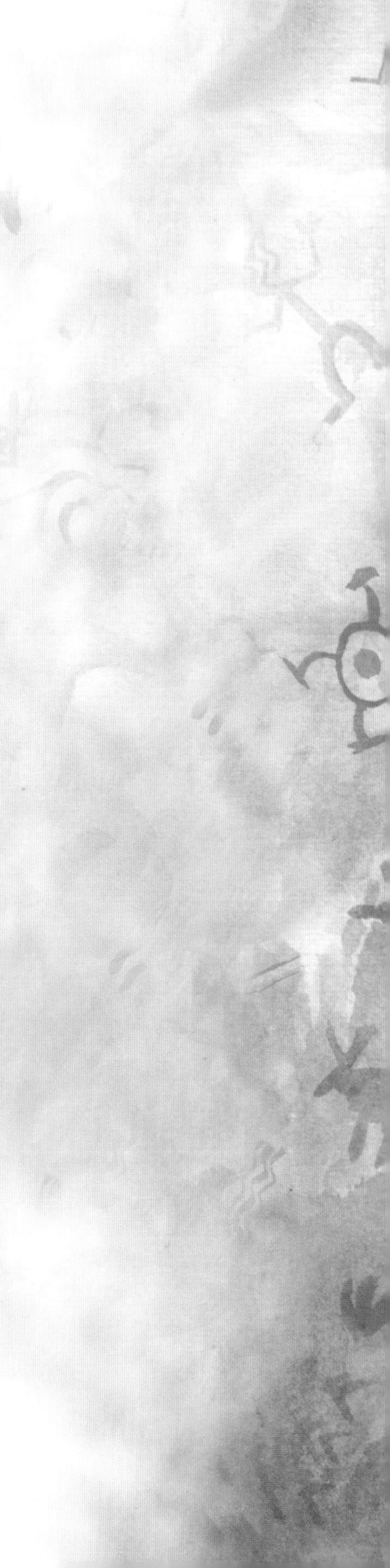

. . . if it gets too cold I will light a

fire,

because I have a fireplace,

people need to experience fire.

People in Europe only see

a fire when their house

is burning. Their souls wither

because

they do not see fire. After all,

how often will a house be on fire,

and who will take the time

to look into the flames untroubled.

Merian, from Janosch, *Canary Islands*

1 Sitting at the Fire

How It All Began

Outside, a snowstorm is whipping through the trees, making the animal skin that covers the entrance to the cave shudder. We moved closer to the fire, feeling its comfortable warmth on our skin. Our faces became warm, but we still could feel the cold on our backs. We got lost during the night. The old people and the children of our tribe would not have survived very much longer. Urak, our healer, was reaching for her medicine bag. It contained fragrant herbs, resins, and seeds which she had carefully collected during the summer. She murmured prayers for the ancestors and the ghosts of this cave. Then she tossed a handful of a mixture of incense on the hot stones. The rising smoke filled the cave with a mysterious fragrance. It began to spread, and all felt gratitude to be here. Tension gave way to a pleasant feeling. Together with the smoke of the fragrant incense, we had arrived. Now the cave was ours, the ghosts accepted us graciously. Urak was satisfied.

Fragrances of the Campfire

The history of incense burning begins with the history of fire. People have been gathering around fires for millions of years. In a cave, in a tent, or in a hut, fire gave them peace and warmth after a hard and dangerous day. Countless stories have been told around campfires, countless songs sung, and countless dances danced. Fire has always brought people closer together because it is a bonding experience. Whenever someone threw a piece of bark, rich with resins, or an aromatic plant into the fire, the mood changed. People noticed how comfortable they began to feel in the presence of the fragrant smoke. They also used it to accompany rituals. The fragrant smoke of the incense carried the request or plea for a successful hunt, for good weather, and for health as a message to beings of another world.

We believe that African tribes first discovered fire for themselves. Objects found in the caves in the vicinity of Johannesburg indicate that *Homo erectus* made use of fire 1½ million years ago. At that time, however, people could not create and control it by themselves. About 400,000 years ago, they discovered how to create a spark with stones or by rubbing pieces of wood together. This might have been the greatest discovery humans ever made, and it is closely connected with the ancient love of burning incense.

The search for the beginning of incense-burning traditions starts in the fireplaces of ancient times. It is there that the first conscious experience with fragrances took place. At that time, the human sense of smell was much more sensitive than it is today because it was essential for survival. People knew the smell that indicated a change in the weather. They smelled the approach of wild animals. They knew the smell of danger and of security. They could distinguish between edible and poisonous food. This keen sense of smell allowed our early ancestors to survive and to make important decisions. The fragrance of the fire also affected this sense of smell. Fragrances became part of the treasure of experiences, stored forever in memories. There, they remained as an archetypal experience for us today.

People began to collect plants according to their fragrances. In the course of time, people discovered that certain parts of a plant had a distinct and specific fragrance. For instance, the fragrance of burning elderberry branches created a comfortable atmosphere, pine resin could cleanse the air, the seeds from datura plants, which belong to the nightshade family, produced

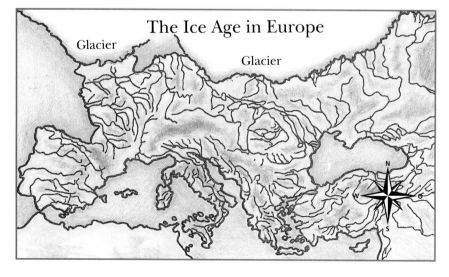

The Ice Age in Europe

Glacier

Glacier

N

W   E

S

visions. At that time, our ancestors probably discovered these effects by accident. Or is it possible that in ancient times plants were still talking to people, telling them about their innate powers? Is it possible that the much larger brain of the Neanderthal people, who lived between 90,000 and 35,000 B.C., had a greater capacity for detecting fragrances? As research in paleoanthropology has shown, Neanderthal people already had ritual practices that had a connection to the plant world. Excavations in Skanidar (in present-day Iraq) discovered Neanderthal caves from approximately 16,000 years ago. The graves found underneath the floors of the caves were covered with plant material, most likely placed there to aid the dead on their journey into the beyond. We still use a few of these types of plants for incense burning.

Shaman Knowledge

During the Stone Age, when people still lived in caves or tents, a shaman culture began to flourish. Medicine men and medicine women recorded their experiences with aromatic incense plants and began to classify them very accurately. This knowledge evolved and began to spread. For the first time, an entirely independent tradition developed. People were able to change the scent in their caves and tents deliberately. They considered fire a gift from the gods. Its smoke traveled visibly towards the heavens. Our ancestors believed the smoke conveyed their gratitude, their prayers, and their requests to the gods. They honored the unexplainable with smoke and fragrance. The shamans were very protective of their knowledge about which kind of incense was to be directed to which godly entity. Ritual activities involving smoke were supposed to help bring prayers and requests to the heavens and to the gods. People had learned how to use resins and different parts of plants to create fragrant mixtures. They connected incense burning to ritual as a message sent to the heavens. The shamans handed down this wisdom from generation to generation, and we have been able to find very definite evidence of it.

One of the oldest findings, which points to a particular incense-burning tradition, dates back to 7200 B.C. Incense cakes, found in Denmark and in the southern part of Sweden, reminded us of the fragrance of frankincense and myrrh.

During ancient times, the shamans also knew the secret of which plants were able to open the gates of consciousness to increase awareness of other worlds. The ancient shamans also discovered the power of plants to induce hallucinations. They worshiped these plants and honored them as gifts from the gods. These plants served as transportation for a journey into a different reality and as a bridge to a mystical place beyond time. Shamans used the smoke from very specific plants, such as the the thorn apple (datura), mandrake, and poppy, to reach a trance (during which the gods would speak to them) and also for healing ceremonies. Probably the first community gatherings

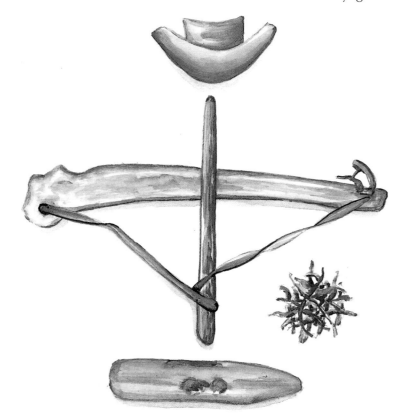

Implement for lighting a fire

for worship purposes took place around the rising smoke created by burning holy plants. Incense burning connects us to an archetypal knowledge that resides in each of us.

The development of healing ceremonies is closely connected to incense burning. We are probably correct to assume that when plagued by pain and rheumatism, our ancestors held their limbs over smoke to induce healing and that they tried to soothe the effects of a cold by burning resins. Most likely, they used resins from the pine tree as well as twigs from juniper, cedar, or thyme for this purpose.

From the Rhythm of Nature

After thousands of years, fire still fascinates us. We are still trying to connect to it because of its smells and fragrances. None of our senses touches us as deeply as that of smell. Janosch may have been correct when he said that our souls will wither without experiencing the element of fire. After a day's work, we are still drawn to a source of light. Only it is not the light of a crackling and fragrant fire anymore but the pale, electronic light of

the television, and this light is not fragrant. We've broken the healing connection to the fire and surrounding nature.

But burning incense, the way our ancestors did, can reconnect us to nature. It allows us to experience the changes of the seasons, the state of Earth's vegetation, and the sound of nature. Orienting ourselves to the cycle of nature can strengthen our inner balance and help us overcome the anonymity of modern life. Visualizing the rhythms of nature may also be very healing.

The ancient tradition of incense burning, using an individual plant, a resin, or a mixture, is particularly wonderful for incense burning outdoors. We need a crackling fire when burning fragrant twigs, which by itself is healing for our soul, given that we are so far removed from nature. We touch the stones that surround the fire, we touch the wood as we arrange it in the fireplace, we take in the flash of the first spark. Flames licking, dancing in shades of orange, yellow, blue, and red reach upwards to the sky. We throw dry juniper twigs into the fire or place resin on the hot stones.

The fragrance of the ancient

Cave painting in Altamira

24

forests and the breath of nature touch our souls and inspire us again to tell stories, to dance, and to sing songs connected to fire and fragrant smoke.

Aromatic Resin of Pine Trees

Since ancient times, people have used the balsamlike, fragrant resins of evergreens for incense burning because the wood contains more resin than that of deciduous trees. We do not know the specifics about how these fragrances were used for ritual or healing purposes, but we may assume that the ancients knew about the healing power of the resins. For example, the resins of these trees help disinfect and heal wounds. We know that people used resins to prepare medicinal remedies. And in earlier times, people made a salve from resin to cover wounds, a practice still in use at the beginning of the 20th century. Today, salves made from resins are only used in veterinary medicine.

We can still let the fragrance of pine resins carry us back to ancient times when forests completely covered our continent and when we still understood the powerful, healing language of trees. The resins from pine trees, spruce, larch, and juniper all have slightly different fragrances. Today, you can find resins for incense burning that are the same as those used in ancient times. Walking through a pine forest, you can discover trees where resin is seeping through the bark. A tree reacts to an injury by excreting resin.

Theophrastus, an ancient philosopher and naturalist, suggested collecting tree resin during the ascension of Sirius, the Dog Star, a star in the constellation of Canis Major. This period is also known as the dog days, the hottest days of the year (in the Northern Hemisphere). Collecting resin during the summer makes sense because the water content of the resin is particularly low because of the high evaporation. The less water in the resin, the more delicate the fragrance during incense burning. You can easily remove the resin by scraping the bark with a knife or a spatula and then wrapping it in aluminum foil. The quality of the resin is highest when allowed to dry for at least a year. Only then will it develop its balsamlike fragrance. Because natural resins create a considerable amount of smoke, use them outoors or, if you are using them indoors, open windows. For incense burning, place a small piece of the resin in the glowing charcoal or on a hot stone.

Pine trees

Effective Incense Substances of Ancient Times

The Pine Tree

Abies alba Mill.

We still practice many of the ancient customs connected with the majestic pine tree. We can assume that during the Stone Age people knew about the healing power of the pine tree, used many substances from it for healing purposes, and greatly revered it. To this day the pine tree is still a symbol of light and life in the Christian world. For our Celtic and Germanic ancestors, the pine tree was a tree of protection, shielding them from the influences of demonic powers. Eight hundred years ago, the abbess Hildegard von Bingen wrote in her book *Natural Science*: "The pine tree is more warm than cold and contains many energies and powers. The tree is a symbol for strength. Ghosts hate pine trees and avoid places where they grow."

Today, we still use substances from the pine tree for protective incense burning. When burning pine, we ought to ask those helpful higher powers to protect us, and we should imagine that we are surrounded by a shield of light and safety.

Pine resin has a balsamlike, green fragrance. It cleanses and improves the air. According to old herb books, incense burning with pine resin strengthens the nerves and gives energy, courage, and emotional strength. Our ancestors burned pine incense in sick rooms in order to support and strengthen the healing process. Excavations of prehistoric sites have revealed that incense substances included pine resin. We can well understand that people in those times also used pine resin as a strengthening medium. Native American tribes in Canada used resin from pine trees for incense burning. The resin collects in the bark, creating a swelling into which you insert a spoutlike container that allows the resin to drip into a can. When exposed to the air, this honey-colored, clear liquid solidifies into a clear mass of resin used for incense burning. It creates a very comfortable, woody, green fragrance. Native Americans in Canada chewed the resin of this balsam tree (*Abies balsamea L. Mill.*) when they had a throat infection, but they also used it to treat cuts, contusions, and bruises. They considered the smoke to be a remedy for arthritis. Today, we use balsam resin in industry as an embedding medium in microscopes, for making liquor, and as an adhesive for lens systems.

Europeans used a turpentine called Alsace turpentine, or Strasbourg turpentine—a product of the white pine—as a remedy for wounds and rheumatism. This cleansing pine resin, which has a particularly delicate citruslike aroma, acts as an antiseptic and dissolves mucus. People burn it to cure coughs and rheumatism. It is still available today.

You can also use the dried needles instead of the resin. Pick the fresh needles off the twig and dry them by spreading them on a piece of cloth for about two weeks. Then, chop or crush them and add them to frankincense or mastic resin. Always store dried needles in a tightly closed container. You can also pulverize the needles and add them to an incense mixture.

Larch

Larix decidua Mill.

The larch tree, which has existed since ancient times, is particularly conspicuous in a pine forest. The larch is the only pine tree that sheds its needles in the fall. This is the reason ancient people considered this tree a symbol of new beginnings, spontaneity, courage, and renewal. Our ancestors used the wood, resin, and needles from this tree for ritual incense burning, particularly during ceremonies in spring or for renewal, when they were symbolically discarding the old and welcoming the new. They felt that the fragrance of the larch tree stimulated the powers of renewal and helped free blocked energies. When you look at a larch tree, pay attention to the fact that a rich ground flora surrounds this tree. The needles that the tree sheds in the fall turn into a very nutritious mulch for many plants. The delicate construction of the branches allows light to penetrate the ground so plants can thrive. On the other hand, the acid ground below pine trees prevents any flora from flourishing.

In contrast to the pine tree, the larch tree has a delicate and sensitive expression. In the spring, it radiates beauty when its light green needles sprout from their delicate branches. In the fall, branches glow with deep yellow colors. These delicate branches seem to be antennae that communicate with unseen energies. During the Stone Age, our ancestors were probably aware of this special radiance. And to this day, old customs and stories about the larch tree abound. Fables tell us that forest elves, well disposed toward human beings, live around the larch tree. These are the good elves that always appear in a story (and sometimes even in real life!) when they are desperately needed. Thus, our ancestors thought that incense burning with larch resin would bring luck, creating an atmosphere of success, well-being, and good fortune. Many recipes that use larch still exist.

Many people considered a larch tree growing on their property an indication that good spirits occupied the house. Whenever bad luck and sorrow visited a house, people would burn the resin of the larch tree in the evening. They felt that the fragrant substances of this tree would sharpen their awareness and their contact with the world of elves and natural beings. People believed that certain incense-burning practices that mixed larch resin with other ingredients produced clairvoyance. In addition, people valued the resin of this tree for its enormous healing properties. Larch resin relieves muscle cramps and soothes and strengthens the respiratory tract. It is helpful in dissolving severe mucus accumulation in cases of a cold and in cases of chronic respiratory and sinus infections. Herbal therapists use it for treating chronic illnesses of the respiratory tract.

Refined larch resin is available on the market. You can harvest it by drilling holes into the tree. After you gather the resin, you close the openings with wooden dowels. You can remove the dowels at certain intervals to collect additional resin. Larch resin is a yellowish, clear liquid and has a delicate balsamlike fragrance.

Scotch Pine

Pinus sylvestris L.
Pinus mugo Turra
Pinus cembra L.

In the middle of the Stone Age (85,000–12,000 B.C.), the forests in northern Europe consisted primarily of pine trees surrounded by birch trees and hazelnut bushes. We believe that this was when people discovered the balsamlike, warm, fragrant resin of the pine tree and began to use it. The bark of these trees also contains a reddish resin which, when burned, produces a pleasant resinous fragrance. For that reason, ancient people shredded or pulverized the bark and used it for incense burning. To this day, pulverized pine bark is the main ingredient in Japanese incense sticks, giving them their basic fragrance. In Morocco, people use the resin of the Aleppo pine, called the "Mother of the People," for magical and medicinal incense burning.

Some people believe that the fragrance of this pine resin protects them from magic practices that cause illnesses. They feel that the smoke strengthens their heart. Today, we only think of this resin as a treatment for violin strings, which is why we also call the resin of the Scotch pine violin resin. You can buy it in many different qualities, from very light to very dark. The color is light yellow to light brown, and when broken apart the surfaces have a glasslike shine. Today, the resin we use is manufactured from Scotch pine balsam by a process of distillation. The remnants of the process are heated until all the water has evaporated and only a resinous substance remains.

Incense burning with Scotch pine has warming and strengthening effects. When boiled, the steam strengthens the lungs and increases the energy of sickly children. The smoke also has antiseptic properties and strengthens the circulatory system. If you have a fireplace or can make a campfire, burn a handful of small pieces of pine bark. This is a wonderful way to enjoy the fragrance.

Scotch-pine resin

Spruce

Picea abies (L.) Karst.

In the last century, people sold spruce resin as a cheap replacement for frankincense. Our ancestors called spruce resin "common frankincense" and used only the purest and driest pieces of the liquid resin. They improved the resin mentioned in old herbal books by placing it for a specific amount of time in an anthill. The acid secreted by the ants produced a chemical transformation in the resin. Spruce resin was used to dissolve mucus in the lungs, to treat eczema, and as part of the treatment for rheumatism. Spruce resin has bacteria-killing properties and can disinfect the air in a room. Its fragrance is much stronger than that of the fir tree, but it is missing the fresh, often lemonlike scent peculiar to fir resins.

Burning spruce-tree resin cleanses indoor space. In the olden days, long before frankincense was available, people thought that the smoke of this resin protected them against disrupting influences and helped them discover inner peace.

Spruce resin is easy to find. As with all resins, it needs to mature before you can use it for incense burning. The burgundy-colored resin, *Pix burgundica* or *Resina Pini burgundica,* available in specialty stores, is a spruce resin of high quality obtained through a melting process. It has a strong, forestlike fragrance when it is burned. Burgundy spruce resin has strengthening and regenerative properties. Since it creates a considerable amount of smoke, you should burn it outside. During the Middle Ages, people frequently used this light yellow resin for medicinal purposes, for incense burning, and as a salve. During the Middle Ages, people used the simple, cleansed spruce resin, also known as scrap resin, as a medication. Both qualities were available on the market then.

Juniper

Juniperus communis L.

All ancient shaman cultures that knew juniper trees or shrubs honored them as sacred plants. The shamans believed that the juniper tree had certain magical powers that served as protection. They knew juniper as the "tree of life." In fact, the last shamans in Siberia still called it by that name. Since prehistoric times, people have used the wood, branches, and berries for ritual and medicinal incense burning. From the earliest history to this day, the juniper has remained the tree that provides protection.

Juniper

times in history, people thought juniper possessed very specific life-strengthening energies that could be transferred to people as well as to indoor spaces. Even today, people feel that incense burning with juniper is particularly good to support convalescence and to recharge people and their living space with new energies. Juniper strengthens our ability to be attentive and awakens us.

For incense-burning purposes, mix juniper needles and berries with resins from spruce or sandarac. Dried sage is a good addition to a mixture that contains juniper and combines well with the effects and fragrance of juniper.

Old herb books contain many juniper descriptions that combine ritualistic, magical, and medicinal uses. Many old texts include this phrase: "Wherever there is the fragrance of the juniper, the devil cannot be found." Ancient people used juniper for incense burning to keep away influences that caused illness. Juniper resin, however, is very rare because this tree neither produces nor relinquishes much resin. However, the resin needs less time to mature, usually no more than half a year. Its fragrance is very delicate.

Because it has disinfecting properties, people often use it for incense burning to cleanse sick rooms. It also has warming and mucus-dissolving properties. In the late Middle Ages, people used juniper resin to treat rheumatism, contusions, paralysis, and tumors. They suspended the affected part of the body above the juniper smoke.

An 1874 book about herbal remedies states that incense burning with juniper berries and juniper wood was helpful for tumors and rheumatoidlike afflictions. The book suggested that you suspend a flannel cloth above the smoke and wrap this cloth around the affected parts of the body.

In earlier times, people considered incense burning with juniper a protection against infectious illnesses. During the times of the great epidemics, for instance, people would burn juniper. In antiquity, people thought that the smoke of the juniper bestowed the gift of prophecy. From the very earliest

Juniper Berries

Archeologists have found the small black-blue berries from the juniper tree near Stone Age fireplaces. The berries served as food, as a spice, and as an ingredient for incense burning. We believe that these ancient people also used dried juniper twigs for incense burning. Allow the berries to dry for three weeks before using them for incense burning.

1. Juniper berries
2. Scotch resin
3. Spruce resin
4. Pine needles
5. Ledum
6. Burgundy spruce resin
7. Larch
8. Juniper

Ledum

Ledum palustre L.

Ledum is an evergreen plant similar to a shrub. Depending on its location, it grows 8 in.–5 ft. (20 cm–1.5 m) tall. It is an archaic shaman plant of the North and grows in bogs in regions as diverse as East Asia, Central Asia, and the Alps. Shamans in Siberia used ledum as a rub to treat joint pain and for incense-burning ceremonies to induce a trance. They often mixed it with juniper. Although the plant is similar to rosemary, it is smoother, softer, and more delicate. For that reason, people sometimes refer to it as wild rosemary. However, ledum is not related to the rosemary plant. In fact, it belongs to a totally different species. In some European countries, it is a protected plant.

In the Middle Ages, people considered it a magical plant. We don't know much today about its

Ledum

Ledum

inner and submaterial energies. Today ledum is primarily used in homeopathy. People use this herb, also called Labrador tea, to treat rheumatism and whooping cough. It also stimulates kidney function and perspiration. In the past, women used the herb to induce abortions. Unfortunately, it frequently had harmful

effects. Pregnant women should not use this plant for incense burning.

For medicinal incense burning, ledum is used to treat coughs (together with sage leaves) and to induce sleep in the evening. Recent experiments have discovered that this plant also prolongs sleep. When used for this purpose and for relaxation, people mix it with other herbs, such as sage, pine bark, and hops. In ancient times, people thought this plant was a magical substance used to connect with the sublime powers of nature. In those shaman cultures that still exist, people use this ancient healing plant. We can as-

sume that our ancestors knew of it during the Stone Age and used it for visionary and other shamanistic practices.

Recipes for Archaic, Natural Incense-Burning Mixtures

These recipes work particularly well outside.

Ayla

Pine resin	1 part
Pine	2 parts
Juniper berries	1 part
Mastic resin	3 parts

Crush dry resin and bark or cut them with a knife. Also cut dry pine needles. Crush juniper berries with a mortar and pestle. Mix all the ingredients well. Place the mixture on a hot stone or on glowing charcoal.

Fundamental Essence

Sage leaves	3 parts
Ledum leaves	1 part
Juniper needles	1 part
Spurge	½ part
Mastic	5 parts

Crush dry sage leaves between the palms of your hands. Pick off the dried ledum leaves from the branch. Crush dried *mercurialis* herb. Mix all ingredients together well. Burn small amounts (a pinch at a time) either above the fire of an incense-burning vessel or on charcoal. This particular mixture releases the more delicate energies of nature. It is helpful for people who use plants for healing purposes. Don't waste this incense-burning mixture of the shamans. Use it with care, economy, and gratitude. Some people believe that when properly used, it can produce healing dreams, which suggest remedies from the plant world.

Guardian Spirit

Fir wood	1 part
Fir bark	1 part
Juniper wood	1 part
Clove root	1 part
Frankincense resin	4 parts

Dry the woody parts of the ingredients and finely grate them. Also grate the dried clove roots. Mix all the ingredients together well. Burn a pinch of this mixture directly in the fire, on a hot stone, or on charcoal. The fragrant smoke creates a vibration for a subliminal, invisible protective shield. In addition, this mixture has a cleansing effect and supports inner strength. It unites with the positive energies of surrounding space.

Lupuleda

Ledum	1 part
Pine bark and resin	4 parts
Hops	½ part
Juniper berries	1 part
Frankincense	2 parts

Cut the dried ledum into small pieces with a pair of scissors. Crush the pine bark and resin. Break the frankincense into small pieces. Add the hops (see also chapter on *Northern Europe*) and juniper berries. This is a mixture with a balsamlike, natural fragrance. It improves inner balance. Because it is very calming, it can also provide a good night's sleep, particularly in times of anxiety and stress. At the same time, this combination of ingredients can connect us to the healing powers of nature.

I am a reindeer: with seven antlers

I am the flood: covering the ground,

I am the wind: moving across a deep lake,

I am a teardrop: falling from the sun,

I am a falcon: above a cliff,

I am a thorn: under the nail,

I am the magic: between the flowers,

I am the magician, who but me

Can light a cool head with smoke?

Song of Amergin—early Celtic

from Robert Graves, *The White Goddess*

2 NORTHERN EUROPE

INCENSE-BURNING NIGHTS AND BUSHELS OF HERBS

On the first night after Christmas, Grandfather brought a great iron frying pan from the kitchen and suspended it over a candle. He lit pieces of a tree mushroom which he had dried during the summer. He held them there until they glowed deep red. Then, he threw a handful of an herbal mixture that he had kept in a little bag on the glowing mushroom. Thick smoke now began to rise from the frying pan. A warm and aromatic fragrance from the herbs and the resins began to spread throughout the room. Moving his arms in large circles, grandfather walked through the house, mumbling prayers in the process. Each room had its own very special atmosphere and its own scent. Everything that had happened during the year seemed to linger in every room like an invisible veil. As we were walking with this incense-burning pan through the house, it seemed as if the rising smoke was lifting this veil from every room. Something was changing.

Stone Age Journey

The nomads of the Stone Age in northern Europe never allowed their fire to die. The magical power of that fire, the fragrance of the rising smoke, and the age-old knowledge of the shamans connected with it have remained deep within us and subconsciously influenced our souls. In modern Europe, where old myths and symbols seem to have disappeared, some rituals of this ancient incense-burning tradition have survived. As we follow the traces of incense-burning practices from the shamans of the Stone Age, through the prehistoric Celtic and Germanic settlements, to ancient national traditions, and to the present, we feel the power of the immense stone circles, such as those at Stonehenge and the rock formation in Germany's Teutoburg Forest, which our ancestors considered to be holy places, along with the dolmen graves and feen houses in Ireland.

People in northern Europe are particularly sensitive to the changes of the seasons: ice-cold winters, which were often fatal; the promise of life-renewing

Altar in the Extern Stone

spring; the fertile, warm summers; and then the colorful, fruit-producing fall. The incense burning and the rituals connected to it in northern Europe were profoundly influenced by this awareness. Many of these holy places, the stone circles and dolmen graves, were built so that their orientation coincided with the cosmic rhythm of the seasons. The knowledge of the interaction between heaven and earth formed the foundation for these ancient cultural places.

Ancient people considered themselves to be part of the rhythm of the cosmos. In early European cultures, our ancestors saw the smoke rising to the sky in these holy places as a connection to and a message for the heavens. For instance, at the Extern Stone, the holy place in the Teutoburg Forest, on the day of the summer solstice, the first rays of the morning sun fall through the opening in the rock directly on the altar placed behind it. This ancient place is approximately 10,000 years old. It shows the profound connection the people of that time had with nature. Those ancient mystical traditions and rituals most likely included burning incense. Unfortunately, details of the rituals and the recipes used for incense-burning ceremonies remain lost

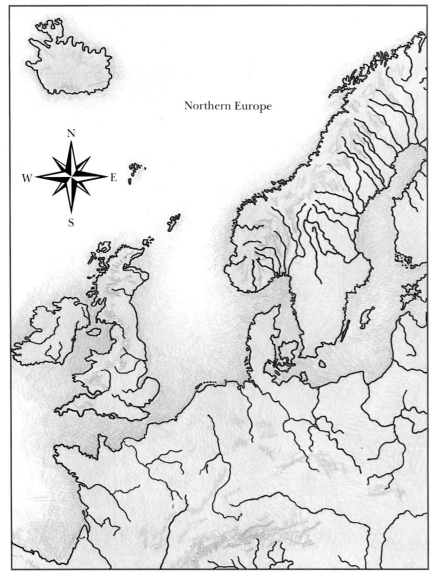
Northern Europe

N
W   E
S

Extern Stones

in the darkness of history. However, a few things have been passed on to us, and we've been able to reconstruct some others. For example, we know that burning incense using native plants connects us to the ancient wisdom of the European plant world.

The Ancient Forests

The Celtic people, who moved into western Europe from 5000 to 4000 B.C., continued the tradition of worshiping the magical power of nature practiced by the first inhabitants of northern Europe. The enormous granite altar stones of the Neolithic culture later became places of worship for the Celtic people. But before the invading Celts integrated the traditions of the native people, they had to become involved with the magic and the power of trees.

They came from an area that consisted almost entirely of tree-less prairies. Now, they found themselves surrounded by a wall of huge, powerful, and almost impenetrable forests. The Celtic people distinguished themselves with their tremendous curiosity, their joy of traveling, and their courage. And these characteristics largely influenced their explorations. They were not only able to find their way through the forests, which at that time covered almost the whole of northern Europe, they also became great admirers of the natural force and wisdom of the trees. They even went as far as using some of the names and characteristics of trees in their calendar. The tree, rooted in the earth and stretching toward the sky, became the Celtic symbol for life. The bizarrely shaped, powerful oak and the small ash made deep impressions on the Celtic and Germanic peoples. They

even considered one type of mistletoe to be a holy, mythical plant. For the Celts, trees had a religious meaning, and they would hold their worship services under them.

We still have much of the exceptional knowledge the Celtic people had of healing plants. The plant world was a source of wisdom, always seen in mystical, even spiritual, terms. They honored the spirit of plants in so-called plant elves. The elves were the ones who breathed life into the world of plants, and they possessed secret healing powers that could be made available to people. The Druids and the seers had direct access to the power and energy of a plant. They communicated through mediums to discover the secrets of nature. Through incense burning, they freed secret messages from the plants and then conveyed the messages to the people. In fairy tales and fables,

Stone formation in an ancient Celtic area

37

we've preserved the knowledge that plant beings and helpful ghosts abound in nature. In fairy tales and fables, elves, gnomes, dwarfs, and water nymphs always appear as helpers in difficult situations. Kitschy garden gnomes are the last remnants of these ancient beliefs.

Wisdom of the Druids

For Celtic people, spiritual guidance was in the hands of Druids, whom they considered to be particularly versed in healing matters. The priest or priestess guided the people in their efforts to live in harmony with the energies of the cosmos. To receive messages and advice required a connection with another world. For this, they would consult oracles, such as throwing runes. They experienced so-called truth dreams, in which they entered other worlds. They gained access to those worlds through fairy or elf plants that would appear during incense-burning ceremonies or with magic drinks.

Once the Celtic people became settled, they lived on large individual farms, almost like islands in the midst of a huge ocean. These farms, often housing up to 200 people, also in-

cluded a Druid priest or priestess whose responsibility was to establish a connection to the spiritual energies of the earth and the heavens. They maintained a house altar for sacrifices and incense burning. They also used this altar to burn incense mixtures in small pottery vessels. Even after the Celtic people had settled, the fires of ancient Neolithic times continued to flourish on their farms.

Each house had an open fireplace in its center. The rising smoke from a village was a sign of peacefulness, protection, and nourishment. The smoke was the center of everyday human existence. During rituals they burned very specific plants. The Celtic people did not build temples or churches; they preferred to make contact with their gods in sacred groves surrounded by nature. They used specific wood for their sacrificial fires. We have also found evidence of fragrant wood and resins in burial sites. Excavations of graves show that the Celtic people gave their dead precious fragrant substances for the journey to the beyond. Archeologists found frankincense, resins, and small stoneware vessels used for burning incense.

Through contact with other peoples, such as the Etruscans, Romans, and Greeks, the Celtics learned of many different incense-burning substances and incorporated them into their own customs.

Once settled, people began to experience the seasons and their different qualities much more intensely. As reconstructed in the book *The White Goddess,* by Robert Graves, the Celtic calendar consisted of 13 months, or moons, with 28 days in each. Each month was named for a tree, and each name stood for a consonant of the Celtic "tree alphabet." They also gave the nights of the solstices and equinoxes the names of plants:

The Night of the Silver Fir
December 21

The Night of the Gorse
March 21

The Night of the Heather
June 21

The Night of the White Poplar
September 23

In this same way, they connected every seasonal feast to a certain plant, and each had a different purpose.

Incense-Burning Culture in the North European Steppe

Our journey in search of traces of incense-burning traditions requires that we leave the protection of the big forests that covered the land in ancient northern Europe. Today, of course, much of northern Europe is a sort of treeless industrial landscape, similar to what the Celts left behind.

The ancient forest has disappeared. But we should continue our search in places where we can still find something of the ancient knowledge, for instance, in places where forests have survived or in the mountains. In the

"Tinder mushroom"

Alps in Germany, Austria, and Switzerland we can still find ancient traditions that are alive and well.

In primarily Catholic and rural areas, people still keep the tradition of the 12 days between Christmas and the Day of the Three Kings, January 6th. They still practice the custom of fumigating the house, stalls, and barn with red-hot coal in an iron pan. Originally, they used the "tinder mushroom." This fungus, *Polyporus fomentarius*, shaped like a large plate, grows on the trunk of beech trees or birches, but seldom on other trees. When dried beforehand, it burns for a long time and doesn't create sparks. They spread the incense generously on top of the burning medium and carry the pan through the house, stalls, and barn. In earlier times, people would recite prayers during this ceremony. The incense mixture used for this purpose had a particularly strong and cleansing effect. It contained frankincense and juniper. Special incense-burning pans with a lid with many holes are still available in Austria today.

In contrast to the native people who lived in Europe, the

Celtic people knew frankincense resin well. Many Celts had been members of the army of Alexander the Great. They had accompanied him all the way to Persia, where they confiscated rich sources of frankincense and myrrh.

The original Celtic custom of cleansing ceremonies during the winter solstice stemmed from the belief that an important transformation in the cosmic earth year took place during this time. The natural year begins at the winter solstice with the longest night and the shortest day. The sun reaches its deepest point and begins to rise again, indicating that the power of light has triumphed. The days grow stronger and longer.

These times of change and transformation can also be dangerous for people when they give rise to chaos and a loss of orientation. As we know all too well today, depression can be particularly severe when the nights are long and the days short. We also know today that illnesses often increase around Christmas and during the changes of the seasons. According to ancient tradition, we need 12 nights in order to adjust to new situations, to leave the old year behind, and to get ready for the new. During the night, the unconscious is open and able to adjust the inner clock. In order to remain in harmony with this cosmic event, the Celtics would fast during this time of important transformation. Fasting served to make people more sensitive to the energies created during incense burning. People believed that the dreams they had during these nights were meaningful. To this day, people believe that nightmares experienced during these 12 nights are an indication of what is ahead for them in the next 12 months.

Twelve Nights for Cleansing

Why shouldn't we make use of the mystical nights between Christmas and the Day of the Three Kings (January 6th) to bring our internal clock into harmony with the rhythm of the universe? We could, for instance, use incense burning around this time to cleanse and put he events of the past year behind us. Supported by a strong mixture that cleanses the atmosphere, we might want to go through our house or apartment and imagine that we are dissolving everything that was burdensome and unhealthy during the past year. During the first six nights, we should let our thoughts walk through the old year once again, sorting it out, evaluating it, and bringing it to a close. For the last six nights, we might want to imagine the coming year in positive terms. As we are walking through the rooms or sitting in

front of the incense-burning vessel, we might want to contemplate what we desire and "paint" a totally new picture of the new year, as we would want it to be. Incense burning creates a new and positive field of energy where new things can emerge. Prayers or songs are very helpful during these ceremonies.

Incense burning may make us more attentive to our dreams. Ancient cultures used specific incense substances to accomplish this. During these 12 nights, pay attention to your dreams. Write them down. The unconscious wants you to pay attention during times of change; it is eager to convey the messages that come from the depths of the soul.

Another tradition still alive involves incense burning at the end of the 12 nights. In rural areas in Germany, particularly in Bavaria, children go from door to door dressed as the Three Kings, waving a bowl of burning incense as they walk through people's houses. The pure frankincense fragrance cleanses the air and is a fitting conclusion to the rituals just completed and a wonderful preparation for what is to come. Let the new year begin!

The Herbal Bouquet

During the 12 magical nights, but also during the times when people are ill, the inhabitants of southern Germany still use an "herbal bouquet" for incense burning. On August 15th, the Day of Assumption, they collect special herbs. Usually, they collect nine, 15, or even 77 different herbs. All of these are

medicinal herbs, and we can trace their use back to Celtic-Germanic times. They braid the herbs together in a very special bouquet and decorate the base with ribbons. After the priest consecrates the herbs in church, they place the bouquet on the house altar, next to the crucifix. They pick off a few herbs at a time from this bouquet and use them for incense burning together with frankincense. This particular mixture is supposed to have special healing powers, which is why people also burn it in sickrooms. People still insist that this practice speeds up the healing process. They also use this particular mixture again on the Day of the Three Kings

Some herbs in this bouquet are called weather herbs because in early times people believed

Herb bouquet

that these plants could change the weather. As late as the beginning of the 20th century, whenever a thunderstorm threatened, people in rural areas would pick a few herbs from this bouquet and burn them to protect the house from lightning. We've also traced this practice back to the early times of the shamans. Some people believe that the Druids were able to influence the weather and that they most likely used similar herbs in their practices. The different herbs contained in this herbal bouquet work particularly well for incense burning during the winter. Incense burning frees the energy of the healing plants collected in the summer.

These herbs are very helpful in reducing depression during the long nights between November and February. When burning incense plants, try to imagine the sun-drenched beauty of the summer meadow where plants grow and consciously try to absorb their energies.

Where Elves Dance with the Gnomes

Where are the elves and gnomes of the Celtics? Are they hiding high up in the North, in the forests of Sweden and Norway, or do they live in the moors and mountains of the foothills of the Alps? The ancient Celtic belief in plant ghosts is buried deep in our subconscious, and every now and then it resurfaces. Iceland, for instance, has a very official elf map that identifies the places where natural beings are at home. In Findhorn, Scotland,

ghosts and natural beings seem to have found a place where they survive. People living in the Findhorn community have seen them in their gardens, where they give advice while the people are at work.

The conviction that plants are elves, gnomes, and elemental beings has survived to this day. We find traces of this in today's traditional and popular herbal medicine. Many of the common names we have given plants indicate the connection we still have with secret plant beings. The Celtic people believed that using specific plants could be helpful in getting in touch with these plant elves. Is there a chance that this custom would be effective today? Why don't you burn some these elf herbs and see for yourself?

Seers and Wise Women

The Roman emperor Tiberius persecuted the Celtic people and pursued the Druids relent-

lessly. For a time, Celtic seers had been responsible for the spiritual guidance of their people. The tradition continued in the Germanic era. Here, too, it was the wise woman, the seer, and the prophet who used plants for incense burning during rituals, prophecies, and prayers. This knowledge became part of Germanic tradition. Women healers of the early Middle Ages continued using it. Often acting as midwives, they used incense burning to make birth easier, to speed it up, or to reduce pain. They also burned incense to increase a woman's fertility and to act as a contraceptive. In the *Edda*, we can read about specific fruits from trees that are supposed to increase a woman's fertility when used for incense burning. These wise women also used incense burning to control painful menstruation, uterine prolapse, and menstrual bleeding. Women passed this knowledge on from generation to generation.

A medical book from the 13th century lists an incense-burning remedy for treating menstruation that is too weak or has ceased. The remedy contains myrrh, larch wood, and deer horn. The patient was to stand directly above the incense-burning vessel. A highly developed knowledge about incense burning for healing was alive and well during this time. However, the Inquisition destroyed much of this knowledge when the Church burned wise women as witches. Only a few written references from that period still exist. *Natural History*, written by the abbess Hildegard von Bingen, accused of witchcraft by the Church, is one of the last references to an ancient knowledge of the magic and healing power of plants.

Smoke and Magic

A few centuries later, physicians, philosophers, and alchemists in Europe began to pay attention again to plants used for incense burning. They were, however, primarily interested in the cult and magical effects of incense burning. A hunger for power seems to have influenced them. In the book by Agrippa von Nettesheim (1486–1535), *De occulta philosophia*, we find many recipes for incense-burning mixtures. These include plants such as hemlock, which can cause very severe hallucinations and possibly fatal consequences. These herbs create a poisonous vapor when burned. The scientist Carl Eckhartshausen (1752–1803), in his book *Magische Aufschlüsse (Magical Disclosures)*, describes incense burning that creates magical effects—conjuring up ghosts, calling on the dead, and making

the invisible visible. I don't think it is advisable to experiment with these recipes. They are difficult to control. Many of the herbs listed have very strong hallucinatory effects and can have considerable side effects. On the other hand, the herbs, plants, and mixtures discussed in *The Complete Incense Book* have absolutely no side effects on the physical, psychic, or subliminal level.

What Still Exists Today

We have now come to the present and will examine what we know about incense burning. You will be astounded! In Germany until a few years ago, the *German Apothecary* listed almost all the plants discussed in this book, and you could purchase or order them from specialty shops. Wholesale companies that provide the products for apothecaries or drugstores carry almost all resins and plant materials used for incense burning, primarily for the treatment of asthma. Remnants of the age-old art of incense burning have survived to the present day.

And now we notice a growing interest in incense burning as

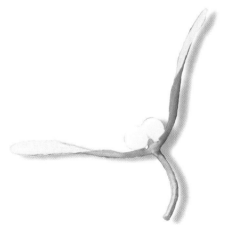

more and more people discover its balancing, healing, and soothing powers.

Inulin

Inula helenium L.

The real inulin plant belongs to the Asteraceae family. Originally from central Asia, it now grows only in the wild in Europe, Japan, and North America. We assume that the Celts brought this plant with them from central Asia as they migrated to Europe. The inulin plant is easy to cultivate in the garden. It is a stately plant with sweeping branches and grows up to 52 in. (130 cm) tall. It has large leaves, and from June to October it produces golden yellow, sun-shaped flowers on the tips of strong stems. Many different names are in use for this plant. All say something about its special healing power and suggest its use in the past during ritual practices. The inulin plant is among the oldest healing plants in Europe, known to Hippocratic practitioners, who called it *helenion*. The root of the plant played a large role in the Middle Ages as a universal remedy. Because it has strong mucus-dissolving properties, strengthens the lungs, soothes an irritated throat, and reduces coughing, it is an ideal remedy for bronchitis and tuberculosis.

As scientific research has shown, inulin reduces the growth of the tuberculosis bacillus even when diluted 1:10,000. The fresh root, a rhizome, has a bananalike smell. In the past, people ate it raw or cooked. The root is brownish red on the out-

Inulin

cense-burning substance. People there add it to mixtures used for cleansing, harmonizing, and healing.

Verbena

Verbena officinalis L.

side and light on the inside. When dried, the root has a delicate fragrance reminiscent of frankincense, subtle violet, and camphor. People have used the roots for incense burning throughout history. The roots were part of a mixture used for the summer solstice ceremonies and festivities. The plant symbolizes·the energy of the sun. People believe that incense burning frees the plant's innate power. Inulin also works well if you burn it during the short days of winter, when sunshine is rare.

Burning inulin is helpful in times of grief, melancholy, and depression, or even when you are just feeling low. Its fragrance

is calming in times of tension and stress. Nomadic people used the root to calm the horses that pulled their wagons, because they knew even then of the harmonizing energy of this root. Some people also say that burning inulin provides effective protection against illness-causing influences. They also say that it activates inner strength. Ancient writings describe inulin as a magic remedy and a defense against demons. Today, we would probably call these demons depression, melancholy, and gloom. Inulin creates an atmosphere of protection particularly during the dark days of winter. The type that is native to India, *Inula racemosa*, is highly regarded as an in-

Verbena grows everywhere in Europe. It belongs to the Verbenaceae family and reaches 20 in. (50 cm). The leaves are similar to oak leaves, and the small flowers are white-blue to blue. The traditional, common names still used in Europe point to a Celtic past. Verbena was one of the favorite incense-burning plants of the Celts. They used it during prophecies and for blessings during different sacred ceremonies.

Druid priests and priestesses used verbena to induce "truth dreams." In his *Natural History*, Pliny reported that Druids used this plant when they made their prophecies. And to this day, many people believe that verbena can influence dreaming and can be helpful in remembering dreams. In addition, they believe that verbena can prevent nightmares when used for incense burning or when suspended over the bed. In ancient times, it was part of recipes for a magic drink. People felt that verbena gave them courage and was helpful when they were fearful. Using verbena for incense burning helps in finding inner strength and developing new strengths. It is also helpful in times of exhaustion. It strengthens and supports centering when you are overwhelmed. Verbena is a good remedy for reducing the effects of shock. Many people believe it induces a good night's sleep and produces dreams that help solve problems.

Propolis

Propolis is a waxy resin produced by bees. It has a dark brown, viscous, solid consistency. Naturopathic medicine uses propolis in the form of tinctures to strengthen the body's own immune system, especially in cases of infectious diseases. Usually, you can buy propolis in health food stores. For incense burning, scrape off a few small pieces with a knife. The resin has a warm, balsamlike, honey fragrance that is very relaxing. When used in incense burning, propolis helps you reconnect with the healing power of nature.

Mugwort

Artemisia vulgaris L.

Mugwort belongs to the Asteraceae family. It is a tenacious plant that reaches a height of 5 ft. (150 cm). The plant grows in Europe, North America, and Asia. In Europe and Asia, people consider it a very important magical plant. Its various common names point to the role it once played in rituals and witchcraft. In the Anglo-Saxon witchcraft ceremonies, *Lacnunga*, which honors nine sacred plants, mentions mugwort first:

Remember, mugwort, what you have proclaimed,
What you have announced at the solemn demonstration.
Your name is Una, the oldest of all the herbs;
You have power over Three and Thirty,
You have power over poison and infections,
You have power over the evil that ravages the land.

This text goes on to describe the magical property of a belt woven from mugwort roots, the so-called midsummer's belt. Throwing such a belt into the fire, after someone has worn it, transfers the person's suffering to the fire. In other words, mugwort transfers through magic. People believe that it has cleansing powers. Therefore, incense burning with mugwort works well in situations that demand decisions and represent a turning point. It is helpful for letting go of the old. That is why, in ancient times, people burned mugwort at incense-burning ceremonies for the summer solstice. It is the time of year when the sun has reached its highest point and is beginning to draw back. Mugwort is very helpful in gaining introspection, discovering inner resources, and receiving advice from the unconscious. Traditionally, women used mugwort for incense burning during changes in their lives because it has balancing effects. As an ancient female herb, mugwort is something women should have on hand during puberty, birth, and during times of transition.

Mugwort is part of the traditional herbal bouquet and belongs with those substances that are protective. In addition, it also has relaxing, warming, and calming effects. Together with herbs that serve similar purposes, mugwort works particularly well for incense burning in the evening as a preparation for a good night's sleep. Mugwort, also called the "mother of herbs," can be helpful in activating a person's innate healing powers. It can initiate self-healing in cases of physical or emotional illnesses. Mugwort also strengthens the healing power of people in the health professions. Ancient tradition indicates that healers themselves used certain plants for strengthening, and mugwort and sage were two of the plants they used.

Hops

Humulus lupulus L.

We know hops primarily as one of the traditional ingredients for making beer. The hops used to make beer is a farm product. Originally hops was a wild plant that grew in Middle and Eastern Europe. It is a creeper that can grow up to 20 ft. (6 m) tall. The female plant produces cone-shaped flowers covered with scales like roof tiles. On the inside are small lymph nodes, called hop glands (*Glandulae lupuli*). Delicate yellow powder, called lupuli, falls out of the cone when shaken. It has a spicy,

valerianlike fragrance. In naturopathic medicine, it is a remedy for ailing nerves. It is calming and has a mildly sedative effect. In that regard, lupuli is an appropriate addition to incense burning when you need a good night's sleep. In herbology, people use hops to get in touch with the sublime energies of nature.

Fragrant Grass

Hierochloe odorata (L.) Wahlenb.

This sweetly scented European grass grows in northern Europe in the wild. The grass smells somewhat like coumarin and has the unmistakable scent of hay. This intense fragrance only develops during the drying process. In its dry form, you can finely chop it and add it to an incense-burning mixture. You can easily substitute sweet grass, which has an even more intense fragrance, for it. Both grow in North

America (see also chapter on *North America*). You can purchase both of these grasses as potting plants from a nursery. They work well in wildflower gardens.

Additional plants for incense burning used by the Celtic and Germanic people are: ash seeds, bead lichen, goldenseal, mistletoe, and elderberry pith.

Hops

1. Ash seeds
2. Inulin root
3. Elderberry pith
4. Verbena
5. Mugwort
6. Mistletoe
7. Hop gland
8. Propolis

Recipes for Popular Incense-Burning Mixtures Used by the Celts and the Germanic Peoples

Twelve Holy Nights

Frankincense resin	3 parts
Mastic	1 part
Herbal-bouquet mixture	2 parts

The herbal bouquet mixture should onsist of the following dried herbs: mugwort, verbena, sage leaves, mullein, balm leaves, inulin root (cut into fine pieces), St.-John's-wort, yarrow, mint, and chamomile flower.

Traditionally, you collect the herbs for this mixture between August 15th and September 8th. During this time, they have developed their optimum healing power and fragrance. Collect these plants around noon and allow them to dry on a piece of cloth. You can also tie them into a bouquet and suspend them in the air to dry. Dig up the inulin root, cut it, and allow it to dry. After approximately three weeks, when the plants are thoroughly dehydrated, crush all of them well. Mix with the pulverized resin and store the mixture in a dry place. This herbal mixture has a balsamlike fragrance. Use it for incense burning at the end of the year to cleanse and clarify the house and inside space. This mixture also works well for incense burning celebrating the change of seasons.

St.-John's-wort

Avalon

Frankincense	5 parts
Mastic	5 parts
White pine needles	1 part
Juniper berries	1 part
Mistletoe leaves or wood	1 part
Verbena	1 part

Pulverize the resins with a mortar and pestle. Cut the dried pine needles into small pieces. Lightly crush the dried juniper berries with a mortar and pestle. Mix everything together well. This mixture has a sharp, aromatic fragrance. It awakens the ancient spirits of the Celtic Druid and speaks of Avalon, the paradise island of the Celts. It hearkens back to Merlin the magician, King Arthur, and the seers living among the Celts. The mixture strengthens, reinforces, and helps to reconnect with the powers of nature. It is an aid to finding inner stability and the source of your own power.

The Game of the Elves

Mastic	5 parts
Propolis	2 parts
Elderberry pith	½ part
Fragrant grass	1 part
Lupulin	1 part

Propolis has a resinlike consistency. Scrape it with a knife. The inside of the elderberry twig is whitish and light. Scoop it out with a knife and cut it into small pieces. Dry the fragrant grass well and then cut it into small pieces. Instead of the fragrant grass, you may also use lemongrass. It is available in dried form in health food stores. Hops flower, *Glandulae lupuli*, also called lupulin, is available in pharmacies. Pulverize the mastic resin with a mortar and pestle. Add propolis and mix well. Next add the rest of the ingredients. This mixture has a fine, gentle, warm fragrance that inspires creativity and inspiration and makes us cheerful and relaxed. It is the door to the gentle powers of light and the secret powers of nature's plant world. This mixture is an invitation to dream and fantasize.

Duir
Summer solstice

Inulin root	1 part
Myrrh	1 part
Mugwort	½ part
Frankincense	4 parts
Sage	3 parts

Inulin root is available in health food stores and in shops where you buy other herbs or similar products. Cut the inulin root, myrrh, and mugwort into small pieces. Crush the sage leaves. Native American white sage is particularly good for this mixture (see also the chapter on *North America*). It is available in stores that sell incense-burning products. Crush the resin with a mortar and pestle and add it to the herbs. This mixture has a full, warm, balsamlike, and herbal-like fragrance. Use only a small amount, a pinch at a time. Place it on charcoal or in an incense-burning vessel. It works best outside. Traditionally, people used these herbs used during the summer solstice. The fragrance connects us to the high point of the earthly year and to the special energies of that moment in time. It connects us to the fullness of nature, encourages us to discover our inner wealth, and urges us to see and enjoy the body as a gift. It also connects the feminine and masculine.

Druid
Winter solstice

Frankincense	3 parts
Mastic	3 parts
Cinnamon blossoms	1 part
Pine needles	½ part
Clove	½ part
Sandarac	2 parts
Ash seeds	½ part

Cut the dried needles of the white pine and the ash seeds into small pieces. Pulverize the resins, cinnamon flowers (possibly also the bark of the cinnamon), and the clove in a mortar and pestle. Mix everything well. This mixture has a fine, ethereal, sacred fragrance that connects to the special energies of the winter solstice. It is an invitation to reflection, meditation, and prayer. It is helpful in letting go of the heaviness of earth. It works particularly well if you are searching for inner balance when your emotions are taxing and heavy. This incense mixture is powerful for cleansing the atmosphere in a room.

An offering I bring to the mountaintop:

Incense-burning vessels, seven times seven in number,

I place on the ground,

And into them I place sweet grass, cedar wood, and myrrh.

The gods have smelled the fragrance,

The gods smelled the pleasing fragrance,

The gods, like flies, came and surrounded the offering.

from "The Epic of Gilgamesh"

(written approximately 1200 B.C.)

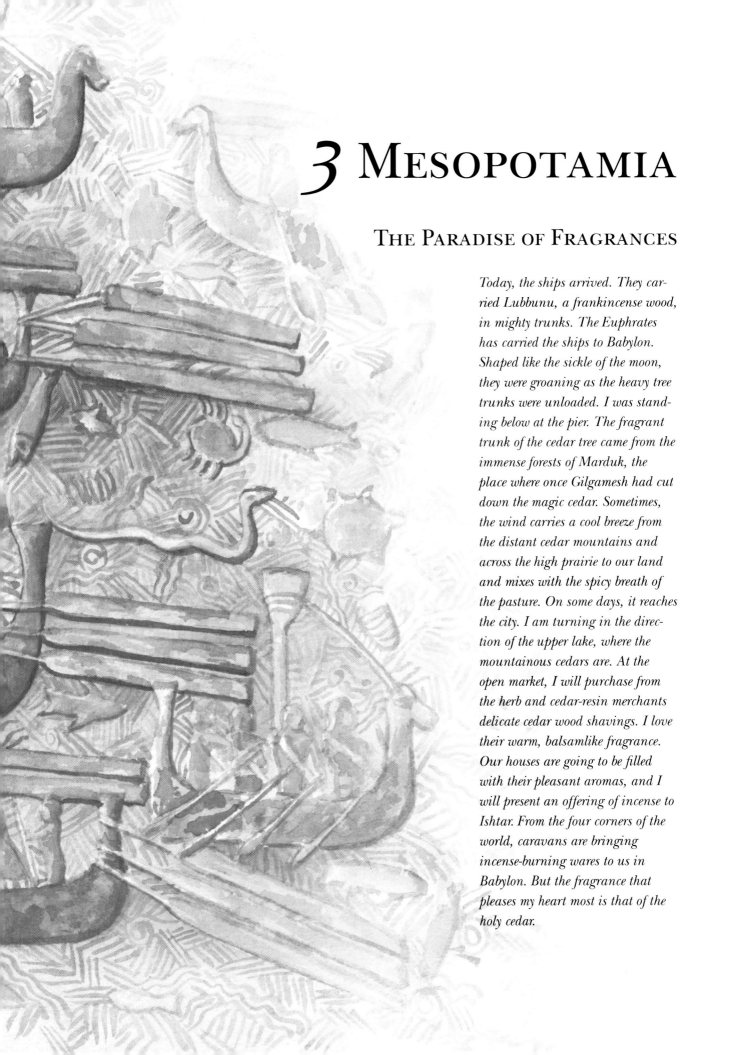

3 MESOPOTAMIA

THE PARADISE OF FRAGRANCES

Today, the ships arrived. They carried Lubbunu, a frankincense wood, in mighty trunks. The Euphrates has carried the ships to Babylon. Shaped like the sickle of the moon, they were groaning as the heavy tree trunks were unloaded. I was standing below at the pier. The fragrant trunk of the cedar tree came from the immense forests of Marduk, the place where once Gilgamesh had cut down the magic cedar. Sometimes, the wind carries a cool breeze from the distant cedar mountains and across the high prairie to our land and mixes with the spicy breath of the pasture. On some days, it reaches the city. I am turning in the direction of the upper lake, where the mountainous cedars are. At the open market, I will purchase from the herb and cedar-resin merchants delicate cedar wood shavings. I love their warm, balsamlike fragrance. Our houses are going to be filled with their pleasant aromas, and I will present an offering of incense to Ishtar. From the four corners of the world, caravans are bringing incense-burning wares to us in Babylon. But the fragrance that pleases my heart most is that of the holy cedar.

Pleasing Aromas from the Garden of Eden

The Tigris and the Euphrates, the two mighty rivers in Asia Minor, are the boundaries of the land that has always inspired people to dream about Paradise. Every story about the Garden of Eden originated in Mesopotamia. Here, in this "Land of Two Rivers," nature was well-disposed toward the inhabitants. The fertile ground provided food for them, and nature surrounded them with magical beauty.

Sir Austen Henry Layard, the English geologist and discoverer of the ancient Mesopotamian city of Nineveh, was very touched by the beauty of nature in this two-river land, despite the exhausting excavations:

Meadows displayed flowers in every imaginable beauty; they were not just sparsely strewn about in the grass, like in the northern climate zones. They grew in such thick, dense patches that the whole valley seemed like a quilt of many different colors.

Here, in the Garden of Eden in ancient Mesopotamia, every fragrance seemed to have found a home. Could you possibly imagine a paradise that smelled bad?

This description of the fragrant Garden of Eden appears in the Bible, in Genesis:

> *. . . and when God visited his angels Adam and Eve, . . . all the leaves in Paradise began to move, so that all the people, fathered by Adam, were lulled into sleep by this fragrant aroma.*

In other words, Paradise really did exist, at least until the invaders came from the East and destroyed it. One culture followed another: the Hittites, the Sumerians, the Akkadians, the Babylonians, and the Assyrians. They all disappeared. Where once flowering gardens and cities flourished, only sand, shrubbery, and the ruins of once proud cities are left today. But Paradise lingers in our memory, a place we still long for. And the fragrances of Mesopotamia can be the glimmer we need to dream about Paradise, where plants and fragrances bring gentle stillness. Ancient stories report that people have exported all the healing and fragrant plants from the original Garden of Eden, the "Land of Two Rivers," throughout the world. Thus, every pleasant aroma created during incense burning represents a piece of Paradise.

The Cedars of Gilgamesh

In order to discover which of the incense-burning fragrances was available to the people of the ancient cities, we need to decipher the countless stone tablets covered in cuneiform script. What we find is the first written evidence of mankind. Archeologists discovered it 93 miles (150 km) south of Baghdad at the beginning of the 20th century. It originally belonged to the library of Nineveh. The Sumerians wrote the heroic saga of Gilgamesh, the king of Uruk, who searched for everlasting life. Together with is friend Enkidu, he cut down the magic cedar, Chumbabs, actually the demon with a fatal breath, in order to break his power. When we read the *Gilgamesh Epic*, we discover the most favored, fragrant plant of that time. To thank the gods for having survived the great flood, Utnapishtim, the primeval father of the human race and the Babylonian Noah, holds an incense-burning ceremony using a recipe that he passes on to Gilgamesh: calmus, cedar, and myrrh. Ut-

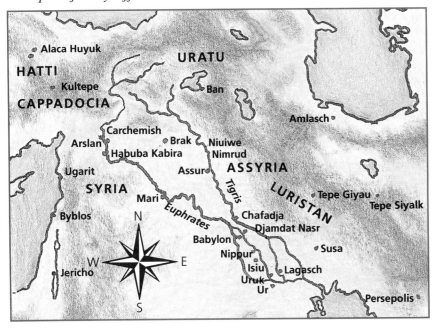

Cypress relief in Nineveh

napishtim says that the gods were so pleased with this incense-burning mixture that they surrounded the offering bowl like flies.

The people in the "Land of Two Rivers" had a variety of incense-burning and fragrant substances that have never been duplicated. Babylon, once the pearl of the Orient, and other cities in the "Land of Two Rivers" sat at the juncture of the most important connecting routes between the Far and Near East. As a result, these cities were important trade centers for precious incense-burning ingredients and spices. Caravans from all four corners of the world reached these cities. The earliest reports about the export of incense came from the Babylonians, whose merchants sold these fra-grant substances on their own streets as early as 2250 B.C. The city trade lists, carefully recorded on stone tablets, mention 200 va-rieties of fragrant substances. Herodotus reported that 29 tons (26,000 kg) of frankincense were burned on the altars of Baal-Marduk every year. The stone tablets tell us that the gods and the people favored very specific fragrances. These were the seven fragrances of Mesopotamia.

First mentioned on the list was the cedar, honored as a sacred tree. The word for frankincense was identical to that of the Lebanon cedar. The word "Leba-non" comes from the Akkadian word *Lubbunu,* which is also the basis for frankincense and cedar. The Mesopotamian cul-ture commonly used cedar and its resin for incense burning. They used the majestic cedar, the tree of power, magic, vitality, and immortality, for offerings, prayer, cleansing, healing, and many other purposes.

From the once enormous cedar forest that covered the mountains of Lebanon during the time of Gilgamesh, only 400 trees remain today. Over the course of the last few centuries,

Cedar tree

people would go there on pilgrimages to renew their energy and vitality in the shadow of these trees. As was the tradition in ancient times, the pilgrims were also searching for the holy oracle trees, hoping that they would reveal prophecies through the sound created by the wind as it moved through the treetops. They leaned against the powerful trunks of these trees hoping that the trees would cure their chronic illnesses. Today, people have reported that at an elevation of 4,000–6,000 ft. (1200–1800 m), they've found cedar trees with circumferences of 50 ft. (15 m). The oldest trees are at least 2,500 years old.

In the *Gilgamesh Epic*, Inanna, the goddess of love and vitality, invites the hero to:

> *Be my lover!*
> *Come into my house,*
> *Surrounded by the fragrance of*
> *the cedar wood.*

Let's take a closer look and try to reconstruct the recipe handed down to us by Utnapishtim, called the "Primeval Father." The recipe tells us to combine cedar, delicately grated and pulverized, with fragrant reed. Most likely, here, reed means calmus, which is very similar to reed or bamboo. Its roots provide a powerful, strong, cinnamonlike fragrance. A third ingredient in Utnapishtim's recipe is myrtle leaves, which added a fresh, gentle aroma reminiscent of eucalyptus. Herodotus has reported that myrtle was a particularly favored fragrance in the "Land of Two Rivers." People used it for incense burning as well as for oils, salves, and perfumes. Reports in the archives of the palace of Mari (1800 B.C.) tell us that during Abraham's journey, people pur-

Relief of winged deity, in Nineveh

chased huge amounts of myrtle oil to anoint priestesses and priests during ceremonies honoring the sun god Shamash. The myrtle plant, dedicated to Shamash, was a holy plant and a symbol of purity and love. The Bible often uses this symbolic meaning for myrtle. Even today, we give a bride a bouquet of myrtle on her wedding day as a symbol of purity and love.

In addition to the three plants mentioned above, people living in the "Land of Two Rivers" also loved to use cypress, labdanum, galbanum, and storax for incense burning. They used these seven aromatic plants in mixtures and individually.

Incense-burning altar in Mesopotamia

The Spirituality of Fragrances

The land between the two rivers had many different rulers, but the people never neglected the use of fragrances. Pleasant aromas always filled temples, houses, and streets. The inscription on one of the stone tablets reads:

During the procession, pleasant aromas overwhelmed the heavens like a huge hurricane.

People had elaborate incense burnings because no one wanted the gods to think they were petty and stingy. During Babylonian times, people burned frankincense by the ton on a golden altar in honor of the god Baal-Marduk, making sure that the message of fragrance would reach him. While people used fragrances to communicate with the gods in heaven, they also used them to communicate with the underworld. They believed that the ghosts of the underworld loved only bad smells and that pleasant aromas would keep them away.

Incense burning was also an important part of their burial ceremonies. They believed that the fragrance of frankincense, burned by their children, nour-

ished the deceased. Fragrances were also part of everyday life. The Greek historian Herodotus reported that people burned fragrant incenses in abundance during festive meals and that the Babylonians used fragrant salves generously as an integral part of their daily routine. They treated indoor spaces with pleasant aromas through incense burning. What we have then is a very refined, elegant, and well-developed tradition of using fragrances.

Abraham brought much of the knowledge about incense burning to the Holy Land. And later, incense-burning traditions,

Mesopotamian incense bowl

Mesopotamian bowls

developed in Mesopotamia, permeated Christianity. Indeed, Christian rites of worship owe much to Ur, a city established in the third century B.C. in Mesopotamia. The Catholic Church still practices incense burning during worship, and we still use incense burning in a room where someone is dying and during blessings and dedications. Many cultures have preserved varying uses of fragrances, lending a touch of Paradise even to our modern industrialized world.

Here, in the "Land of Two Rivers," the cradle of civilization, we find the oldest recorded instructions about the spiritual meaning of fragrances and the subliminal powers which they develop when burned as incense. People did not use incense substances indiscriminately; in fact,

they were very careful about using them. That is easy to understand when we remember that it was during the early Mesopotamian period that writing, mathematics, the codification of law, astronomy, and many other sciences developed. The practice of magic became more complicated, and incense burning accompanied each magical venture. Magic was common in Mesopotamian life and still exists today in superstitions that may be difficult to understand. A highly differentiated science of incense burning, far older than that of Egypt, developed in Mesopotamia. The culture of Mesopotamia is the source of many of our present traditions, and the basis for a great deal of our thinking and feeling originated there.

Want to see the present correctly? View it from afar. How far? Very simply: far enough So that the nose of Cleopatra can't be recognized.

—Ortega y Gasset

Let us then go past the beautiful nose of Cleopatra and put our own into the fascinating culture of incense burning in this land between the two rivers. Astrology began here during the time of the Sumerians. People worshiped the planets, stars, and constellations as gods. They considered these gods as the distant energy centers that influenced the earth and each individual person. They assigned each energy and each deity a specific fragrant substance. Here, we find the incense-burning rituals for planets that continued to be practiced in ancient Rome and Greece, even after Cleopatra. Mesopotamians believed that fragrances had the ability to awaken special cosmic energies or to bring them into contact with specific energy centers. This is not difficult to understand when we observe how fragrances can create an atmosphere in which specific things can or cannot happen.

The Sumerian people were the first to give soul to matter and to detect the purest essence in perfumes: their spirituality. The spiritual meaning they gave to flowers and plants . . . to daily life, gave new value and aesthetic sensibilities to their lives
—Prof. Paulo Rovesti

The delicate magic that fragrances can give to our lives, that can stir our most intimate feelings, was described first time by Sumerians. One of the stone tablets from their era states:

This little container contains hundreds
of rose blossoms from my garden.
Each petal reveals
a message of love for you.

Cedar

Effective Incense-Burning Substances from Mesopotamia

Cedar

Cedrus libani A. Rich.
Sumerian name: erinnu

The powerful cedar, often as tall as 130 ft. (40 m), came to Mesopotamia from Lebanon on the Euphrates and Tigris rivers. It grew in the mountains near the city of Ugarit in today's Lebanon. People used cedar for incense burning in the form of dried, finely chopped shavings, pulverized wood, resins, and the dried tips from branches. They used it by itself and added it to mixtures.

The cedar is a stately, majestic tree that has always been a symbol of strength, dignity, power, and vitality. From the very beginning of the incense-burning tradition, people wanted these qualities for themselves. By burning incense, they hoped to extract those qualities from the tree and absorb them. The cedar was the tree for magical, ritual cleansing, frequently practiced in Mesopotamia. People used cedar fragrance to cover up the unpleasant odor of animals burned in sacrificial fires, placing the carcass on top of cedar branches. For the Greeks and Romans, who also practiced animal sacrifices, the fragrances used during the incense burning were intended to make the ceremony more comfortable for the noses of the gods, as well as for the people present.

We have inherited many cleansing and atonement rituals

from those times, usually in connection with specific incense-burning ceremonies. For instance, ancient people followed lovemaking by burning incense. Here, the fragrance of the cedar was to provide mental cleansing. The balsamlike fragrance of the cedar would infuse a room, creating a mood of confidence and inner strength. Incense burning with cedar cleanses the atmosphere in rooms and spaces and cleanses objects suspended in the smoke. It supports self-confidence and trust during difficult situations in life. For example, incense burning with cedar is very relaxing during times of great anxiety and stress. The ancient Egyptians, as well as people in Mesopotamia, used cedar fragrance to create detailed dreams that could be helpful in finding solutions to critical situations. Cedar fragrance is ideal to support meditation and reflection. Since early times, people have considered the cedar to be the tree of knowledge that could awaken the inner counselor and healer during difficult times. The fragrance aids breathing and is effective in clearing respiratory passages of viscous mucus.

You can burn cedar on charcoal or small incense stove. The wood should be dry, finely grated, or pulverized. For incense burning, use the wood, resin, needles, or bark. You can purchase cedar wood shavings in herbal stores. They usually come from the Atlas cedar or the Virginia cedar. The cedar of Lebanon is almost impossible to obtain. The fragrance is woody, warm, balsamlike, and deep. The fragrance of the needles is lighter and more delicate.

Myrtle

Myrtus communis L.
Sumerian term: asu

The myrtle is a shrub 3–10 ft. (1–3 m) tall. The leaves are small, evergreen, lanceolate, and shiny. The brilliant flowers are a delicate white with eight petals

Myrtle

and small juniperlike berries. People used the delicate balsamlike fragrance for incense burning and added it to fragrant oils and salves. Every ancient culture considered the myrtle a sacred plant. Different cultures dedicated myrtle to a different goddess, including Janna, Astarte, Aphrodite, Venus, and the Virgin Mary. The plant was also the symbol for female purity, grace, and love. To this day, many Asians consider the myrtle to be very beneficial, equipped with very special powers. The fragrance reminds us of Paradise, and, so the story goes, myrtle is a particular favorite of the angels.

As an incense-burning substance, myrtle is used in many different situations. Myrtle creates a leaflike fragrance when burned. The dried berries are similar to juniper berries. They work well for incense burning and give mixtures a fruity fragrance. Dry the berries thoroughly and crush them with a mortar and pestle before burning. You can also use dried myrtle leaves in incense-burning mixtures. According to ancient beliefs, burning myrtle and using it in the form of essential oils, preserves love and youth. Burning dried myrtle mixed with mastic resin cleanses the environment. The fragrance of the myrtle contributes to a pure and clear atmosphere. It works well during prayer and meditation. It is helpful for healing old emotional wounds and supports forgiveness. Because of these attributes, it is a wonderful way to prepare for a happy new beginning.

Calmus

Acorus calamus L.
Sumerian term: Kanu babu

This aromatic, spicy, cinnamon-like fragrance of "the sweet reed," as calmus is also called, was a great favorite of the people in ancient Mesopotamia and Egypt. In the *Gilgamesh Epic,* they use calmus in an incense-burning mixture with cedar and myrtle to please the gods. Calmus, like cedar, is a nerve tonic. When burned, it produces a strong, spicy and warm fragrance. It strengthens nerves and is helpful during times of emotional exhaustion. The fragrance is a guide to the center of our own power. For incense burning, dry the root and finely grate it. Calmus is mainly used in mixtures (see also chapter on *Egypt*).

Labdanum

Cistus ladanifer L.

Sumerian term: ladunu

The fragrance originates from the rockrose, which emits a resinous dark brown mass from its leaves and twigs. In Mesopotamia, labdanum came from three different kinds of rockrose (see also chapter on *Crete*).

Cypress

Cupressus sempervirens L.

Sumerian term: surmina

People in many countries considered the cypress a holy tree and a symbol of long life, determination, and thoughtfulness. It was also their tree of life and death. A cypress tree can live 2,000 years. Mesopotamian stone-tablet inscriptions list the cypress as an ingredient for incense burning. Even today, people use cypress for healing purposes, including the treatment of problems of the respiratory tract. In ritual ceremonies, however, people use it for its psychological effects. Its strong, balsamlike fragrance can be helpful when trying to get a fresh start, set goals, and make decisions with more clarity. It can also resolve old griefs and disappointments. Ancient people saw the cypress as a threshold. They saw the fragrance as helpful when crossing the inner, hidden frontiers in their lives, making it easier to understand the reason for suffering and to integrate the experience. They burned dried cypress tips like grated, dried wood on charcoal. They also used the resin from the African sandarac tree, for incense burning (see also chapter on *Arabia*). It has a very delicate balsamlike fragrance.

Galbanum

Ferula gummosa Boiss.
Ferula rubri caulis Boiss.
Ferula galbaniflua Boiss. Buhse

Sumerian term: baluchu

Galbanum, also called "Mother Resin," is a plant similar to fennel. Originally it grew in the Mesopotamian area. From there, traders exported it to India, China, Israel, and Egypt.

1. Storax
2. Myrtle
3. Cedar
4. Galbanum
5. Labdanum
6. Lugal Banda
7. Calmus root
8. Cypress

Today, galbanum comes almost exclusively from Iran, where the plant grows in the wild. The dried milky substance inside the stem, called oleoresin, has a green, leaflike, woody fragrance that is reminiscent of spruce needles. The plant grows up to 5 ft. (1.5 m) tall and belongs to the Apiaceae family. The perfume industry still uses galbanum for its fresh scent. Galbanum comes in two different qualities: the galbanum from Afghanistan has a mild, grassy fragrance; the galbanum from Iran has a stronger scent. At this point, only galbanum from Iran is available on the market. Galbanum extends the burning time of an incense mixture. Many years ago, Pliny pointed out in *Natural History* that galbanum is a fixative that extends the life of the fragrance.

Galbanum has a glutinous, sticky consistency. You can form it into small pellets the size of a pinhead and burn it on charcoal. It has a heavy, sweet, balsamlike fragrance. For medicinal purposes, people use it for its antispasmodic effects and to relieve muscle spasms, for instance, during childbirth. They also use it in cases of colic and to relax the muscles of the respiratory system. One reason why it is called "Mother Resin" may be because people also use it to treat female conditions. Galbanum is also effective on a psychological and emotional level. It is very effective in relieving tension due to anxiety and severe restlessness. Here, it is used in combination with the kava kava root (see also chapters on *Egypt* and *Israel*).

Storax

Liquidambar orientalis Mill.
Liquidambar styraciflua L.

Sumerian term: balukku

The storax tree, also called the Oriental amber tree, is native to the area of Mesopotamia. Today, it grows wild in Asia Minor, Iran, Lebanon, on Cypress and Rhodes, as well as in the southwestern part of Turkey. We distinguish between four different types of storax. Two of these grow in China and Japan, one in Central and North America, but the tree discussed in this text grows in Asia Minor. The storax tree reaches a height of up to 33 ft. (10 m), usually as a shrub. It sheds its maplelike leaves at the end of the year. Using a tool shaped like a spoon, you can extract the light, liquid balsam from the trunk and collect it in sacks. Exposed to the air, it becomes glutinous and sticky. It turns a yellowish brown color. For cleansing purposes, thoroughly cook the balsam in water. When it rises to the surface, remove it and place it in a horsehair sack. Peel off the fragrant bark and boil it. Press it to remove the water. You should use alcohol extraction to produce pure resin from this glutinous balsam. It is dark black and offered on the market in pieces or as fine shavings.

Early on, people in Mesopotamia used storax gum as a substance for incense burning. From there, Phoenician traders exported the precious incense to Egypt. As they did in Mesopotamia, people in Egypt used storax gum as a fragrance on festive occasions that honored a dignified fragrance. Ancient

Storax tree

peoples knew that adding storax gum to an incense-burning mixture would intensify the fragrances of all the other sweet and flowery substances in the mixture and make the whole more brilliant. They also used storax as a substitute for true ambergris—a substance harvested from whales. Storax also preserves the fragrances of other substances. You only need a small amount to preserve the fragrance of an incense-burning mixture.

Storax gum is an ancient incense-burning substance used for medicinal purposes. People in the West have known this and used it this way for a long time. Because of its mucus-dissolving properties, people used it to treat bronchitis. Externally, they used it for skin conditions and scabies. Orthodox churches also used the wood of the storax tree in incense-burning mixtures (see also chapter on *Egypt*).

In addition to the seven favorite fragrances known in the Mesopotamian region, people used many other incenses including: juniper, frankincense, myrrh, mastic, rose, Dutch-pine resin, henna flowers, spikenard, cypress grass, mint, ambergris, cinnamon, Nagarmotha, costus, jimsonweed, benzoin, and opoponax.

Recipes for Incense Ingredients from Mesopotamia

Gilgamesh

Cedar wood, shaved	1½ parts
Cedar tips	1 part
Myrtle leaves	1 part
Calmus root	1 part

Remove the dried cedar needles and dried myrtle leaves from their stems. You can also buy them as a commercial mixture. Grate the dried calmus and mix all the ingredients together. Place the mixture in an incense bowl or use small amounts and let them burn on a hot stone close to the fire. This particular mixture produces strength and is uplifting. It works well in times of melancholy, doubt, or depression. It strengthens the inner hero, guides the eyes, and opens up the respiratory tract. This recipe is well suited for men.

Cedar branch with typical cedar cones

Lugal Banda
A festive fragrance of kings

Galbanum	½ part
Storax	1 part
Labdanum	½ part
Mastic	1 part
Myrrh	1 part
Tree honey, in liquid form	

Pulverize the mastic, myrrh, and storax. Add the galbanum and labdanum. Work the mixture well with a mortar and pestle. Add small amounts of honey until you can form the dough into small pellets, about the size of a pea. Place the pellets on a piece of cloth or a sieve and allow them to dry for seven days. Use on charcoal. This mixture creates a strong, sensuous fragrance. It is like giving your senses a special gift. It relaxes on a very deep level. Because it stimulates sensuality, it is ideal for a beautiful hour for two.

Ishtar
For the great goddess

Cedar wood, shaved	2 parts
Opoponax	1 part
Benzoin	1 part
Cinnamon bark	½ part

Pulverize the resins and bark and add the finely grated wood. This mixture has a powerful, warm, balsamlike fragrance. It connects to the power of the divine feminine and is a benediction presented by the great goddess, regardless of whether you call her Ishtar, Astarte, or Mary. The fragrance creates an atmosphere of vitality and inner strength. It is particularly suited to women.

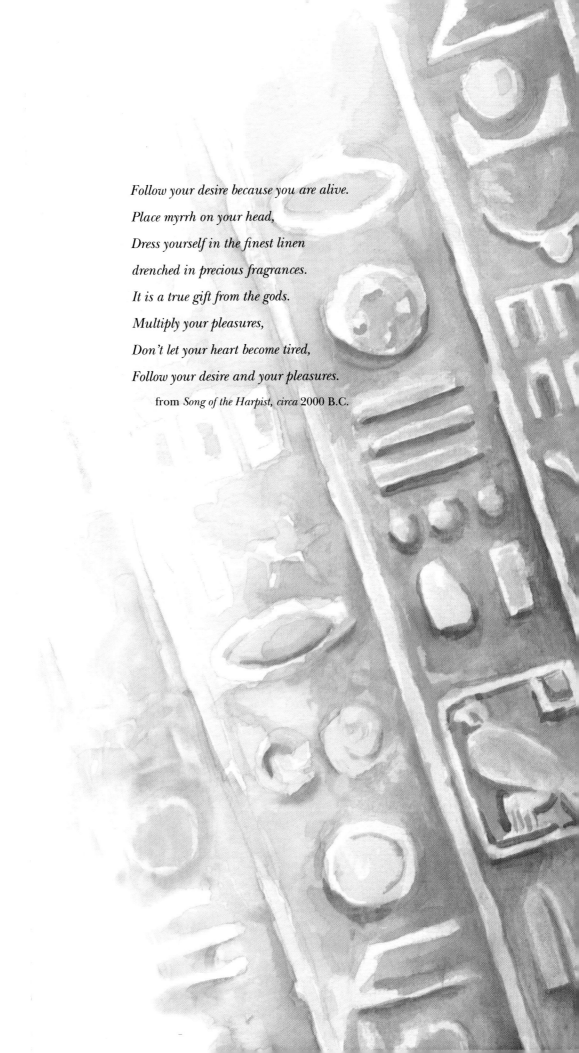

Follow your desire because you are alive.

Place myrrh on your head,

Dress yourself in the finest linen

drenched in precious fragrances.

It is a true gift from the gods.

Multiply your pleasures,

Don't let your heart become tired,

Follow your desire and your pleasures.

from *Song of the Harpist, circa* 2000 B.C.

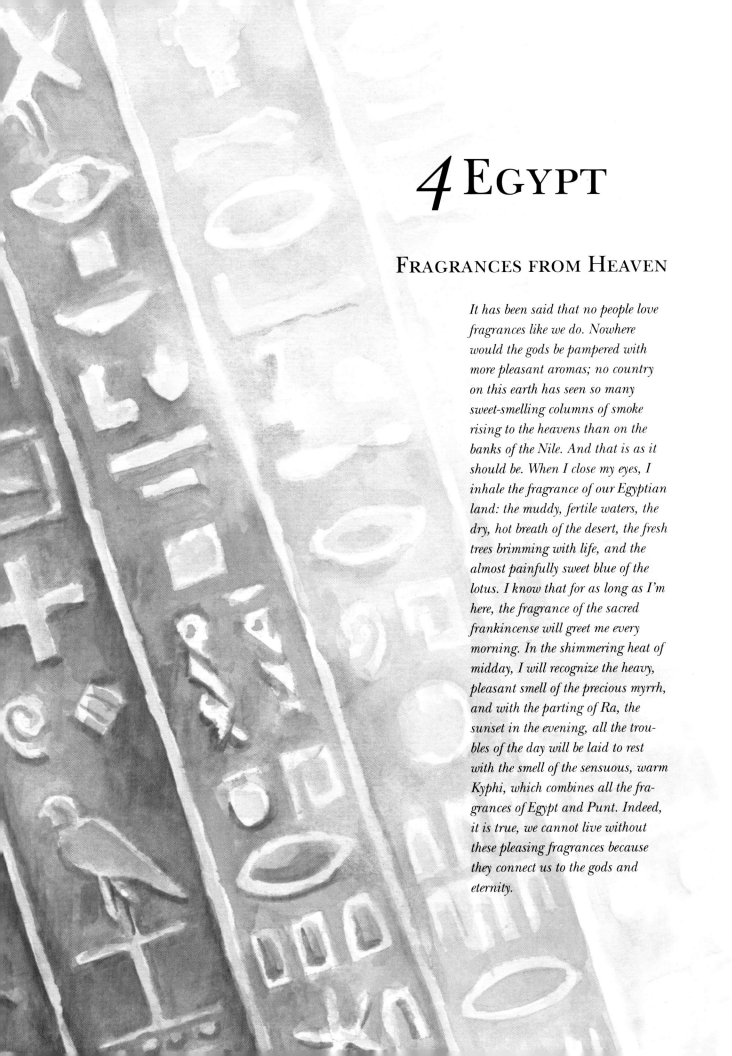

4 EGYPT

FRAGRANCES FROM HEAVEN

It has been said that no people love fragrances like we do. Nowhere would the gods be pampered with more pleasant aromas; no country on this earth has seen so many sweet-smelling columns of smoke rising to the heavens than on the banks of the Nile. And that is as it should be. When I close my eyes, I inhale the fragrance of our Egyptian land: the muddy, fertile waters, the dry, hot breath of the desert, the fresh trees brimming with life, and the almost painfully sweet blue of the lotus. I know that for as long as I'm here, the fragrance of the sacred frankincense will greet me every morning. In the shimmering heat of midday, I will recognize the heavy, pleasant smell of the precious myrrh, and with the parting of Ra, the sunset in the evening, all the troubles of the day will be laid to rest with the smell of the sensuous, warm Kyphi, which combines all the fragrances of Egypt and Punt. Indeed, it is true, we cannot live without these pleasing fragrances because they connect us to the gods and eternity.

The Route of Fragrances

The Egyptian incense-burning tradition began 6,000 years ago. During the time of the early, predynastic Badari culture (4500–3200 B.C.), it was a common practice to place fragrant tree resins in burial sites. Trees, with their roots buried deep in the soil and their crowns reaching dramatically to the sky, appealed to people's religious sensibilities during primeval times. They considered trees the seat of the gods. Their chances of survival in the hot climate of Egypt and Africa often depended on trees. In that sense, they saw the fragrances of the resins as the trees' breath and energy, which were aides for the soul. Burning resins

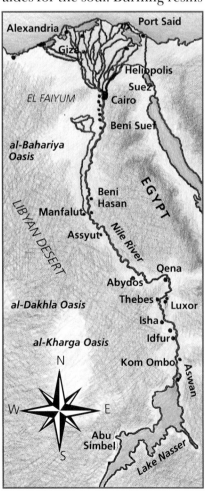

was an attempt to transfer a tree's magical life force to people. Families buried fragrant gifts with the dead to assure the deceased person's survival in the next world.

The tradition of giving the dead an incense-burning gift on the journey to the beyond was a custom that continued until the end of the ancient Egyptian culture. Many centuries later, when archeologists opened grave sites, they found burial chambers with ebony chests and marble urns filled with beautiful fragrances. Scientists analyzed the air in these burial chambers and found evidence of fragrance particles from incense-burning ceremonies that took place more than 2,500 years ago!

Merchants from India passed on the tradition of burning of frankincense and myrrh, two of the most favorite fragrances in Egypt. Indeed, the Egyptian people copied the tradition of incense burning from India. They believed it connected them to the gods. Most likely, the merchants from India were responsible for establishing the frankincense trade route, one of the most important trade routes in all of history. But traders carried more than incense-burning substances from Arabia on this route. The route itself connected different cultures with one another, which allowed trade to flourish. Beginning in the fifth century B.C., this road through the desert, 2,200 miles (3,500 km) long, became easier to use because of the domestication of camels. These replaced travel on donkeys, the "beasts of burden."

Travel from Asia to Europe became possible because the frankincense trade route connected to seaports.

As soon as the Indian merchants introduced Egyptians to the wonderful fragrances of frankincense and myrrh, the Egyptians were determined that they would never be without them again. They were fascinated, and no price was too high, no trouble too great to possess these precious incense-burning wares. Throughout the Egyptian empire, frankincense and myrrh became the most precious objects one could possess.

The Pharaoh queen Hatshepsut

Expeditions to the Land of Happiness

The appetite of the Egyptians for incense-burning substances grew rapidly, and people were not willing to wait until a merchant arrived with his wares. To honor

Terraced temple Deir el Bahri

the Egyptian gods and to sacrifice frankincense and myrrh to them, King Assa, Tet-Ka-Ra (3580–3536 B.C.), of Dynasty XI, went on an expedition to Punt, called the "Magic Land of Happiness," where balsam trees grew in abundance.

Punt is located at the southern end of the Red Sea. Frankincense and myrrh trees, although native to the region, were already rare. The most important route for world trade during antiquity began among these trees that flourished in that particular hot climate.

King Assa reached Punt by ship. Everything went beautifully, bringing honor not only to the gods but to the king himself. From then on, expeditions to Punt took place on a regular basis during this ancient kingdom. These events were so important, scholars recorded them in great detail on temple walls and in burial chambers. One of the expeditions particularly well documented took place in the year 1500 B.C., during Dynasty XVIII. Pharaoh empress Hatshepsut, the Daughter of the Sun, organized it. She was the first woman to occupy the throne of the pharaoh. Ever since this expedition took place, her name, her fame, and her beauty have been closely connected to the precious fragrances of Punt. Reports indicate that she was personally involved when the myrrh was taken off the ships.

Her Majesty herself is working with her hands.
The most precious myrrh is all over her body.
Her fragrance is mingled with that of Punt.
Her skin is wrapped in gold.

This wise pharaoh, the first extraordinary woman in world history, wanted more than the precious resin. She also gave orders to bring whole trees intact. This is the first reported botanical expedition. Five boats laden with frankincense, myrrh, gold, and 31 balsam trees re-turned years later. The trees were planted in honor of the god Amon-Ra and of Hathor, the goddess of love, at the terraced temple Deir el Bahri. This was the temple Empress Hatshepsut had built in the vicinity of Luxor. Hieroglyphics on the temple walls report:

Never has there been undertaken a transport like this by any queen since the beginning of the universe.

The myrrh trees themselves were also carefully painted on the rock walls. The people who carried them spoke the following words:

Myrrh tree come with us,
Come to land of the gods,
to the kingdom of Amon.
That is where you belong.
You will thrive like Maat
in the temple of Amon.

Frankincense tree

Flattering the Noses of the Gods and the People

Fragrant incense burning accompanied almost every facet of Egyptian life: sacred, medicinal, and aesthetic.

Sacred Incense Burning

"Gods love fragrances" is a frequent saying in Egypt, and ancient Egyptians burned them very generously during their incense-burning ceremonies. They burned something fragrant on a daily basis in every temple and on every household altar. Outside the temple, they sacrificed frankincense to the gods in flat, open, bowls that were often golden. The pharaohs burned incense even while conducting government business. A granite tablet shows Thutmose IV above the burning incense. In Heliopolis, the city of the sun god Ra, priests performed incense-burning ceremonies daily, according to where the sun was in the sky: frankincense at sunrise, myrrh at noon, and Kyphi at sunset—the latter a mixture of precious ingredients. The Egyptians considered fragrances so powerful, they were a sign the gods were near. They even thought fragrances were the breath of eternal life. Surrounding oneself with fragrances was to be close to the gods and eternity.

They burned incense as a sacrifice every day. They placed the incense mixtures in small clay bowls that had lids. Frequently, they removed the lids so the fragrant smoke could escape. Later, during Dynasty XVIII and Dynasty XIX, the Egyptians used beautifully carved pipes with small metal bowls on one end to burn small incense pellets on charcoal. Inside the house, they sacrificed incense on small cube-shaped altars. Outdoors, they used incense to mask unpleasant smells and keep insects away.

Incense Burning for Medicinal Purposes

Priests, as well as medicine men and physicians, had great knowledge of the healing powers of incense burning. We've found proof of this on medical papyri. Healers exposed sick people or at least the painful parts of the body to the smoke. Sometimes the treatment was followed by massaging the respective region of the body. This type of incense burning for the ill is one of the oldest reported healing practices.

The ancient Egyptians also used incense burning to drive illness-causing demons from the body. Some native peoples still follow this practice. Today, we know that intense fragrances,

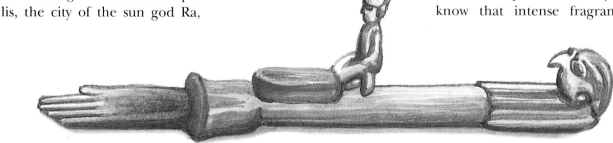

Arm-shaped incense-burning tool

such as the ones created by incense burning, have a strong effect on the human psyche. We can, for instance, easily imagine that incense burning can reduce, neutralize, or even dissolve illness-causing mental situations. Today, we call these demons fear, stress, restlessness, and depression. Specific incense-burning fragrances can lessen the effects of all of them.

Visionary Incense Burnings

The ancient Egyptians used incense-burning ceremonies to create visions of oracles, trances, temple sleep, and divination. The ceremony freed psychoactive substances in the plant, and the participants inhaled these. We find recipes for such incense mixtures recorded in books about magic and inscribed on temple walls. A few very specific recipes can be found in the *Leidener Magic Papyrus*. Ancient Egyptians often used visionary incense-burning plants such as alraune, blue lotus, poppy, harmala, and jimsonweed together with frankincense resin. Since these plants have hallucinatory properties and, when used improperly, can have strong physical and emotional side effects, you should not use them. The oracle shrine in Egypt, very similar to that of Delphi in Greece, was located in the Libyan desert near the Siwa oasis. The use of plants that had psychedelic, magical effects was always limited to occult practices and was supervised by experienced priests or priestesses. Visionary incense burning goes back to the primeval shaman times. It reached another high point in ancient Greece.

Incense Burning for Love and a Beautiful Day

Enjoying wonderful fragrances was not only for the gods. People, too, had the capacity to use fragrances for well-being, vitality, and sensuality.

For Egyptians, death was always present. They had a highly developed tradition of giving fragrances to the dead for their journey into the world beyond. They embalmed the bodies of the deceased with large amounts of myrrh and other fragrant substances.

But the fragrance of myrrh was also a symbol for love, sensu-

Incense burning using the incense "arm"

Incense burning using a cup

ality, and eroticism. Their awareness of the impermanence of life was a source of inspiration for the Egyptians and gave rise to the desire to experience the beautiful side of life consciously and to cultivate it to their heart's content. They expressed death, love, eroticism, impermanence, and pleasant fragrances in lyrics with unparalleled beauty and a deep magical and timeless wisdom. Shadow and light, awareness of death, and the pleasures of life were all part of incense-burning ceremonies. Against the backdrop of death, the joys and pleasures of life became more and more colorful and unique for the people of Egypt.

Nobody has returned
To make known their condition,
To make known their needs,
Which would comfort our heart,
Until we reach this place,
Where they are now.
Therefore, celebrate the beauty of
the day
And don't tire!

People used beautiful fragrances to increase joy and aesthetics, as well as for amusement and sensuality. Incense burning brought elegance and lightness to the life of the people of ancient Egypt. They wrote erotic instructions on papyri, lyrical poems of love, and even inscriptions on gravestones, all encouraging people to celebrate the beauty of the day. Fragrances, such as myrrh, sandalwood, cinnamon, benzoin, labdanum, storax, and Chinese cinnamon, increased beautiful hours, making them even more precious.

Birds of Punt appear on my horizon.
I am catching them, one after another, with my net.
One is saturated with myrrh, the other with frankincense,
Another again with cinnamon.
O loved one, I am longing for both of us to set them free,
One after the other,
So the movement of their wings will bathe us both
in the paradise of fragrances.

The above comes from a stone tablet found in a grave in Egypt dating from the third century B.C.

Ancient Egyptians often said, "A day without fragrance is a lost day." Even today, we have sensuously sweet incense at our disposal. Why not do as the Egyptians did: create a beautiful day that allows you to forget your troubles?

Soul bird

In the Laboratory of Fragrances

The highly developed Egyptian art of fragrances began with burning incense. The priests and priestesses prepared the incense-burning mixtures and stored

them in the back rooms of the temples. Priests competed with each other, trying to come up with the most beautiful mixture. They kept the recipes very secret

Hand-held incense bowl with Kyphi pellets

and wrote them down in "magic books" or chiseled them in code on the walls of their laboratories. During the first centuries, the practice of incense burning was strictly limited to religious ceremonies carried out by the pharaohs. Ramses III established the priesthood. Among the priests' responsibilities was selling precious substances to upper-level society. But over time, incense substances and other fragrant concoctions, such as salves and perfumes, became an important part of daily life.

The walls of the laboratories tell us about precious recipes for mixing incense and salves. Other sources are papyri, an offering pillar in the museum of Leiden, in Holland, and notes from Greek historians as they traveled through Egypt, including meticulous records of what they saw, heard, and smelled. These industrious reporters, who deserve our thanks for passing on the traditions of incense burning, were Theophrastus (fourth to third century B.C.); Herodotus, the

Egyptian man savoring incense

Greek historian and student of Aristotle (fifth century B.C.); Pliny the Elder, a natural scientist from Rome (first century A.D.); as well as Plutarch, the historian (first century A.D.).

The supreme patron of the art of incense mixtures was Toth, the god of pleasant aromas and wisdom. Special rites and prayers designed to maintain contact with this god accompanied the creation of incense-burning mixtures. Over time, the recipes became increasingly complicated and cumbersome. We have reports that one particular incense-burning mixture took a whole year to create. Each event and each time of the year had its own unique incense mixtures because the priests knew which fragrances had what effects. Each priest reached true mastery in incense burning. Never since has the knowledge of the use and effects of incense burning reached such a high level.

Kyphi for the Troubles of the Day

Ancient Egyptians burned some substances individually, such as frankincense, myrrh, opoponax, cedar, and juniper. Some favored mixtures that contained cleverly combined and coordinated ingredients which created whole new fragrances and new effects. Kyphi was the favorite incense-burning mixture created in Egyptian fragrance laboratories. Widely used throughout Egypt, it was also exported.

Trying to reconstruct Kyphi today requires us to piece together many different and partly incomplete notes. The best and most famous Kyphi was produced in the temple of Edfu, the temple erected in honor of the falcon god Horus. The priests of Edfu wrote the recipe in hieroglyphics on the walls of the temple. The *Papyrus Ebers* records other Kyphi recipes. In addition, papyri found in the pyramids of Cheops (Khufu) also lists recipes. Plutarch (first century A.D.) left instructions for a Kyphi recipe given to him by Maneton, an Egyptian priest. The recipe contains 16 different ingredients. Dioscurides, a military physician under Emperor Nero, wrote down a recipe that includes 10 ingredients. When we look at these recipes, we can assume that the following ingredients were part of the Kyphi mixture: frankincense, myrrh, cinnamon, sandalwood, cypress grass, juniper, calmus, coriander, mastic, storax, raisins, and wine. Rituals and prayers accompanied the creation of the mixture, which took several months. And we can imagine the praises about the pleasing effects of an incense-burning ceremony with Kyphi.

Plutarch enthusiastically states:

Kyphi can rock a person to sleep, create pleasant dreams, and chase away the troubles of the day. Burning Kyphi in the evening is sure to bring the gift of peace and quiet.

Horus at the temple of Edfu

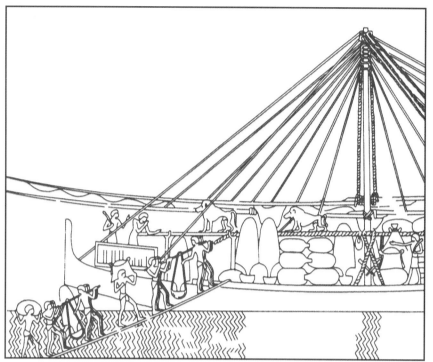

Loading frankincense trees

make use of the monsoon rains. During the warm weather, the ships drifted towards India. The cold winds that followed literally blew the merchant ships back in the direction of Egypt—laden with precious commodities.

The following is a list of the most commonly used incense-burning substances that were part of the recipes created in the laboratories and used in temples and in homes: frankincense, myrrh, opoponax, balsam, labdanum, benzoin, cinnamon, mastic, cedar, juniper, white cedar, galbanum, storax, calmus, cypress grass, henna, spikenard, aquillaria wood, coriander, Scotch-pine resin, jimsonweed, and henbane.

The most sought-after ingredients for precious incense-burning mixtures such as Kyphi were frankincense and myrrh. Initially, they were so expensive, only the pharaoh and his family, bureaucrats, and very rich Egyptians were able to afford them.

Because of its geographical location, Egypt was able to import a great variety of incense-burning plants from Arabia and the Near East, as well as Asia. More and more of these plants came from India because the pharaoh's seafarers were clever enough to

Measuring myrrh, imported from Punt

Effective Incense-Burning Substances from Egypt

Frankincense

Boswellia carterii Birdw.

Egyptian mythology tells us that the mysterious bird Phoenix brought frankincense to the land of Punt in its claws. This gives us an idea of why ancient Egyptians felt that frankincense resin was a special gift of the gods.

For the Egyptian people, its elegant, balsamlike, bright fragrance was the holiest, most precious, and most divine of all. In their language, frankincense meant "becoming godly." They used frankincense for sacred purposes conducted to immerse themselves in the spheres of the gods. Prayers and offerings accompanied the burning of this incense during funerals, official acts of state, coronations of the pharaohs, and daily rituals performed by priests. Pure frankincense has a balsamlike, spicy, citrusy scent (see also chapter on *Arabia*).

Myrrh

Commiphora myrrha Nees
Commiphora abyssinica Engl.
Commiphora schimperi Berg

Egyptian mythology tells us the tears of Horus, the falcon god, created myrrh. People were promised that,

Whoever partakes of this pleasant aroma has escaped death and will become part of the eternal life of the gods.

In ancient Egypt and later cultures, people perceived the heavy, earthy, aromatic fragrance of myrrh as sensually stimulating. Lyrical love poems use the characteristics of myrrh to describe feminine eroticism. But people also use myrrh for a quiet and healthy night's sleep. Plutarch reports:

Not only the air is changed by this pleasant refreshing steam. A stressed body is also given the pleasure of sleep. The troubles that have burdened us throughout the day are dissolved, and even our fantasies become as smooth as a mirror.

Egyptians used myrrh resin for hygiene, medical treatment, worship services, and magic. The Egyptians called myrrh *bal,* which translates to "driving out insanity." They used myrrh to calm the sick, to make salves, and to produce perfumes. Frequently, they mixed it with frankincense, benzoin, and cinnamon. It was a common remedy for wounds. Pure myrrh has a warm, balsamlike, earthy, spicy fragrance (see also chapter on *Arabia*).

Opoponax (Sweet Myrrh)

Commiphora Erythraea var. glabrescens
Commiphora kataf Engler
Opoponax chironicum Koch

Opoponax, also called sweet myrrh or bisabol myrrh, is a close relative of myrrh. Both belong to the family of the balsam tree, Burseraceae. In ancient times, people obtained opoponax from the *Opoponax chironicum Koch* family. But opoponax has almost been forgotten and is not available on the market anymore. Today we use the opoponax resin from bisabol myrrh instead. Both seem to have very similar fragrances. The resin is in the form of a rough, almost unsightly clump. But smell it, and you will be in for a surprise. This unsightly, dirty brown clump has a very gentle lavender fragrance! During the burning process, it develops an aromatic, sweet, balsamlike, pleasant aroma that is reminiscent of the cork of a red wine bottle or of old libraries filled with secrets. The aroma is lighter than that of the original myrrh.

Different cultures used opoponax in incense burning against negative influences. People believed that the fragrance of opoponax created a shield that protected against disasters waiting outside. Traditionally, they also believed that opoponax was capable of increasing intuition. Using this resin for incense burning works well to strengthen the senses and increase awareness. It supports intuition and inspiration. Opoponax strengthens exercises for balancing one's aura. Opoponax resin should not be too old, because it loses its gentle fragrance over time. To determine its quality, break off a piece and see if the surfaces are slightly oily and wet. Opoponax (bisabol myrrh) is available on the market now. The reddish brown solid resinoid is made from the raw gum resin of the opoponax through alcohol extraction. This is the form you want to use for incense burning. As with all resins, make sure it is free of any remnants of the solvent. If remnants remain, they will evaporate during the incense burning and the fumes may be detrimental to your health. Burn the resin on charcoal.

Balsam (Mecca Balsam)

Balsamodendron gileadensis Knth.
Commiphora opobalsamum (L) Engl.
Balsamodendron meccaensis Gled.
Commiphora kataf Engl

Balsam, also called "Balsam of Gilead," was a very precious substance in antiquity. Balsam was often part of the Kyphi recipes. Judea had the monopoly on balsam trees, and Egypt imported its resins from there. During the wars between the people of Judea and Rome, all the forests were destroyed. At the same time, the Egyptians attempted to start plantations of these trees. Balsam from Gilead is almost never available on the market (see also chapter on *Israel*).

Labdanum

Cistus creticus L.
Cistus ladanifer L.

This resin is from the rockrose shrub. The best aroma of labdanum comes from a plant originally found in Crete and imported by the ancient Egyptians. They used this gum for incense burning but also as perfume and for embalming. The resin was primarily used in mixtures. It was an ingredient used in Kyphi recipes. The Egyptians added the waxlike gum to other pulverized substances and shaped the mixture into the pellets that were extremely popular at the time (see also chapter on *Crete*).

Benzoin

Benzoin Siam-Storax tonkinensis Craib.
Benzoin Sumatra-Styrax benzoin Dryand.

This fragrant resin originally came from Sumatra, Thailand, and Laos. At first, Indian merchants brought it to Egypt via the ocean, but later merchants transported it on the frankincense route. Benzoin resin has a sweet, balsamlike fragrance that resembles vanilla. Since it has the same makeup as vanilla, the Egyptians used it for incense-burning mixtures they considered to be joyful. Benzoin from Thailand has a sweeter fragrance than benzoin from Sumatra. Both resins are available today. Benzoin from Thailand is very expensive and is considered the more precious of the two. The Egyptians preferred the fragrance of benzoin from Sumatra.

Because it does not develop a very pleasant aroma when burned individually, people use the resin primarily in mixtures. It burns very quickly, and the smoke is rather biting. If you want to experiment and use it by itself, cut it in small pieces and place them on aluminum foil on the charcoal or on top of an incense-burning stove. The effect is relaxing, calming, expanding. Incense burning with benzoin is good in the evening when it is usually mixed with sandalwood and cinnamon. It stimulates imagination and inspiration and is, therefore, appropriate when involved in creative work such as painting and playing music. In addition to its sensuous components, benzoin fragrance is also very comforting and very appropriate during bouts of sadness and when nurturing emotional injuries. It conveys a feeling of inner peace. For these purposes, mix it with frankincense and cedar (see also chapter on *India*).

Cinnamon

Cinnamomum zeylanicum Breyn.

The fragrance of cinnamon was very popular in Egypt. Egyptians imported the bark of the cinnamon and the dried blossoms from Arabia. Originally, the fragrance was produced from the bark of an African tree, *Amyris kataf.* Not until later did the people of ancient Egypt import cinnamon from Ceylon. The essential oil of cinnamon, used for medicinal purposes, cosmetics, and embalming, was also obtained from the bark of this tree. Cinnamon is highly effective in killing bacteria and for conservation, both of which were well known to the people of Egypt at that time. The fragrance is warm, spicy, and sweet. Today, cinnamon bark is easily obtainable as a spice. You can buy dried cinnamon blossoms in specialty shops carrying incense ingredients. The bark and the flowers work well for mixtures that need to be warm and sweet. You can burn the flowers alone over charcoal or in an incense-burning stove. (See also chapters on *Israel, India, Japan.*)

Cinnamon

Mastic

Pistacia lentiscus L.

The transparent, tear-shaped resin from the mastic tree generally comes from the Greek island of Chios. Egypt imported this popular incense from that island. It was an ingredient used in Kyphi recipes, but people also used it individually. Mastic has a gentle balsamlike fragrance. It is clarifying, cleansing, and balancing. In ancient Egypt, mastic was also called "the fragrance that pleases the gods" (see also chapter on *Crete*).

Cedar

Cedrus libani, A. Rich.
Cedrus deodora G. Dan
Cedrus atlantica Manet

Burning incense with cedar twigs and finely grated cedar wood was a very common practice in ancient Egypt. In the hot Egyptian climate, the fragrance of these evergreen trees created a comfortable, refreshing, and woody atmosphere. The most favored cedar was the Lebanon cedar. Ancient Egyptians considered the wood of the cedar tree to be indestructible. They used cedar oil for mummification. In the early days of the Egyptian empire, they often buried kings with cedar wood and branches. Today, we use the dried needle, the resin, or the wood. Because cedar creates a great deal of smoke when used by itself, you should only use it for incense burning outside. It creates less smoke when added to mixtures in powdered form. Cedar provides a warm, balsam-like fragrance. Good substitutes for Lebanon cedar are the Himalayan cedar, *Cedrus deodora*, and the Atlas cedar, *Cedrus atlantica*. Ancient Egyptians used the resin of the pine tree, *Abies cilicia*, to make rare salves. The resin and wood of *Abies cilicia* were a substitute for cedar.

Another evergreen used for incense burning in ancient Egypt was the avar tree. When dried, the tips of the branches have a resinous, spicy, somewhat strong fragrance. The resin of this tree, also called sandarac, is very similar to frankincense resin.

Juniper

Juniperus phoenicea L.
Juniperus oxycedrus L.
Juniperus drupacea Labill.

The juniper plant provides berries, twigs, and wood, as well as resins for incense burning. All were part of the Kyphi recipes. The Phoenician juniper, used in Egypt during the time of the pharaohs, grows as a tree or shrub. It is seldom taller than 16 ft. (5 m). It can, however, live for several hundred years, and this is why people in that area have always considered it to be a symbol for longevity and strength. Incense burning with Phoenician juniper has strengthening, cleansing, and revitalizing effects. The ancient Egyptians also used the resin from the Greek and Asia Minor juniper, *Juniperus drupacea*. It has a balsamlike, coniferous fragrance. However, the dried twigs and needles are very difficult to obtain today. You can use the one from North America instead. (See also chapters on *North America, The Himalayas, Sitting at the Fire.*)

White Cedar

Thuja occidentalis L.

Archeologists found pieces of white cedar in charcoal vessels in the tomb of Tutankhamen. We believe that incense was burned before the tomb was closed. White cedar has a warm, woody fragrance. However, you should only use it in small quantities or add it to mixtures. White cedar works well for outside incense burning.

Galbanum

Ferula galbaniflua Boiss
Ferula gummosa Boiss
Ferula kokanika Reg. et Schmalh.

This plant belongs to the Apiaceae family. The roots and the lower part of the trunk discharge the gumlike resin when cut. Galbanum looks like a thick, milky juice. It dries when exposed to air. When used for incense burning, it creates a spicy, woody, balsamlike fragrance that was very popular in Egypt. Galbanum, also called "Mother Resin," is usually used in mixtures. The Egyptians imported galbanum from Asia Minor, where it was also a popular incense-burning substance (see also chapters on *Mesopotamia* and *Israel*).

Storax

Liquidambar orientalis Mill.
Liquidambar styraciflua L.

Storax balsam is obtained by cutting the bark of the tree. It belongs to the Hamamelidaceae family. During ancient Egyptian times, as well as today, the plant was native to Asia Minor. Storax had to be imported through the Phoenicians. In the *Magic Papyrus*, Abraxas (fourth century A.D.) described storax as a pleasant incense-burning substance and recommended it as a substance for sound sleep. People in Egypt and Mesopotamia call storax *miniaki*, which means "festive fragrance." Black storax produces a balsamlike, sweet, flowery, feminine, intense, and

slightly grassy fragrance when burned. It adds a sweet, sensuous, and seductive note to any mixture. Storax has a calming and relaxing effect and works particularly well for incense burning in the evening. It is helpful in combating insomnia.

Poorly prepared storax creates a rubberlike odor when burned. People often mix storax with calmus; they seem to belong together, like frankincense and myrrh. Ancient Egyptians believed that this combination supported mental strength and self-realization. You can burn storax on charcoal or in incense-burning vessels, but you should only use it in small amounts and not too frequently. It creates its fragrance best when added to other mixtures. Storax is available as gum from Honduras, Iran, and Turkey. Turkish storax is considered the finest quality (see also chapter on *Mesopotamia*).

Calmus

Acorus calamus L.

Calmus belongs to the Araceae family and looks very much like a reed. The root stock (rhizome) has a strong, herbal fragrance. It grows on ponds, marshes, and at the edges of small rivers. The Egyptians preferred calmus that came from Phoenicia. They also used calmus roots in Kyphi mixtures and in homes for cleansing and sanitary purposes.

Together with cinnamon, calmus was the main ingredient in *Egyptium*, the famous Egyptian salve used throughout antiquity.

Calmus

In Ayurvedic medicine in India, people added calmus to incense burning for medicinal purposes to prevent side effects from medicines that were too strong.

Add calmus directly to charcoal or burn it in an incense-burning vessel placed on top of a metal grid or on a Japanese mica leaf. By itself, calmus is very strong, but it is less so when you add storax and mastic. Cut up the dried root into very small pieces and grate or pulverize them. Burning calmus as incense can strengthen self-confidence as well as create a better attitude for success in life. The substances in calmus strengthen the nervous system and improve energy. In antiquity, the tangy, aromatic, intense cinnamon fragrance was considered a symbol of masculine vitality and worldly success (see also chapter on *Mesopotamia*).

Cocoa Grass

Cyperus rotundus L.
Cyperus longus L.

For incense burning, people used the root of the grass, which grows in swampy areas in Egypt. It has an intense, aromatic, camphorlike fragrance, very similar to that of vetiver. The plant grows anywhere from 1½–4 ft. (40–120 cm) tall. It is similar to the papyrus plant and grew wild in ancient Egypt. Many of the Kyphi recipes use the roots of this kind of grass. Other grasses used for incense-burning mixtures are:

manna grass, *Cymbopogon confertiflorus*
spikenard grass, *Cymbopogon nardus (L.)*

Cyprus grass

citronella grass, *Cymbopogon martinii (Roxb.)*
Egyptian fragrant grass, *Cymbopogon schoenanthus L.*

Cocoa grass roots give incense-burning mixtures a long-lasting, intensive fragrance. They are very difficult to find today. Nurseries sell the grass as a plant for the edge of ponds. For incense-burning purposes, dry the root for at least three weeks before using it. A fragrant grass very similar to cocoa grass, called Nagarmotha grass (*Cyperus cariosus*), grows in the swampy marshes of India. Its fragrance is very similar to that of the cypress grass used in Egypt and can be a good substitute. The dried root of Nagarmotha grass is available on the market. It adds an earthy, aromatic, fragrant base to your incense-burning mixture.

Sandalwood

Santalum album L.

The clever use of winds during the monsoon enabled the Egyptian seafaring merchants to import much of India's precious incense-burning substances, including the fragrant sandalwood. This has a warm, sweet, woody fragrance and was an important ingredient for the Kyphi mixtures (see also chapter on *India*).

Henna

Lawsonia inermis L.

The henna bush is known mainly for the red dye it provides. In antiquity, its flowers were sought after for their fragrance, which is reminiscent of roses and lilac. In ancient times, the best quality henna flowers came from Cyprus and Sidon. They were a part of Kyphi recipes. Henna flowers are available today.

Spikenard

Nardostachys Jatamansi (Wall) D.C.

This plant was imported to Egypt from the Himalayas. The roots are the part of the plant that was used. The plant is similar to valerian. It was also part of some Kyphi mixtures (see also chapter on *Israel*).

Aquillaria Wood

Aquillaria agallocha Roxb.

This aromatic wood comes from northern India. Its dark, warm, balsamlike fragrance was very popular in Egypt. It was a particularly precious ingredient of Kyphi mixtures (see also chapter on *Japan*).

Coriander

Coriandrum sativum L.

This plant belongs to the Apiaceae family. In antiquity, people used the plant as an herb. Its seeds (fruits)—the part used for incense burning—have a spicy, sweet, and warm fragrance. The seeds add warmth to incense-burning mixtures. Coriander seeds have always been part of Kyphi recipes. The Egyptians probably adopted the tradition of using coriander from the Minoans (see also chapter on *Crete*).

1. Opoponax
2. Calmus
3. Myrrh
4. Sandalwood
5. Frankincense, first quality
6. Cinnamon
7. Cocoa grass
8. Labdanum
9. Frankincense, cleansed
10. Mastic
11. Storax
12. Kyphi
13. White cedar

Egyptian Incense-Burning Recipes

Now that we have looked at the long history of the art of Egyptian incense burning, you might want to get a feeling for what you have read and to create your own experience. The art of Egyptian incense burning can serve different purposes: meditating, finding inner peace and harmony, celebrating, worshiping, accompanying a ritual, and creating a spiritual atmosphere. Maybe you are longing for sweet dreams and better, healthier sleep? Or would you prefer to create sensuous, erotic nights? Do you want to experience a wonderful day, one that you wouldn't consider a waste? Choose among the following recipes or experiment with the individual ingredients that we have listed. Buy an incense-burning vessel, charcoal, and a few of the Egyptian ingredients and let yourself be carried on the wings of fragrance and time to the land of happiness!

Amon-Ra

Incense burning with frankincense

Pure frankincense has a balsamlike, fruity, transparent, and spicy fragrance. Use only frankincense of the highest quality (see also chapter on *Arabia*). Arrange small pieces of the resin, about the size of the head of a pin, but no larger than the size of a pea, on burning charcoal or a metal sieve placed on top of an incense vessel. Do not use too frequently, only two or three times and only use small amounts.

The effect is cleansing, clarifying, harmonizing, elevating, and balancing. Frankincense stimulates the mind, supports inspiration, and protects by removing negative influences. It also supports inner reflection. Use frankincense for meditation, prayers, centering, spiritual inspiration, or for cleansing indoor spaces or objects. You can use it in the morning as well as during the day (see also chapter on *Arabia*).

Isis and Osiris

Frankincense	1 part
Myrrh	1 part

With a mortar and pestle, crush both resins and mix well. Burn the pulverized resins on charcoal or in an incense-burning vessel. Isis and Osiris is balancing, harmonizing, and comforting. It creates a peaceful atmosphere that is helpful during meditation, Reiki treatments, and energy-balancing massages. It is helpful in creating empathy, especially when two people want to get in tune with each other. It is very effective as a remedy for stress and works well any time of the day. The fragrance is like a mystical wedding, one that connects opposites. It creates a harmonious atmosphere in a room where people get together for sharing. It supports therapeutic treatments whose goal is to harmonize body and soul.

Hathor

Incense burning with myrrh only

Ancient Egyptians used myrrh exclusively for incense burning during midday when the sun was at its zenith. It has an earthy, heavy, and warm fragrance. It is relaxing, centering, and grounding. It connects to the energy of the earth. Hathor is helpful when you are suffering from anxiety, stress, or insomnia. It helps when you have a lack of imagination or when you have too much intellectual work to do. Pulverize pieces of myrrh and burn them on charcoal or in an incense-burning vessel. Use it only in small amounts. Myrrh is for people unable to accept their body in a positive fashion. It is helpful in treating cases of chronic sensation of cold. It is relaxing and helpful for the nerves. In addition, it helps dissolve mucus in the respiratory tract (see also chapter on *Arabia*).

Pleasure of the Heart

Frankincense	3 parts
Myrrh	1 part
Benzoin Sumatra	1 part

Pulverize the resins individually and then mix them together. Burn the mixture on charcoal or in an incense-burning vessel in small amounts, not to exceed a pinch. The mixture helps create pleasure wherever people gather together making music or painting. The fragrance increases creativity, inspires, and creates a magical atmosphere that produces harmony. Burning this mixture fills the heart with pleasure and opens the senses.

Egyptium

Mastic	1 part
Frankincense	1 part
Opoponax	½ part
Myrrh	½ part
Cinnamon bark	1 part
Calmus	½ part
Storax	½ part

Pulverize cinnamon bark with a mortar and pestle and add the other resins. Then add the calmus, which you've cut into small pieces or grated beforehand. Continue to work until pulverized. Add the mixture to the charcoal in small amounts, about a pinch at a time. This full and spicy mixture is balancing and harmonizing. It is suitable any time of the day to create a pleasant atmosphere in a room. Ancient Egyptians also used this mixture for perfumes. You can enjoy this fragrance alone or in a group. It inspires dreaming and well-being.

Maneton

Storax	1 part
Calmus	½ part
Frankincense	4 parts
Galangal	½ part

Pulverize all four ingredients with a mortar and pestle. The mixture has an intense, warm, powerful, balsamlike, spicy fragrance. It encourages mental activity and self-development.

Kyphi

Frankincense	4 parts
Mastic	2 parts
Juniper berries	½ part
Calmus	¼ part
Galangal	¼ part
Cardamom	½ part
Cinnamon bark or flower	1 part
Myrrh	1 part
Lemon grass	1 part
Rose leaves (dried rose buds)	½ part
Benzoin Siam	1 part
Sandalwood	1½ part
Aquillaria wood	a pinch as needed
Forest honey, liquid	½ part
Red wine, heavy and full-bodied	a tablespoon at a time, as needed
Sultana raisins, unsulfured	8 parts

Soak the raisins overnight in red wine. Pulverize the frankincense, mastic, myrrh, and benzoin with a mortar and pestle. Pulverize the cinnamon flowers, juniper berries, calmus, galangal, cardamom (with the skin), sandalwood (may be in powder form) individually with a mortar and pestle. Mix all the ingredients together with the resin powder. Crumble the rose buds and cut the lemongrass. Mix everything together well. Use ½ tsp. (2.5 ml) of aquillaria wood powder to 1 cup (¼ l) of this mixture. (If the aquillaria is not available, do without.) Remove the raisins from the wine. Blend everything in a mixer. Add the honey. Add the pulverized mixture and knead well. Crumble in the palm of your hand. Spread on a piece of cloth and allow to dry in a warm place. Do not dry in an oven or direct sunlight. Turn often. After seven to 14 days, depending on the temperature and the weather, this Kyphi mixture is dry and ready for incense burning. Ancient Egyptians formed pellets the size of peas and used them for incense burning. This fragrant mixture banishes the troubles of the day. It works well in the evening.

Crete, an island fertile and graceful,

Surrounded by the dark waves of the ocean,

Countless people call it home; ninety cities in all.

People from many tribes, of many languages:

Achaens, Kydonians and

Dorians, the native born Crete,

Sharing the land, with the aristocratic Pelasgeans.

The city of their kings is Knossos,

Where once Minos ruled,

The nine-year-old with Zeus,

Who spoke to the gods.

from Homer, *The Odyssey* 19:172–179

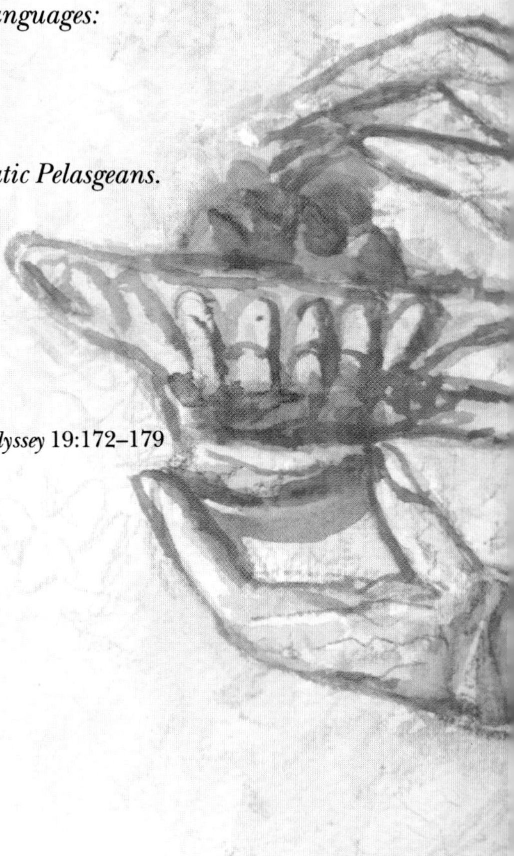

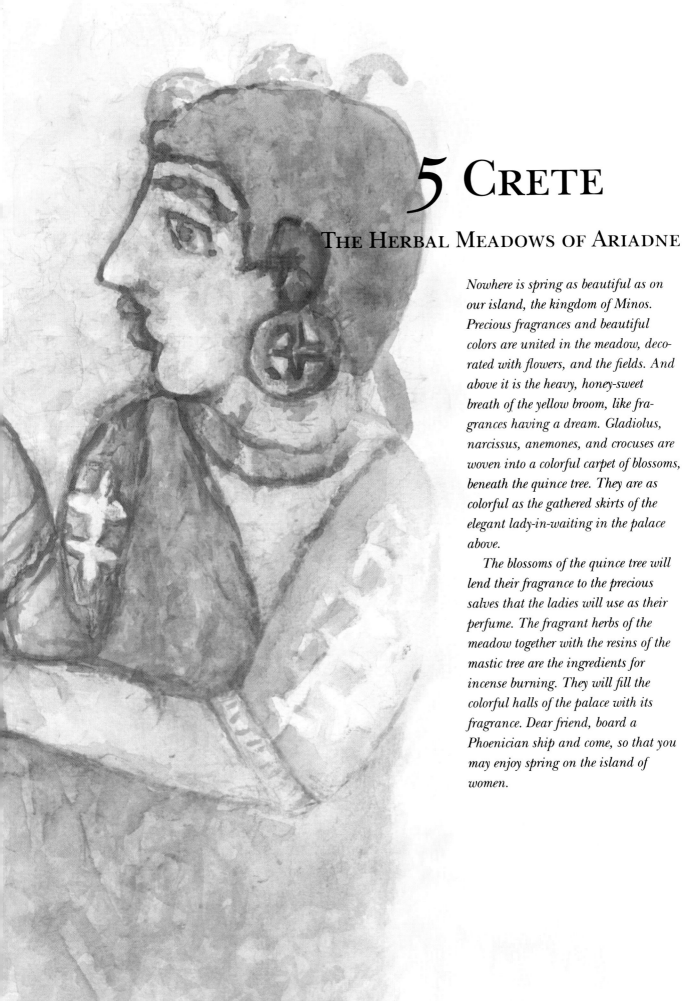

5 CRETE

THE HERBAL MEADOWS OF ARIADNE

Nowhere is spring as beautiful as on our island, the kingdom of Minos. Precious fragrances and beautiful colors are united in the meadow, decorated with flowers, and the fields. And above it is the heavy, honey-sweet breath of the yellow broom, like fragrances having a dream. Gladiolus, narcissus, anemones, and crocuses are woven into a colorful carpet of blossoms, beneath the quince tree. They are as colorful as the gathered skirts of the elegant lady-in-waiting in the palace above.

The blossoms of the quince tree will lend their fragrance to the precious salves that the ladies will use as their perfume. The fragrant herbs of the meadow together with the resins of the mastic tree are the ingredients for incense burning. They will fill the colorful halls of the palace with its fragrance. Dear friend, board a Phoenician ship and come, so that you may enjoy spring on the island of women.

Fragrances from the Cradle of the Occident

According to Greek legend, Zeus, disguised as a bull, abducted the beautiful Europa, a Phoenician princess, and took her to the sunny island of Crete. The culture that was to become the cradle for today's Europe began there 5,000 years ago. Crete, located at the intersection of Asia, Europe, and Africa, plays a very important role in the history of fragrances and incense burning. The Minoan traditions and customs that involve fragrances

The abduction of Europa

grances had a great influence on Greece, which developed much later. Greece and Rome did not really develop new incense-burning traditions but adapted those of Crete, Phoenicia, Mesopotamia, and Egypt.

For the longest time, the Minoan kingdom of Crete was only a series of legends from a time

far removed. These legends reported that Theseus, the son of a Greek king, had killed the terrible Minotaur, a monster shaped half like a human and half like a bull, who lived in the labyrinth beneath the palace of King Minos. But Theseus was only able to carry out this heroic deed with the help of Ariadne, the beautiful daughter of King Minos. She gave him a thread that allowed him to find his way out of the labyrinth. The story of the fabled palace of Minos moved out of the dark world of legends into the light of reality when Sir Arthur Evans started excavating the palace of Knossos in March of 1900. The excavation uncovered gigantic buildings that bore witness to a great matriarchal culture and discovered the fragrances that the Minoans seemed to favor most.

The Island of the Blessed

A papyrus from the 16th century B.C. includes an Egyptian recipe that discusses the fragrant ingredients of the land of Keftin, today's Crete. We learn about the harvest of the Crete iris and about narcissus plants that have different fragrances. The papyrus speaks about fragrant substances obtained from coriander, juniper, and wild fennel, as well as the aromatic resin of Scotch pine, storax, and rockrose—all of which were known at that time.

As we walk through the airy halls of the reconstructed palace of Knossos, not far from Heraklion, and look at the colorful, beautiful frescoes, we get a fleeting awareness of time long past. We are touched by the deliberate grace of the people depicted, their alluring elegance, and the beguiling pleasure of their lives. A culture shaped by women with feminine allure gives us a sense of the peace that surrounded them. The rigidity and oppressive nature of Egyptian and Mesopotamian architecture, which conveys a sense of a heavy, religious narrowness, is totally absent here. We see no sign of aggression or brutality. This kingdom, shaped by women, existed because of trade and maintained no army, no military base, no fortress. Most faces of the people have satisfied smiles. We get a sense that they feel comfortable in their surroundings and that they are moved by the magic and wonders of nature on their island.

We can still sense those feel-

Prince with lilies

ings today. Long after the demise of Crete, people still talked about this "Island of the Blessed." Each fresco portrays plants and people equally. We know that the people of Minos loved flowers. They grew narcissuses, hyacinths, irises, and tulips in colorfully decorated pots. Indeed, they even created "inside gardens." People who love flowers also have a great regard for pleasant aromas. The Minoans brought the fragrance of the surrounding nature inside by burning incense. The extensive flora of Crete provided plenty of inspiration and raw material. All of this lent itself well to creating a highly developed art of fragrances and an aesthetic sense. Fragrant oils, salves, and incense-burning substances from Crete were known throughout antiquity and were much in demand. They shipped these luxuries to faraway countries. Even in the fragrant land of Egypt, people

praised the aromatic products from Crete and used them whenever they could afford them, especially the fragrant salve made from the Minoan quince tree.

What fragrances did the elegant ladies—in the frescoes depicted lasciviously reclining in garden lounge chairs—wear? What was it that the athletic prince preferred as he walked through the lily fields? What kind of fragrance did they create from the incense-burning substances that filled the bedroom of Ariadne, the daughter of the mighty King Minos, the ruler of the palace of Knossos? As we learned when we visited Mesopotamia, inscriptions on stone tablets can satisfy our thirst for knowledge. A great number of these tablets have been found in Crete. Stone tablets were the books of their time. They were the means by which these highly sophisticated people recorded their knowledge. Where books made from paper would have been lost long ago, the stone tablets survived the fires that destroyed palace and libraries. This is the way the people of Crete preserved their knowledge about fragrant plants and the traditions of their time. These tablets allow us to reconstruct the Minoan tradition of incense burning and get a sense of what life was like on the "Island of the Blessed."

The Pleasant Aromas of Minoa

While they were searching for stone tablets, archeologists also came across objects of an ancient fragrance culture. French arche-

Goddess of the snakes

ologists discovered an incense-burning vessel in the eastern part of the island. The vessel contained charcoal that hadn't burned and remnants of coriander seeds, juniper berries, and the seeds of an umbelliferous plant: galbanum, anise, or fennel. Herbs for incense burning were also mentioned on the stone tablets. We learned that the Minoan kingdom used incense burning for sacred purposes. They assigned specific fragrances to certain gods. Which fragrances might have found favor with the famous goddess of the serpent? We do not know. What we do know is that six to seven different fragrances honored the gods and that huge amounts of fragrant oils and salves were sacrificed to them.

In Kato Zakros, remnants of a late Minoan salve kitchen were excavated and reconstructed in such a way that it was possible to determine which fragrant plants

the Minoans used in what way. People combined saffron, marjoram, mastic, labdanum, and many other aromatic plants to create fragrant salves, oils, and incense-burning substances. In their frescoes, the Minoan culture expressed what is divine and ever-present in nature in the way the painted flowers in bloom, in the way they depicted frolicking dolphins, and in the way they expressed the joy of beauty and the allure and lightness of the present moment. Incense burning was part of daily life and an expression of joy, the aesthetic of the Minoan people. Every house had a niche with an altar where they placed god statues and incense-burning vessels. The stone tablets also contained lists of other fragrances that people liked, such as rockrose resin, mastic "pearls," anise fruits, and many fragrant plants growing wild in the meadows.

People owned container vessels for incense burning. The elegant lady from Santorini, who appears in a fresco with a chic, short haircut, large earrings, and lips painted bright red, holds a small incense-burning bowl covered with an awkward-looking lid. Another version of this was an incense-burning barrel, a vessel in the shape of a semicircle with holes on one side. This incense-burning vessel, the so-called *thymiaterion*, had its own inscription. Inside the vessel Minoans would place hot charcoal and the fragrant substance they wanted to burn on it. Collecting our own incense-burning containers and a few fragrant herbs and resins, we are now ready to embark on a journey into the joyful life of the Minoan.

Effective Incense-Burning Substances of the Minoans

Labdanum

Cistus creticus (L.) Heyw.
Cistus ladanifer L.

The grayish white, hairy rockrose from Crete is a member of the Cistaceae family. It is a shrub that grows to about 4½ ft. (130 cm) tall. In the spring, the plant produces delicate, large, pink or yellowish flowers which are similar to the wild dog rose or wild rose. At the height of the summer, when the sun is hottest, it excretes a resinous substance from the leaves. The plant looks as if it is perspiring. The highest quality of this resin comes from Crete. Labdanum that grows in Crete has a particularly strong ambergrislike fragrance. Today, however, most labdanum comes from Spain, France, and Morocco.

The historian Herodotus was so impressed with the way people obtained this resin that he made special mention of it in his writings: "Labdanum has the most beautiful fragrance; but it comes from the most foul-smelling place: the beard of a goat." And to this day, the people on Crete drive their goats, not known for their pleasant scent, into thick forests overgrown with labdanum bushes. The goats eat their fill from the branches. And, coincidentally, the sticky resin from the leaves gets stuck on

their beards. When they return to the pen in the evening, their owners carefully comb out the beards. Then, they press the wax-like resin into small sticks and sell them. From the Middle Ages to today, people have collected labdanum resin with a rakelike instrument, a so-called *ladaniste-rion*. They drag the rake, with long strips of leather attached to it, across the bushes.

This deep brown, waxlike, fragrant resin was highly valued by the women of Crete. They burned incense with labdanum in the morning so that their clothes and body smelled wonderful. Bathrooms also had an incense-burning bowl in which they burned resin on charcoal. A famous cream that the women of Crete applied to their skin just above their low-cut dresses also contained labdanum, which was "framed" by lily, jasmine, and quince perfume.

The fragrance of labdanum resin is very complex. You can detect a new component each time you burn the resin: balsam-like, woody, earthy, marshy, ambergrislike, smoky, leathery, flowery, honeylike, mintlike, sometimes a scent of raspberry or ripe plum, celery, like oak moss after a rain, or fresh-cut grass. This fragrance, opening many doors, has fascinated people for centuries. It reaches deep into our subconscious and stirs memories, brings back pictures, feelings, and moods.

Someday, allow images to pass in front of your eye, allow secret, hidden strings to vibrate gently. Burn a small piece of labdanum resin, the size of a wheat kernel or pea, on hot charcoal. Close your eyes and follow the fragrance on your imaginary journey. Labdanum resin also works well for a simple Ko-doh ceremony, a ceremony described in the chapter on Japan. You will be surprised how much this experience unfolds.

The warm fragrance of labdanum is for people who feel an inner coldness and want to find inner warmth and sensuality. The fragrance strengthens body awareness. It is particularly good for grounding and for times when we've done too much intellectualizing and have lost touch with ourselves.

Ancient traders exported labdanum resin from Crete to all civilized countries. The fragrance captivated everyone. People wanted it to create their own symphony of fragrances. The Egyptians used it in Kyphi mixtures, and the Hebrews burned it in the Temple. Later, the Greek Orthodox church used it. A so-called "cardinal incense mixture," consisting of labdanum resin, calmus, storax, and myrrh, was well known in Europe during the Middle Ages. Today's perfume industry would hate to be without labdanum. It uses this inimitable fragrance to add a note of moss and leather to its products.

Labdanum is very glutinous. It is difficult to break and divide into portions. Try putting a clump of resin in the freezer and using the back of a knife to shave off whatever you need. Sometimes, labdanum is available in a more liquid form, which makes it easier to form into small fragrant pellets. Throughout the Minoan kingdom, labdanum resin was one of the basic fragrances for incense-burning mixtures. People usually combined it with mastic resin. They also added small amounts of other herbs whenever special and gentle nuances would be called for. Labdanum resinoid, cleansed in a solvent, is available in specialty stores.

Mastic

Pistacia lentiscus L.
Pistacia lentiscus var. Chia

Pellets or "pearls" of mastic resin, also called pistachio resin, come almost exclusively from the Aegean island of Chios. Physicians and natural healers of the past, who worked intensely with mastic, had nothing but high praise for its healing properties. In Egypt, mastic was a part of Kyphi mixtures and was used for mummification. The resin has disinfecting properties and strengthens the gums around the teeth. It was always a popular and healthful chewing gum. At one time it was even used for dental fillings. Because of its healing effect, mastic has remained an official part of natural medicine. People in Greece still use it as a spice for baking goods. In addition, it gives the Greek liqueur *mastika* its characteristic aroma. People use mastic to conserve wine, to produce liqueur, and to restore antique furniture. Traditionally, people have used it as glue for hanging posters.

Mastic grows up to 20 ft. (6 m) high. To obtain the resin, you cut the bark between June and Au-gust. Collect the resin, a natural oleoresin, which the tree excretes as soon as it solidifies. Scrape the resin off the tree trunk every two weeks. Each tree produces about 11–13 lb. (5–6 kg) of mastic during a collecting period. In the past, women sorted the resin according to size and purity, readying it for the market. The color of mastic "pearls" is light to lemony, often crystal clear. When burned, it creates a light, balsamlike, fresh, lemony, gentle fragrance. It is cleansing, clarifying, and mentally refreshing. People in northern Africa use mastic for incense burning as a tonic for exhaustion.

Mastic works well during meditation and reflection, and its bright radiant energy is helpful when you need clarity. The fragrance guides your view to the heavens and provides a sense of lightness. Burning mastic makes us clairvoyant and strengthens intuition and visions. Mastic works well for incense burning during times of depression, when you are feeling heavy and burdened. Experience the joyfulness of life as it was on Minoa: a life spent in meadows with abundant flowers. In ancient Greece, as well as in some of the Arabian countries, people burned mastic for medicinal purposes, and its effectiveness increased through visualization. The people present at a ceremony helped by visualizing that illness was being washed away, cleansing the soul and the body. For example, in Morocco, as a healer performs healing ceremonies for sick children using mastic, she imagines the plant's aura surrounding the child like a protective shield.

Mastic resin is available in the form of so-called "tears" or powder. You can burn it individually on charcoal or add it to a mixture.

Mastic blends with the individual components and reinforces

Mastic tree

the other ingredients of the incense mixture, giving it a special note. *Pistacia vera*, which produces those wonderful pistachio nuts, is closely related to the tree that produces the mastic resin.

Herbs from the Meadow

The Minoans used many of the fragrant plants found in abundance on the island for incense burning, perfumes, salves, and spices. Vegetation thrived, and the island was like a paradise. The barren landscape of Greece and Crete today is the result of clear-cutting the forests, which took place in later times.

Dried medicinal plants and herbs from the fields usually have a grassy scent when burned by themselves. They burn quickly and create a great deal of smoke. You should only use them for incense burning outside. You'll produce the best results if you add resins to an herbal incense-burning mixture, usually at a ratio of one part herbs to two or three parts resin. This is the ratio used in antiquity. The herbs discussed in the following pages are all combined with mastic resin. You can also combine pulverized and dried herbs with mastic powder. Work them in a dough with soft labdanum and form them into small pellets the size of a pea. Burn the pellets on charcoal. Make sure to dry the herbs well if you have collected them yourself. Try making a mixture with the herbs from the "Meadows of Ariadne."

Coriander

Coriandrum sativum L.

We use the fruits, mistakenly called "seeds," from the coriander plant for incense burning. Originally, this plant was not native to Crete. It was imported to the island from Egypt. Over time, it grew wild and spread throughout the vegetation in the meadow. Actually, coriander is not native to Egypt, either. Coriander came from India. Medical papyri list coriander as a treatment for joint pain. Arabian merchants spread the use of coriander throughout the ancient world. They brought it from India and sold it to Egypt. Some Phoenician merchants shipped it throughout the Mediterranean region. Coriander is still a valued incense-burning substance in Arabian countries.

People burn coriander to combat severe cases of tension, depression, and chronic headache pain. The people of North Africa believe that it lessens the effects of and defends against supernatural illness-causing energies. Coriander is able to restore inner balance and serenity. People often mix coriander with benzoin resin. Moroccan nomads conduct an incense-burning ceremony with coriander seeds and other substances for 14 days after the birth of a child. In the Arabian world, people believe coriander is a magical remedy to defend against disaster and to balance a distressed atmosphere. Although nothing conclusive has been found yet, we believe that the Minoans of Crete had similar traditions of burning coriander as an incense. However, what we are sure of is that coriander was a substance that the people of Crete used in abundance. They burned the fragrant fruits individually or as part of a mixture in small ritual bowls on the house altar for the pleasant fragrance and comfortable atmosphere.

Today, we can burn coriander by itself or mix it with substances that have similar effects, for a relaxing, balancing, and calming experience. Coriander, combined with frankincense, myrrh, and mastic, works well indoors when things seem out of balance in houses or in apartments where different people move in and out frequently, in places where there is a lack of peace and harmony, or where much arguing has taken place. The fragrance of coriander creates an atmosphere of harmony and works well whenever people want to make peace with each other. Coriander is available in stores that sell herbs or spices used in the kitchen. This is a plant that you can easily cultivate in your garden.

Anise

Pimpinella aniseum L.

Anise comes from the eastern part of the Mediterranean and from western Asia. It belongs to the Apiaceae family. The fruit has a hairy covering. When dried, the stem is 0.08–0.4 in. (2–10 mm) long. Anise is a very common spice. It aids digestion and reduces bloating. We use the dried fruit for incense burning. The fruit adds a sweet, spicy, somewhat fruity fragrance to any mixture. It is calming, increases well-being, and complements heavy or sharp fragrances in a mixture. We seldom use anise by itself. A good substitute for anise is Japanese anise, *Illicium verum*, which has a somewhat fuller and sweeter fragrance. It is available in stores that sell herbs and spices. The fragrance of anise is helpful for people who do a great deal of intellectual work. It creates a relaxed, comfortable atmosphere after work.

Quince

Cydonia oblonga Mill.

The name quince and its botanical name, *Cydonia*, came from the name of a Crete city, Kydonia. According to Greek legend, the Minoans planted the first quince tree in Kydonia. Evidently, the Minoan people were charmed by the fragrance of the fruit and blossoms of the quince tree. Quince salve from Crete was known throughout antiquity. The fragrance of the fruit is pleasant and fruity sweet. We use grated and dried quince for incense burning. Adding the fruit to an incense-burning mixture gives it a very elegant Minoan flair.

Mugwort

Artemisia vulgaris L.

The herbal fragrance of this plant is comforting and warming. Mugwort provides energy and strengthens vitality. For incense-burning purposes, we mix it with hop marjoram and add it to mastic (see also chapter on *Northern Europe*).

Hop Marjoram

Origanum dictamus L

Hop marjoram, called dictamus, is one of the mysterious plants of antiquity. During that period, people considered it to be a divination plant, helpful in getting in touch with the gods and predicting the future. Even today, many people still consider it a magical plant. Madame Blavatsky, the founder of Theosophy, considered it to be one of the most powerful of all magical plants. Hop marjoram belongs to the large family of Lamiaceae. Throughout antiquity, almost all reports praise the magical power of this plant. In Crete, hop marjoram grew in the mountains at elevations up to 5,300 ft. (1,600 m). Even in ancient times, it was one of the most desirable exports of Crete. Aristotle wrote that the wild goats of Mount Ida ate dictamus and became immune to poison arrows.

Hop marjoram from Mount Dicte (where it is said Zeus was reared) is supposed to have particularly healing effects. Those who use it for incense burning say it drives away all illness-causing influences. The dried plant creates a warm, herbal smoke that strengthens the subliminal shield around us. It protects against damaging, negative energy and is able to connect us to our own inner strength. When we have a particular wish, we visualize and concentrate our energies on it. Hop marjoram strengthens such imaginative energies and helps make them come true. (But be very careful what you wish for!) Hop marjoram used for healing purposes is helpful in strengthening the respiratory system. In general, we use it to strengthen our defense system. It is calming and harmonizing in cases of nervousness and fear.

Chamomile

Chamomilla recutita (L.) Rauschert

Use only the dried flowers for incense burning. The balsamlike, herbal fragrance conveys a sense of security and warmth. Use myrrh resin and mastic as a foundation.

Lavender

Lavandula angustifolia Mill.
Lavandula stoechas L.

The blue flowers give a faint blue note and a very gentle fragrance to incense-burning mixtures. Lavender fragrance is invigorating and clearing, as well as cleansing.

Laurel

1. Coriander
2. Quince
3. Hop marjoram
4. Labdanum
5. Mastic

Laurel

Laurus nobilis L.

When added to mixtures, the leaves of the laurel tree provide a balsamlike, spicy fragrance. People believe that laurel intensifies spiritual insights. In ancient Greece, psychics of the Oracle of Delphi used laurel leaves during their incense-burning ceremonies to induce states of trance. For incense-burning purposes, we mix laurel leaves with mastic. It appears that the Minoans used laurel leaves for incense burning. According to the story, the custom of burning incense during fortune-telling ceremonies spread from Crete to Greece. As was true with the Minoans, the ancient Greeks connected fortune-telling to dolphins. This is the source of the term "Oracles of Delphi." The laurel has also been described as the herb of the dolphins.

Marjoram

Origanum majorana L.

When burned, dried marjoram creates a warm, spicy fragrance. The Bible mentions this herb as an incense-burning substance. Later, during the Middle Ages, people said it was helpful in calming a sullen and angry spirit and it brought joy to the heart. It relaxes the central nervous system and, when added to incense-burning mixtures, combats tension and stress. It mixes well with myrrh and mastic.

Sage

Salvia officinalis L.

In every culture in which sage grows, people have used it for incense burning. It is cleansing and works particularly well to clear indoor spaces. It is able to dissolve negative and bothersome energies. Its antiseptic property has been well known throughout history. The burning of incense with sage was a specific practice in sickrooms. The sage that grows on the island of Crete is called *taskomilia*. This sage develops a notably aromatic fragrance (see also chapter on *North America*).

Rosemary

Rosmarinus officinalis L.

You can use rosemary twigs intact or crushed for incense burning. The fragrance is strong and herblike. This herb has always been part of traditional incense-burning practices. The Egyptians, Hebrews, Greeks, and Romans used it to fumigate living spaces and stalls. Rosemary is cleansing and provides mental strength and clarity. To burn sage for disinfecting and cleansing living areas and barns, you tie the twigs of rosemary, sage, and juniper tightly together with a cotton string. Shape the bundle like a cone, 6–8 in. (15–20 cm) long. The herbs must be dry. Light a cone at one end and allow it to burn briefly. Gently extinguish the flames. The herbs continue to smolder, producing a fragrant smoke.

Thyme

Thymus vulgaris L.

Thyme increases strength and endurance. People believe it strengthens willpower and self-confidence. Its strong herblike and warm fragrance creates comfort and boosts motivation. It is supportive in times of crisis when you particularly need assertiveness. Add it to herbal mixtures in small amounts. Thyme mixes particularly well with dragon's blood. Several different types of thyme grow wild on the island of Crete. You can easily grow it in more northerly areas. Nurseries that grow and sell medicinal plants offer several different types, such as lemon thyme or mountain thyme. Both work particularly well in dried form for incense burning.

Hyssop

Hyssopus officinalis L.

The Hebrews considered hyssop to be a sacred plant of mystery. The Bible mentions it 11 times. Its herblike, warm fragrance has strong purifying properties. It blesses and cleanses. For incense burning, mix hyssop with frankincense and mastic. It grows wild on the island of Crete. You can easily cultivate this plant in your garden. The dark blue flowers give a touch of beauty to every herb garden. Use the dried leaves and flowers for incense burning.

Recipes for Incense-Burning Substances from Minoa

The Island of the Blessed

Mastic	2 parts
Labdanum	1 part
Saffron	½ part
Coriander seeds	½ part
Japanese anise	½ part

Crush the mastic with a mortar and pestle. Use a knife to break the labdanum into small pieces. If the labdanum is too soft, use it as a dough and add the other pulverized ingredients. Form small pellets from the dough (see also chapters on *Mesopotamia* and *Japan*).

Crush the coriander seeds and Japanese anise. Mix everything together well. This substance has a warm fragrance reminiscent of a summer day on Crete. It will exhilarate and comfort the soul. It is a bright mixture that cheers you up in time of trouble and is very relaxing after a day at work. Taking a walk on this sunny island is an invitation to joy.

Ariadne's Meadow of Herbs

Labdanum	1 part
Mastic	2 parts

An herb mixture of: dried lavender, mint, sage, and hop marjoram—all 1 part

Crush the herbs, in any combination you like, between the palms of your hands. Crush the mastic with a mortar and pestle. Scrape the labdanum into small pieces with a knife. Use the mixture to accompany rituals and meditation. This recipe is a connection to the healing power of nature.

Blue Bird

Quince	½ part
Lavender flowers	1 part
Mastic	3 parts
Camphor	¼ part

Grate the quince fruit on a cloth or sieve and allow to dry. Crush the mastic with a mortar and pestle. Add the camphor powder and finely grated quince fruit to the lavender flowers. Mix well, but do not overwork. This mixture has a gentle, ethereal fragrance, reminiscent of the blue bird depicted on the famous fresco in Knossos. The fragrance brings cheer. Use it for meditation and reflection. The mixture also works well when burned to cleanse the atmosphere.

Harmonia

Myrrh	1 part
Frankincense	2 parts
Mastic	1 part
Coriander	½ part

Pulverize the resins and coriander with a mortar and pestle. Use only a pinch for incense burning. It has a balsamlike, sweet, and warm fragrance. It harmonizes and creates inner balance. It opens the hearts of those present and allows them to get in tune with each other. In case of restlessness, the fragrance can be helpful in calming emotional turmoil and scattered thoughts.

Stranger, be welcome in this famous land . . .

In whose eternal shade a thousand fruits thrive;

Heavily laden narcissuses composing

Sacred wreath of the gods

bloom day after day

Under the canopy of the heavenly dew,

And crocuses glistening in beautiful gold . . .

from Sophocles, *Oedipus at Colonus*

6 GREECE

ABOUT THE SCIENCE OF FRAGRANCES

We followed the narrow trail for a long time until the brilliant light of midday gave way to the gentle, warm glow of the late afternoon sun. We already had left behind the fragrant shrubs of mastic and labdanum. The trail was leading us through a Scotch-pine forest, the balsamlike, warm aroma of the trees surrounding us. Cinnamon-brown needles covered the warm earth and put a spring in each step. Now we became aware of the scent of damp earth, announcing that the spring must be nearby. In the distance, we could see red flowers glow between the branches. We could hear the murmur of the spring surrounded by oleander trees. The spicy, balsamlike fragrance of laurel was hanging in the sun-drenched air. Apollo was announcing himself: the laurel tree was dedicated to him. How much farther to the sacred Oracles? Yellow bees and sky-blue dragonflies were skimming the surface of the water; a dove sighed, and everything had the fragrance of a luxuriant fall. The reeds whispered their mantra, and I felt as if Pan, the god depicted with goat's feet, might appear at any moment. In our backpacks, we had carried precious myrrh that we wanted to sacrifice at the Oracle. Might we receive answers to our urgent questions?

Fragrances from the East

Long before the Greeks took over the elegant and highly developed tradition of burning incense, the Egyptians, Phoenicians, Sumerians, and Hebrews had been enamored of the fragrance of frankincense, myrrh, opoponax, and other precious resins. The Greeks were eager to embrace the fragrances that came from Asia. We believe that it was the Phoenicians who imported frankincense and myrrh to Greece.

It appears that during the time of Homer (around 750 B.C.), frankincense was not yet known in Greece. Nowhere in his writings does Homer mention this substance. In the early Greek period, people burned animals as a sacrifice to the gods. To cover the awful smell of burning flesh, they added pleasant aromatic woods, such as cedar, juniper, and myrrh, to the fire. They also used sulfur as an incense-burning substance during those times. It was Herodotus who first described frankincense:

Arabia is the only country where frankincense grows. The Arabs burned storax as incense instead, because frankincense trees protect the winged serpents.

It appears that Herodotus believed those horror stories spread by the owners of incense trees in Arabia and by Phoenician merchants. The location where the frankincense trees grew was a well-kept secret during the time of Herodotus.

The Greeks were eager to adapt foreign traditions, ideologies, and cults. From the very beginning, Greek culture was influenced by belief systems and lifestyles of the East. Philosophers satisfied their thirst for knowledge by traveling to the Far East or Egypt. For instance, Apollonius of Tyana went as far as India's borders at the end of the first century A.D. Pythagoras studied with Egyptian priests, and Plato tells us about the cultural exchanges that took place between Egypt and Crete. For the Greeks, the island of Crete served as a connection to the East. Imported Asian incense-burning substances became very popular in Greece. They used a great number of different fragrance substances for incense burning, as perfumes, and for medicinal purposes.

Incense burning played an important role in worship as well as in daily life, as depicted in images engraved on numerous antique vases. The ancient Greeks burned incense in so-called *thymiaterion*, adapted from the Minoans. Flute players often accompanied incense-burning ceremonies. Frequently, the vessel had an engraved image of the goddess Nike. One of the vases, now in a British museum, has a description of the preparation for the Dionysian festival. In the center of the vase sits the god Dionysus, surrounded by satyrs and women figures. One woman stands in front of a large incense-burning vessel in which a small fire is burning. She holds a bowl filled with round objects in her left hand. With her right hand, she is letting a frankincense seed fall into the bowl.

Apollo and Daphne

The Philosophy of Fragrance

The Greeks refined the art of inductive thought and looked at natural phenomena intellectually. They developed the use of fragrances, based on the Eastern tradition, to a very sophisticated level. The word "sophistication" expresses how well the Greeks evaluated and refined the science of olfactory experiences. For the ancient Greek, experiencing a fragrance was an epiphany, an event that revealed the presence of the gods; indeed, the experience was a revelation from the gods. The Greeks coined the term "godliness of pleasant aroma." Bad odors were to be avoided because they had illness-causing characteristics— sent by gods who hated humans. Theophrastus (300 B.C.), in his work *De odoribus*, writes about his philosophical and scientific observations of fragrances. He describes the origin of scent and its connection to taste. In addition, he discusses the use of fragrances, how the famous fra-grant salves were made, and the healing power of fragrant substances. The Greeks didn't need much time to create salve oils that rivaled those of the East, and the enthusiastic Phoenician traders soon began exporting them.

Alexander's Gift of Frankincense

Frankincense was one of the first precious resins that came to Greece from Arabia. It has been in use since the Trojan War. Pliny reports that it was well known as a resin used for sacrifice. From the sixth century on, the Greeks began to use pure frankincense for incense burning. Originally, they used it to cover up the bad odor created when they burned animals as sacrifices to the gods. Eventually, they burned incense at other times.

The knowledge and use of Asian fragrances is closely connected to the work of Alexander the Great. His campaigns to the East resulted in an "orientalization." According to an anecdote, young Alexander once carelessly threw a great amount of frankincense into the fire during a sacrificial ceremony. His teacher, Leonidas of Talmud, punished him severely. In *Alexander and Caesar*, Plutarch reports that Leonidas admonished Alexander to kindly refrain from wasting this precious incense until he had conquered the countries that produced it. This seemed to have affected Alexander deeply, because after he had conquered Gaza, he proceeded to send a whole shipload of frankincense and myrrh (more than 13 tons!) with a note saying:

We have sent to you frankincense and myrrh in abundance; so you can stop being so stingy toward the gods.

Alexander's campaigns in what is today the Arab world greatly enriched the frankincense tradition in Greece. He discovered new fragrances which complemented the ones imported from Crete. Just as in ancient Egypt, frankincense and myrrh continued to be the most highly regarded fragrances in Greece, despite the many different incense substances that were available. The fragrance of both was synonymous with the fragrance of the gods. People believed that burning the resin from these two substances created a message that would surely reach the heavens.

Frankincense and myrrh were both immortalized in Greek mythology. According to Ovid, who mentioned frankincense in his work *Metamorphoses*, Helios transformed the nymph Leukothera into a frankincense tree. Myrrh was originally *Myrrha*, the daughter of King Theias, who transformed her into a myrrh tree after she fled to Arabia. For the Greeks, all aromatic plants originated from the gods, and for every incense-burning substance mentioned in this chapter, we could find a mythological fable. You can find almost all the plants used for incense burning in Greece in Egypt, Crete, or Mesopotamia. Let's discuss them individually now. The use of laurel and amber, as well as incense burning with an astrological flavor, was typical of the ancient Greeks.

Fragrant Incense Burning for Everyday and for the Gods

Alexander gave the very special gift of fragrance to his fellow student, Theophrastus of Athens. This friend received seeds and cuttings from fragrant plants of the East. It was he who created the first botanical garden in Europe. The ancient Greeks used elegant fragrances to celebrate Alexander's triumphs after his campaigns. Incense-burning ceremonies using precious substances became a favored activity for the well-to-do. They burned incense as sacrifice on altars and during celebrations, feasts, rituals, and wedding festivities. But they also used it simply to create a pleasant aroma indoors and to keep insects out. They fumigated their homes, suspending their clothes in the fragrant smoke. Some incense-burning ceremonies were specifically dedicated to the gods. Fragrances were burned for the gods in flat bowls made of iron, bronze, and even gold.

The Orphikeans, who abhorred bloody sacrifices, used many incense substances in their rituals. They considered Orpheus the father of prophecy and the founder of all blessings and mysteries. Therefore, they dedicated frankincense and the practice of incense burning to him. The Pythagoreans, another group that refused animal sacrifices, also preferred fragrant plant substances for sacrifices and prayer rituals. For them, incense burning was the only means by which they could get in touch with the gods. They also connected frankincense with their belief in rebirth. The famous Eleusinian Mysteries, celebrated in honor of the goddess Demeter, included initiation rituals and rites of passage that made use of specific incense-burning substances.

Astrology and Fragrances

Like Plato, the people of Greece also believed in the influence of the stars. They believed that the stars shaped a person and that each person would return to his respective star after death. The planets helped a person to become whole. Fragrances, corresponding to their respective planets, could be useful in that process. It is here that Babylonian sources surface again. These also stated that the stars were the connection between humans and the gods. The Greeks had a tremendous interest in Babylonian astrology. The Babylonian Berosus (340 A.D.) was the founder of the school for astrology on the Greek island of Kos; he achieved great success. Incense burning also played an important role in the ritual celebrating the god Dionysus. The entourage of Dionysus, the ivy-crowned master of wine and divine incense famous for his feasts, included dancing satyrs and forest nymphs. Certain plants and fragrances were dedicated to Pan, the god of nature, and among them most certainly were those that created visionary dreams, because Pan was the ruler of dreams.

This is how the fragrances created during incense burning connected the gods and the stars with human beings in ancient Greece. The energy set free

would accompany a person during his journey on earth and then to the stars.

Greek Incense Burning for Medicinal Purposes

The ancient Greeks had a highly developed tradition of burning incense for medicinal purposes. Like Theophrastus, many other Greek scientists, healers, and philosophers have recorded the beneficial effects of fragrances. Pliny, in his *Natural History*, gave us a wealth of information about incense burning for healing. At the time, people believed that the best recipes for good health were sweet-smelling fragrances. Hippocrates also valued fragrances as healing substances and for prevention.

> *A fragrant massage and a fragrant bath are the best means to achieve good health.*

When pestilence broke out throughout Athens, the citizens burned huge amounts of juniper in the streets in order to prevent the infection from spreading. In the year 430 A.D., Hippocrates ordered that huge mounds of pleasant-smelling woods be burned to rid the city of the illness-causing, foul-smelling odor.

The Greeks burned many different plants to fight health problems: thyme for epilepsy, polei mint for fever, mint for weak memory, caraway seeds for female infertility, anise for pain relief during birth and for insomnia, celery seeds for sneezing and colds. Burning bay leaves and frankincense was supposed to eliminate illness-causing influences. It was believed that the fragrance of apples rid the body of toxins, and the scent of boiling cabbage reduced terrible headaches.

Healing Power of Temple Sleep

In early Greece, incense burning played an important role in sleep therapy. It was the foundation of what we know about medicine from ancient peoples. Because the physician was also a priest, he practiced healing in temples. Healing was still closely connected to spirituality. Sick people underwent sleep therapy in the temple, where incense substances and plants were pre-

pared for the occasion. People seeking help for insomnia went to the temple of Asclepius, where they could expect that Asclepius, the son of Apollo and the founder of medicine, would reveal to them the medicine necessary to cure their illnesses while they slept.

The Asclepius temples were located in particularly lovely places, surrounded by natural springs or in shady forests. People believed that a healing environment supported the health of the sufferer. We have reports of many magical healings from such places, just as we do from today's places of pilgrimage. These particularly charming shrines, built in the quiet of nature, were a reminder of the Kingdom of Chiron, the centaur who had taught medicine to Asclepius.

The Greeks had a special awareness of the beauty of surrounding nature and knew the important influence it had on healing. They even believed that the gods would reside there sometimes. The fragrant world of plants, the abundance of flora, the light playing with the shapes of the plants, all these were the foundation of the incense-burning tradition in Greece, to which fragrances of the East were added. After the priests healed the patient in the sanitariums with sleep therapy, they recorded the history of the illness and the prescriptions given in detail, sometimes even inscribing them on the temple walls. Hippocrates reported that he gained his knowledge and developed his theory about illnesses from these inscriptions.

Native peoples still practice therapeutic as well as visionary dreams. Today, we know about the phenomenon of dreams that confront us with our problems and sometimes present the solutions for them or the methods necessary for healing. The human spirit serves the same functions today as it did in ancient Greece. For that reason, let's burn incense so that we may make contact with the deeper layers of our unconscious. Fragrances have direct access to the base of our brain: the limbic system, the reservoir of emotions, dreams, and archetypal experiences. And science has confirmed that fragrances do influence dreams. We need to give this visual language of the unconscious enough space to unearth something of its richness for our normal everyday awareness. We can prepare ourselves for a healing dream by burning incense before retiring. Have a notepad and pencil on hand to write down upon arising the information gained during a dream.

Incense-burning fragrances are easy to use to uphold certain therapies. They even effectively support regression work.

Prophecies of the Pythia

The ancient Greeks prepared very specific incense-burning ceremonies for fortune-telling and oracle dreams. The word "oracle" also means "answer." The most famous oracle in ancient Greece was that of Delphi. People thought that Delphi, lo-

Aesclepius

cated in central Greece, was the navel of the world. This ancient, holy place of power, originally dedicated to the earth mother, had an opening deep underground from which sulfurous steam evaporated. Many Greek writers of that time described this holy place, which is why we have so much good information about what it looked like and

about the incense burning and oracle rituals that took place there. We know, for instance, that above the entrance to the oracle was the inscription, "Know thyself." Oracle incense burning was supposed to put the Pythia, the seer of Delphi, into a trance so that Apollo could speak through her. Laurel, frankincense, myrrh, and labdanum were probably the ingredients for this secret mixture.

As Greek mythology tells us, the Delphic cult originally came from Crete. In ancient times, people believed that dolphins were holy, mythological animals that lived on a level of awareness that people could only reach during a dream or in a trance. Dolphins were messengers of important information and prophecies that came from a place beyond the stars. We already know that on the island of Crete people used a great deal of labdanum for incense burning. The Minoans may have considered labdanum to be a bridge to the unconscious. We believe that plants with hallucinatory effects, such as henbane and jimsonweed, were among the incense-burning ingredients used by the Pythia. In a trance, sitting on a three-legged stool, the Pythia would announce her prophecies.

The Greeks often used poisonous plants with visionary and hallucinatory effects for magical purposes. They assigned the plants to the goddess Hecate, who was famous for her knowledge of herbs. Together with her daughter, Medea, she grew poisonous plants and magic herbs in a garden surrounded by a

Practice with Astrological Incense-Burning Substances

Incense burning for astrological signs uses individual substances traditionally assigned to the four elements, the planets, and the astrological signs. We may use the substances individually or in mixtures. An incense-burning mixture designed for a specific astrological sign can be supporting, rebuilding, and strengthening. It supports the characteristics of a person and can strengthen positive habits. The fragrant smoke conveys images and energies of the respective astrological sign. Onc might be able to rediscover the self in the mood created by the fragrance. Using an incense-burning mixture for a different astrological sign opens us to the possibility of experiencing a totally different mood, another view, another world connected to the self. In that sense, we become more open to other people, to the unknown, and to the new. We can see astrological incense burning as a walk through astrological signs, and we can experience them on their deepest levels through the fragrances.

high wall. You should not use poisonous plants for incense burning because, used improperly, they can have very severe side effects, such as mental distress and unconsciousness.

Fragrances that Connect Us to the Cosmos

Babylonian astrology was of great interest to the people in Greece and fit in well with Plato's belief that heaven and earth were interrelated. Babylonian astrology, Greek mythology, and the practice of medicinal incense burning became the basis for the development of incense burning specifically geared to the planets and astrological signs. In ancient Greece, people believed they could call on energies helpful for creating harmony and personal growth. They believed that certain plant fragrances stimulated energies that were in contact with the gods of the planets and created an at-mosphere that united the gods, stars, plants, and human beings. The Greeks felt that incense burning created "synchronicity," the concept that things happen that seemingly have nothing to do with one another. Today, our thinking has become increasingly linear, allowing the left half of the brain to dominate the right half. But it is the right half that holds intuitive knowledge. Because our psyche is split, we are out of balance. Burning incense might help us gain access to the closed-off part of our unconscious, to intuitive awareness, and to the reservoir of memories of the whole of human history.

Greek incense arm

The Elements

The study of elements, given precise definition in ancient Greece, states that healing takes place by using opposites. The four elements—earth, water, fire, and air—are divided in two opposite pairs: fire-water and earth-air.

Ancient Greek incense-burning bowl

When attempting to balance yourself or to lower your level of energy, burn incense from elements that are the opposite of yours. If your astrological sign is Virgo (assigned to the element of earth) and you are suffering from severe mistrust and rigidity, you would need the element air to remove these feelings and become flexible again. A Gemini (assigned to the element of air) who has become very nervous and who suffers from a lack of concentration because the air element has become dominant, might well become more grounded, relaxed, and focused by burning an incense that includes plants from the element earth. A hot-headed Aries, whose energetic temperament has turned into aggression and an-

ger, might want to counterbalance these feelings with incense from plants that belong to the element water. We select incense-burning substances according to their elements, making it possible to create mixtures that address each one specifically. These mixtures have strong effects. Burning incense according to the elements strengthens certain qualities, creating the atmosphere of these qualities and supporting and strengthening the rituals assigned to them.

Elements have been assigned certain energies and characteristics:

Element of fire
Energy, power, cleansing, and imagination
Element of earth
Concentration, judgment, and assessment
Element of air
Movement, information, and communication
Element of water
Emotions, cleansing, and healing

Incense-Burning Mixtures for Planets and Astrological Signs

The incense-burning substances discussed in this book have been assigned to specific astrological signs and elements. If you are planning on burning incense for a specific astrological sign or element, you can use one individual substance or create a mixture. They all carry the energies of the 12 hemispheres of heaven within them. You can make rituals designed for specific elements more profound with incense-

mixtures created for that element.

Why don't you experiment with these astrological incense substances and find your very own personal combination? You may want to try to create one for a friend or acquaintance. In the beginning, do not mix more than three different substances. Each mixture should contain at least one resin.

Aries
Fire
March 21–April 20

Thyme, coriander, cinnamon, laurel, red sandalwood, cedar, Scotch pine, tarragon, cardamom, galangal, ginger, clove, aloe, calmus, patchouli, masterwort, angelica root, benzoin, dragon's blood, verbena.

Aries mixtures are powerful and fiery. They strengthen boldness, assertiveness, and courage.

Taurus
Earth
April 21–May 21
Vetiver, spikenard, myrrh, rose, saffron, sandalwood, vanilla, common myrrh, hibiscus seeds, dill, patchouli, cocoa grass, tonka bean, moss, cardamom, propolis, guajak, opoponax, storax, aloe, benzoin, ambergris, Japanese anise.

Taurus mixtures have a comfortable and earthy fragrance. They support stability, endurance, and the ability to love.

Gemini
Air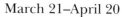
May 22–June 21

Mastic, galbanum, fennel seed, lavender blossoms, camphor, mint, laurel, nutmeg, sandalwood, verbena, storax, propolis, cardamom, coriander, cypress, dammar, galbanum, burgundy spruce resin, rhododendron, golden copal, desert mugwort, inulin, anise.

A Gemini mixture has a light, bright fragrance. It supports an energetic mind and the exchange of ideas.

Cancer
Water
June 22–July 22

Mastic, Scotch pine, jasmine, lavender, camphor, aloe, laurel, cedar, rose, patchouli, myrrh, cinnamon, sandalwood, spikenard, common myrrh, canary tree, ambergris, cherry resin, vanilla, costus, Irish root, elderberry pith.

A Cancer mixture has a sweet and tender fragrance. It supports creativity, intuition, and sensitivity.

Leo
Fire
July 23–August 23

Frankincense, laurel, saffron, benzoin, sandalwood, Chinese cinnamon, cinnamon, clove, aloe, cedar, nutmeg, galangal, angelica, storax, calmus, ash-tree seeds, golden copal.

Leo mixtures have a strong fragrance, supporting self-confidence and autonomy.

Virgo
Earth
August 24–September 23

Sandalwood, cinnamon, benzoin, tonka bean, myrrh, mastic, mint, frankincense, clove, iris root, propolis, storax, opoponax, marjoram, Scotch pine, lark, sage,

pine, guajak, mugwort, Norway spruce.

A Virgo mixture has a clear and pleasant fragrance. It supports purity, clarity, and the ability to adapt.

Libra
Air

September 24–October 23

Saffron, rose, benzoin Sumatra, sandalwood, clove, aloe, Chinese cinnamon, jasmine, hibiscus, galbanum, opoponax, tonka bean, cinnamon blossoms, labdanum, oak moss, coriander, vanilla, ginger lily, golden copal, ambrosia.

A Libra mixture has a sweet and warm fragrance. It supports harmony and the ability to love.

Scorpio
Water
October 24–November 22

Eaglewood, labdanum, rosemary, costus, cypress grass, hibiscus seeds, patchouli, nutmeg, vanilla, lupulin, black copal, asant, spikenard, moss, white cedar, cassia, iris root, dragon's blood.

The fragrance of a Scorpio mixture seems to defy definition; it is dark and strong. It supports sexual magnetism and connects to the darker side of the soul.

Sagittarius
Fire
November 23–December 22

Clove, hyssop, Scotch pine, galangal, coriander, cardamom, cinnamon, ginger, laurel, lavender, cedar, anise, dragon's blood, angelica root, benzoin, calmus, aloe, spikenard, masterwort, herb benet.

The Sagittarius mixture has a

fiery and intense fragrance. It supports resolve and expansion.

Capricorn
Earth
December 23–January 22

Myrrh, calmus, cypress, vetiver, cedar, pine, juniper, bezoin Siam, oak moss, black copal, mugwort, myrrh, frankincense, opoponax, sandarac, burgundy spruce resin, and desert mugwort.

A Capricorn mixture has a dignified fragrance. It supports perspective, calmness, and spirituality.

Aquarius
Air

January 21–February 19

Cypress, marjoram, Scotch pine, rhododendron, mint, canary tree, cardamom, coriander, sage, camphor, sandarac, eucalyptus, calmus, myrrh, Japanese anise, dammar, inulin, burgundy spruce resin, desert mugwort, hop marjoram.

An Aquarius mixture has a lively and expansive fragrance. It supports a thirst for knowledge and spiritual aspiration.

Pisces
Water
February 20–March 20.

Storax, camphor, benzoin, wild rosemary, mastic, Scotch pine, spikenard, lark, jasmine, cassia, opoponax, vanilla, hibiscus seeds, sage, fennel, oak moss, white cedar, lark, propolis, copyba costus, galbanum, toelu, lupulin.

A Pisces mixture has a sensuous, magical fragrance. It supports intuition, empathy, and the ability to dream.

1. Laurel
2. Iris root
3. Myrrh
4. Amber
5. Frankincense

Effective Incense-Burning Substances from Ancient Greece

The following substances were used for incense burning in Greece: frankincense, myrrh, mastic, opoponax, costus, sandalwood, cinnamon, cassia, ambergris, hibiscus berries, common myrrh, myrtle, saffron, cedar, sulfur, ocean onions, and many more. The ancient Greeks used incense-burning substances imported from Arabia, India, and Egypt in much the same way they were used in their countries of origin. For that reason, we will only study plants and substances that had a specific use in Greece. The incense-burning traditions of the ancient Romans were so much like those of Greece, we will not discuss them separately in this book.

Iris

Iris germanicalvar. florentina Dykes
Iris cretica

The iris is the first flower to come into bloom in Greece. The Greeks used the fragrant root stock for incense burning, salves, oils, and perfumes. They also used it to add aroma to wine. According to Greek mythology, Iris, the goddess of the rainbow and the messenger of the gods, escorts the dying along the rainbow into "The Land of Everlasting Peace." The Greeks used the fragrance of the iris to make the journey into the next world easier. Incense burning with irises can have erotic effects when mixed with incense-burning herbs that have similar effects. Together with mastic and frankincense, the fragrance of the root is helpful in cleansing the aura and stimulating the flow of subliminal energies in the body. Many people believe this mixture is helpful in reaching contact with spiritual beings, such as angels.

Laurel

Laurus nobilis L.

The laurel is a typical Mediterranean plant. Its leathery leaves and fruits are particularly rich in essential oils. Greek mythology tells us that Gaia, Mother Earth, changed Daphne into a laurel tree to protect her from Apollo, who was pursuing her. The laurel tree is strongly associated with Apollo, the healing god. It is the plant of cleansing and prophecy. At the Oracle of Delphi, seers slept on a bed of laurel leaves and inhaled the smoke before they announced their prophecies.

The ancient Greeks burned laurel for many sacred purposes: for prophecies, to cleanse the atmosphere, and to induce prophetic dreams. They also used laurel to fumigate in order to diminish the danger of infection during pestilence. They considered laurel an inclusive remedy. Laurel leaves and twigs have a very typical crackling sound when burned. You should only use laurel in small amounts, or better yet, combine it with other herbs. During incense burning, it expands the senses and sharpens awareness. It is part of an incense-burning dream mixture used before retiring. People believe that its fragrance creates dreams that come true. It also allows you to remember more of your dreams.

Amber

Succinum

Amber is a fossil resin that dripped from trees during the Tertiary period (63 million–5 million years ago). It was washed into the ocean and buried there under sediments. After millions of years, the ocean washed out the sediments, and the liquid resin solidified.

In ancient Greece, amber was called *electron*, the root of the word "electricity." When rubbed, this resin becomes electrostatic. Ancient Greeks and Egyptians considered amber to be an important healing remedy against cystitis, mental illnesses, fever, stomach problems, throat infections, pain, and much more. We still have their knowledge about its healing power. You can purchase amber in specialty stores in the form of amber oil, *Oleum succini rct*. We use it as a remedy for rheumatism, in cosmetics, and for revitalizing the skin. The ancient Greeks burned amber extensively as incense resin. They believed the "sun stone," as this resin is called, connected them to the sun god, creating an atmosphere of renewal and mental alertness. Amber was a favorite ingredient in incense-burning mixtures used in temples and for medicinal purposes. Today, you can buy amber in pieces from wholesale companies that sell minerals.

Recipes for Greek Incense Burning

Greek Temple Frankincense

Frankincense	2 parts
Myrrh	1 part
Cedar	1 part
Amber	¼ part

(You may substitute larch or pinion resin for amber.) Crush the frankincense and myrrh with a mortar and pestle. Pulverize the amber separately. Add the cedar shavings. Mix everything together well.

This so-called "temple" incense-burning recipe creates an atmosphere of devotion, dignity, and peace. It works well for praying and meditating. It is very calming and relaxing, particularly at times of severe nervous exhaustion and spastic convulsions. It has a balsamlike, warm fragrance.

Pythia

Opoponax	5 parts
Mastic	5 parts
Labdanum	1 part
Hop marjoram	1 part
Laurel leaves	1 part
Camphor	1 part

The fragrance of this mixture is multilayered. It is spicy, fresh, balsamlike, herblike, and mysterious—like the seer of the Oracle of Delphi. We use this mixture when we want to look into the future. It is a companion when consulting an oracle, or I Ching or Tarot. Its fragrance stimulates dream activities. When used before retiring, it can make us more consciously aware of our dreams. The incense-burning mixture inspires intuition and imagination.

Chiron

Iris root	1 part
Myrtle leaves	1 part
Mastic	4 parts
Strings of saffron	½ part
Sage	1 part

Pulverize the dried iris root. Break the mastic into small pieces with a mortar and pestle. Crush the myrtle and sage between your hands. Mix these and add the strings of saffron. This is a mixture whose fragrance supports healing. In times of inner conflict and vulnerability, emotional pain and grief, this mixture is able to stimulate the body's power of self-healing. Use a pinch at a time on charcoal.

Afternoon of a Faun

Sandalwood powder	4 parts
Hibiscus seeds	4 parts
Storax	1 part
Strings of saffron	½ part
Benzoin	½ part
Herb benet	½ part
Propolis	½ part

Pulverize the hibiscus seeds, propolis, and benzoin with a mortar and pestle. Shave off labdanum using the back of a knife and add it to the mixture. Crush the cloves particularly well. Mix all the ingredients together. If storax gum is only available in a liquid form, knead it into the rest of the ingredients to make a dough you can shape into small pellets the size of peas. Strings of saffron and cloves are available in stores that sell spices. You can find hibiscus seeds in herbal stores that sell incense-burning substances. The fragrance of Pan, the faun (the Greek god of nature with billy-goat feet), awakens the senses. It charms with an erotic and sensuous fragrance and invites you to experience your body sensuously. Close your eyes and allow this fragrance to transport you to the warm countries of the Mediterranean. Snuggle comfortably and enjoy the pleasure. Allow this feeling of well-being to flow through you and warm your body.

I don't feel like writing a poem,

Instead, I will light the incense-burning vessel

Filled with myrrh, jasmine, and frankincense,

And the poem will grow in my heart

Like flowers in my garden.

According to a student of Hafis (15th century A.D.)

7 Arabia

Frankincense and the Desert

I have been riding my horse all day. My body is aching; the sun has parched the skin in my face. The horse is exhausted. We reached the summit. Looking down into the valley I now can see a nomad's black tent. Its walls are made of dark wool and hover above the dry earth like large wings. The horse's nostrils are flaring. A gentle breeze carries a scent of hot stones, dry earth, and camel-dung charcoal from below. And then I smell the gentle, balsamic fragrance of frankincense. The nomads saw us and offered us their hospitality and the protection of their tents. They threw frankincense seeds into the fire, and it was this precious fragrance, carried by the wind, that conveyed to me their welcome.

Traveling to the Land of the Unknown

One of the best-kept secrets of antiquity was the location where frankincense and myrrh trees grew. During the time of the pharaohs, Egyptians seem to have forgotten it, and the journey of the pharaoh queen Hatshepsut was one into a land unknown. The ancient Greeks and Romans didn't fare any better; not even the devotees of these heavenly resins and fragrances knew where they came from. Thus, we can easily understand what fueled so much gossip and so many fantastic stories. Even Herodotus, the otherwise very reliable and well-traveled writer, spoke about winged serpents guarding frankincense and myrrh trees. But behind all this secretiveness was a very clever ploy. Trading in frankincense was a state secret and a monopoly, allowing the countries where these trees flourished to amass great wealth. These countries made up horrible stories just to keep curious people away. A system of very cleverly designed controls, from the point of origin to the consumer, prevented any successful inquiry. All traces of the caravan tracks, indicating where the camels carried the heavy weight of fragrant resins, were lost in the endless desert sands.

Caravans traveled the ancient frankincense route, one of the oldest trading routes in human history. By the time the caravans reached their destinations—Memphis in Egypt, Gaza on the Mediterranean Sea, Aleppo or Damascus in what is today Syria—they had covered an unbelievably difficult and dangerous road through blistering desert sand and over rocky, arid land almost bare of any vegetation.

Exporting resins only became profitable after people learned how to domesticate camels, because the water these animals stored in their humps allowed them to travel long distances without additional water. Donkeys needed water more often, forcing caravans to zigzag from one water source to another. Caravans of camels could use shortcuts, making worldwide trade possible. A caravan consisted of 100 to 400 camels, creating a column stretching for miles on end. These caravans carried incense-burning resins by the ton, but they also brought spices, precious stones, and valuable cloth, such as silk and brocade. Other trade routes, such as the silk routes that originated in distant Asia, linked up and enhanced the resin trade with precious wares from China and India. Sea routes also connected to the frankincense route.

If we want to uncover the secrets of these fragrant resins we must follow the tracks of the caravans of the past into the unknown, to the original source of frankincense. Camels, tireless as they are, will carry us from oasis to oasis. And at every rest stop, we can be sure to find people sitting around a fire fueled by camel manure telling the most

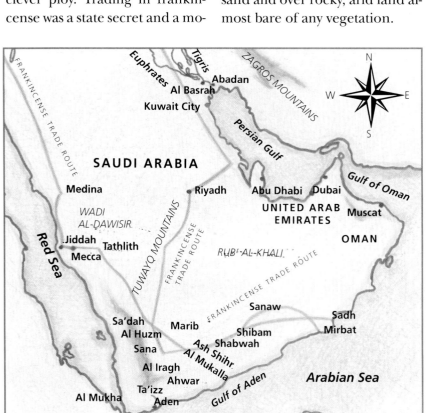

Resting after a long trek through the desert

intriguing stories. We are coming from Gaza, one of the most important trade centers of Arabian wares in the Mediterranean area. We will first learn about Petra, the mysterious city carved from rocky mountains. From there, we will embark on our long journey through the desert. Along the way, we will stop at the oases where Nabataeans will sell us wares and food. They still remember the stories about the exorbitant tolls caravans had to pay for the resins they carried to Gaza. We learn that the price of frankincense and myrrh resins

increases a hundredfold from the beginning of the journey to the end.

We will be traveling for at least three long months; the heat will be almost unbearable; the winds will have blown sand, covering and penetrating every part of our bodies. We will be guests in Bedouin tents, and as soon as they see us, they will throw frankincense seeds in the fire. The farther we travel in the direction of the land where frankincense trees grow, the more generous people will be with these fragrant welcoming gestures. But

the starlit, luminescent night and its endless expanse will be the desert's gift to us, making us forget all the troubles of the journey.

Ours is a journey to the mysterious land of Sheba, where people have amassed unbelievable wealth from the frankincense and myrrh trees that only grow there, in the stony desert, protected from the wind by the mountains, in a soil where nothing else will grow. There, in what is today Yemen and Oman, is the place where these sought-after fragrances grow. And not only

frankincense and myrrh. Balsam and cinnamon were also once native to that area. Later the Romans called the whole Arabian region *Arabia Felix*, meaning "Happy Arabia." Sitting around the fire, we will listen in awe to the stories about Belakis, the queen of Sheba, beautiful ruler of the happy land of frankincense.

In the Kingdom of Belakis

Three thousand years ago, the legendary kingdom of Sheba was located along the southern coast of the Arabian peninsula in what are today Yemen and Oman. This was the domain of the Queen of Sheba, whose wealth was the frankincense and myrrh trees. At that time, the dangerous, cumbersome, exhausting journey through the desert started in Ma'rib, the capital of the kingdom. The camel caravan faced a trip of 2,200 miles (3,500 km) through the desert. Ma'rib, located at the eastern edge of the foothills of the highlands of Yemen, was surrounded by a large desert.

Huge walls enclosed the city, which was built in the center of an oasis that covered 36 square miles (90 sq km). A gigantic dam with walls 50 ft. (16 m) high irri-

gated the area, providing water throughout the year. The dam of Ma'rib was one of the wonders of the ancient world. The clever queen had built this dam with the proceeds from the incense trade, about 1000 B.C. Much later, in the year 24 A.D., the armies of Emperor Augustus attempted to capture the proud city of Ma'rib, but the walls withstood the onslaught. The Roman army withdrew, but not before it took revenge for its defeat by destroying the dam.

Centuries earlier, leaving the protection of the walls of Ma'rib, Belakis, the Queen of Sheba, embarked on the difficult journey to Jerusalem in order to see King Solomon. In the Bible, the Book of Kings reports on her journey:

And as the Queen of Sheba received the message from Solomon, she came to question and to test him. And she came to Jerusalem with camels carrying spices and much gold and precious stones.

As was obvious later, the meeting of the two gave the fragrance trade a considerable impetus. Historians suggest that the queen wanted assurances from King Solomon that he would not meddle in her commerce with the Egyptian kingdom. After all,

Solomon, whose kingdom was at the center of the great trade route, could easily close off the way to Egypt, particularly the one to Memphis. The Arabian peninsula was already under his nominal rule.

Solomon had a strong army at his disposal and, in addition, made Egypt one of his allies by marrying his daughter to an Egyptian pharaoh. Queen Belakis did not invest in a strong army. Instead, she used her enormous knowledge of the effects of fragrances in order to enlist a ruler always ready for battle. Her beauty, wisdom, and fragrances inspired Solomon to one of the most beautiful love poems ever written. When we read The Song of Songs (see also chapter on *Israel*), we can easily imagine how intimate the meeting between these two must have been. Over time, the winds of the desert have covered the trail of her caravan with sand. But even three thousand years later, frankincense is still closely connected to Belakis, the wise woman from Sheba.

Beneath the Frankincense Trees

Let us return once more to the Kingdom of Sheba. Now that we know the secret of where those

trees come from, let's take a closer look. They grow in rocky, desertlike soil. They are seldom more than 20 ft. (6 m) tall, and some have bizarre shapes. Each tree has its own personality. Everything about them is a testimony to the unforgiving sun of this land. They chose a location where the mountains provide protection from the wind, and mountain dew is the only moisture they receive. Average rainfall must be below 4 in. (100 mm) in order for them to thrive.

Frankincense trees are also particular about the condition of the soil. They grow only in the so-called frankincense belt, a strip of land about 9 miles (15 km) wide, where lime deposits in the soil contain very specific combinations of minerals. The trees prefer the rocky slopes along the edge of the canyonlike wadis, or dry river beds. The frankincense tree native to this area, *Boswellia carteri*, is named for the Edinburgh botanist Johann Boswell and the English ship physician H. J. Carter, who, in 1846, was the first to describe the frankincense tree in detail. Of the some 25 different kinds of frankincense that exist, only the following three are now available:

—*Boswellia sacra*, from South Arabia, called *buchur* there
—*Boswellia carteri*, from Somalia and Oman
—*Boswellia serrata*, from India, called "common myrrh" there

These trees grow wild. The owners are usually nomad families that either harvest the resin themselves or lease the trees for profit. Today, Somalia has a frankincense association that organizes the collection of the resin. Ducts inside the bark produce a milky-white, sticky liquid that flows out when the bark is injured. This liquid solidifies into a resin, serving to heal the tree's wound. To harvest frankincense, the owners cut the tree bark in several places. The milky liquid hardens when exposed to the sun. Then they remove the resin with a spatulalike scraper. Usually, the owners don't collect the first and second resins, which appear after a month. It is the third resin that is superior in quality. It is possible to harvest 22 lb. (10 kg) of resin from each tree.

The resin from each of the approximately 25 different frankincense plants has a distinct fragrance. Only a small differ-

ence in location between individual trees produces very subtle changes in the fragrance. We can compare this to the difference in apples growing on different kinds of apple trees. The way the resin is harvested, the way it is dried, and the way it is stored also have a considerable influence on the quality of the frankincense. After a three- or four-month period, the trees produce a particularly pure liquid. The frankincense resin obtained from this late harvest is the best because of its delicate quality. It is seldom available today. The fragrance is light with a clear, citruslike note, while other resin smells somewhat musty and dull. The lesser quality is often due to a quick harvest, during which the resin was not allowed to mature properly. Today, frankincense generally comes from Oman and Somalia.

The frankincense tree loves warmth and dry air, and the same is true of the resin. The best fragrance develops during incense burning in a comfortably heated room or outside on a warm or hot summer's day. Cold temperatures and humidity do not allow the ethereal, gentle fragrance to develop.

Many people have an aversion

Frankincense tree

to the fragrance of frankincense because it reminds them of death and a troubled childhood. Sadly enough, churches don't always use the best quality frankincense. Some even have synthetic aromas. Today, most churches use products made with several different resins. Stores offer 10 to 15 imported incense-burning mixtures for use in churches. These have names such as Three-King Mixture, Spice Mixture, Precious Mixture, Colorful Mixture, Light Arabian Pontificate, Palestine King, Black Lourdes, Gloria, and Angelus. Each pellet of golden frankincense is covered with a bronze layer, adding visual beauty to the mixture. Manufacturers add spices, such as cinnamon and cloves, and flowers, such as

lavender and rose petals, to a base of frankincense, myrrh, and benzoin.

Mixtures made with frankincense resin of better quality are more expensive. Specialty shops also offer pure frankincense resins of different qualities, such as Frankincense Eritrea, Pellets Temperament, Light Powder, First Choice. At this time, Aden Frankincense is the best quality. The resins Somalia–First Quality, also called "Mushaad," and "Oman–First Quality" come highly recommended. The Aden frankincense has the most resinous fragrance. If you can get your hands on good-quality frankincense, make your own frankincense mixture by using spices, flowers, and other incense-burning substances. But

just once, allow yourself the pleasure of citronlike, pure frankincense of high quality. Burn it and enjoy the incredible beauty of this fragrance. But only buy a small piece because it is expensive.

Considering the many benefits and pleasures we derive from burning frankincense, it is difficult to understand why we don't use more of it on many different occasions. Even modern science has found wonderful ways frankincense can affect us. A short while ago, when American researchers burned frankincense indoors, they discovered that the sound of the human voice carried better than when the space had not been exposed to it. This might be the reason why, in earlier times, before electric microphones and loudspeakers, people burned frankincense during speeches and sermons, hoping to improve the sound in churches and temples.

The Healing Properties of Frankincense

The small, bizarrely shaped trees from the rocky desert have given

Frankincense tree with resin

us another gift: a milky-white liquid with unprecedented healing power. Frankincense has properties that help kill bacteria, disinfect, renew cells, heal wounds, kill insects, and relieve rheumatism. During incense burning, it is the psychoactive and disinfecting powers that stand out. Frankincense, for instance, reduced the danger of infection when many people congregated indoors, as was the case in temples

and churches. This was particularly important in times of poverty, when infectious diseases and pestilence were more likely to strike and people visited places like churches and temples more frequently. In Santiago de Compostela, Spain, where pilgrims would sleep in churches, the priests burned incense in huge vessels as a way to lessen the effects of the unpleasant odor of human perspiration and to lower the risks of infection.

In the countries of Arabia, mosques and shrines burned frankincense. In addition, people burned it on a daily basis in living quarters and tents for cleansing purposes and to reduce negative influences.

The fact that burning frankincense increases circulation and is helpful in fighting rheumatism has not gone unnoticed in the West. Older herbal books carry very specific recipes. Mastic, lavender flowers, and frankincense resin were mixed in equal parts and then used for incense burning. People suffering from rheumatism would suspend their painful extremities in the smoke. They would also sit on a chair with a perforated seat over an incense-burning pan. The person was first wrapped in a large piece of cloth, the entire body then being bathed in the smoke.

People in Arabian countries still know about the many different healing effects of frankincense. For instance, they burn frankincense to relieve the pain of toothaches and to lower fever. Avicenna, the famous 11th-century Arabian physician, discovered that frankincense has cooling effects. Thus, he recommended it as a remedy for illnesses that increase the body's temperature and for infections.

In the last few years, Western science has also become aware of the ability of frankincense to lessen the pain caused by rheumatism. A study conducted at the University of Munich was able to prove the effects of frankincense on joint pain. This age-old healing and incense-burning substance can give many people who suffer from rheumatism hope and help. Other experiments, conducted at the University of Tübingen, also have proven that frankincense can reduce infections. According to pharmacological research, frankincense has strong anti-inflammatory properties that could make it a natural remedy for arthritis, rheumatism, psoriasis, and also asthma. People in the past knew much more about the benefits of this precious substance. Frankincense is a natural insecticide. As early as ancient Egypt, farmers fumigated wheat silos to keep wheat moths away. Frankincense steam is able to kill parasitic insects in food.

People still use frankincense for daily hygiene. In Arabia and in parts of Africa, a woman's morning routine includes standing over a vessel of steaming frankincense for its cleansing effects and pleasant scent. In Somalia, people disinfect water tubs and drinking utensils by holding them over the smoke of burning frankincense. To this day, nomads in the Arabian Desert welcome their guests by throwing frankincense pellets in the fire. In some of the African and Arabian countries, people still daub frankincense on a guest's clothing. Many Asian stories remind us that the fragrance of frankincense also has an erotic component. To create this fragrance, we usually mix frankincense with sandalwood, cinnamon, and other sensuous incense-burning fragrances.

Burning Frankincense to Clear the Atmosphere

Frankincense not only removes germs and unpleasant odors, it is also one of the strongest substances for cleansing and clearing the atmosphere. Burning high-quality frankincense will cleanse and clear the atmosphere in places where people have argued, where the air indoors seems thick and heavy, and where people gather to-

Petra, Jordan

gether and leave their troubles behind like a coat on a hook: sickrooms, waiting rooms, and examination rooms. Burning frankincense is also very sensible before moving into a new house or apartment, "cleaning out" the problems left behind by the people who occupied the space before. You can suspend healing stones, crystals, and other objects used for healing purposes in the smoke of frankincense. The objects will regain their original energy and freshness.

For thousands of years, people have considered the heavenly fragrance of frankincense one of the strongest stimuli for a human spirit that wants to be open to the heavens and is attempting to communicate with energies on a higher plane. Today, burning frankincense works particularly well for us during prayer, meditation, and reflection. It cleanses the innermost spaces and sensitive energy channels, allowing spiritual and cosmic energy patterns to heal. In addition, frankincense is also a very effective remedy for stress. It reduces muscle tension and provides a sense of comfort and warmth.

Myrrh: Sensuousness of the Earth

In addition to frankincense resin, the camels of the caravan of the distant past also carried a far more precious resin. Ancient people were just as enthusiastic about myrrh as they were about frankincense. Sometimes, myrrh resin was twice as expensive as frankincense resin. Together with frankincense, people con-

sidered myrrh to be "the divine fragrance." Frankincense symbolizes masculinity, while myrrh symbolizes femininity. They assigned frankincense to the spirit in the heavens; myrrh, to that of earth. They believed myrrh and its fragrance symbolized the sensuousness of the earth. For the sake of comparison, if we held a piece of each, we would notice that, in two pieces the same size, the myrrh is heavier. The resin of the frankincense is light, yellow,

and often clear, while that of the myrrh is dark brown to caramel-colored and is usually not transparent.

In concentrated form, myrrh contains the energy of the earth. For that reason, myrrh resin serves to ground, calm, contract, and condense. Burning myrrh is ideal when we need to get our feet solidly back on the ground and to calm a confused or exhausted spirit. However, never use myrrh when you are suffer-

Myrrh

ing from depression because it would create a melancholy mood.

Many ancient cultures considered myrrh, called "the fragrance of the earth," a symbol for the cradle of the earth and feminine sensuality. Ancient Egyptians believed that burning myrrh would create a sensuous mood in women. In Israel, prospective brides prepared themselves for marriage by massaging their skin with myrrh oil for a whole year prior to the wedding. When burning incense for sensuous purposes, people mixed myrrh with other substances, such as sandalwood, labdanum, benzoin, cassia, and aloe. Ancient people believed that myrrh could be an initiation to feminine divinity and could connect people to this energy. It is the resin of the ancient goddess.

Since antiquity, myrrh has been a well known and highly valued medicinal substance. Some considered it as valuable as gold. It is less well known in the West. Myrrh has healing, tissue-strengthening, and scab-building properties. Therefore, myrrh is a very common remedy for wounds. Myrrh tincture strengthen gums, prevents gingivitis, and disinfects the oral cavity. Myrrh preparations are an effective way to deal with acne. For this purpose, women in Asia once bathed in the smoke of myrrh resin. The fragrant substances contained in the smoke also help cure bronchitis. A number of scientific studies have shown that myrrh resin can slow down tumor development in the human body. It is assumed that this effect is connected to the sesquiterpene-lac-tone content in the plant. Continued research may eventually find that myrrh is a cure for cancer. In any case, we could well find new applications for a remedy used during antiquity.

During the Middle Ages, myrrh resin was processed into so-called "pestilence pills" prescribed for people suffering from this and other infectious diseases. The disinfecting power of the resin was well known. The abbess Hildegard von Bingen considered myrrh to be a fever-reducing medication. Only a few years ago, myrrh was recognized as an effective remedy for treating fungal infections, particularly yeast infections (*Candida*) in the intestinal tract and oral cavity. A series of treatments with myrrh can kill the fungus without destroying the natural intestinal flora. Again, as is the case with frankincense, an age-old healing and incense-burning substance can be helpful to us in the treatment of illnesses so prevalent in our civilization.

The "feminine" myrrh also grows where the "masculine" frankincense does. She loves barren and dry locations on rocky hillsides at medium elevation. She grows as a tree as well as a shrub and reaches up to 33 ft. (10 m) in height. With strong thorns for protection, she defends herself against marauding animals. Similar to the frankincense tree, she has a stunted appearance, looking almost atrophied. The circumference of her truck is no more than 12 in. (30 cm). The gnarled branches are sparsely covered with leaves that are either plain or three-toothed. The flowers of the myrrh tree are small and inconspicuous. They are hanging panicles whose colors range from white to light green. They only appear between the end of August and the beginning of September. The fruits look like small olives. When you cut into the stem a thick, liquidlike, bitter-tasting secretion appears immediately. This taste is what gave the tree its name: in Arabic, *murr* means "bitter." Each myrrh tree produces about 9 lb. (4 kg) of resin every year.

Fragrances from Arabia

The kingdom of Sheba was the "breeding ground" for many Arabian fragrance traditions that are still doing well today. Only a few countries have loved fragrances with as much sophistication as the Arabs. Famous poets and scientists wrote books about fragrant salves, perfumes, and fragrance-induced sensual pleasures. Throughout history, people in the East surrendered naturally to the joy of fragrances because strong religious morals or a narrow interpretation of morals didn't restrict sensual pleasures. On the contrary, people saw the ability to enjoy the manifold pleasures of fragrances as being connected to the profoundly mystical life of the gods. All this made it possible for a highly developed culture of fragrances to flourish.

When reading *A Thousand and One Nights*, we can almost feel those precious and tempting

distance. Burning sweet-smelling fragrances was part of all important events, such as marriage, birth, or the signing of an important contract. For example, on the eve of his wedding, a groom would burn benzoin resin and sandalwood in order to please invisible but good-natured ghosts and ask them to be his guests at the feast. In Arabia, incense-burning or similar traditions involving fragrances usually accompanied prayers. People used one of the most intricate incense-burning mixtures during the 27th night of Ramadan, the month of fasting, because, during Ramadan, negative energies could appear. Particularly pleasant fragrances satisfied these negative energies.

According to Mohammed, the prophet of Islam, the three things he loved most in this world were women, pleasant fragrances, and prayers. The fragrance he loved most was musk, which people used for perfumes, salves, and incense-burning mixtures. Musk originates from the scent gland of the musk deer (*Moschus moschiferus*). When undiluted and still fresh, this secretion smells of urine and ammonia. However, when highly diluted, its fragrance becomes earthy and sensuous.

The musk deer is an endangered, protected animal. Because people were so enamored of this fragrance, the deer almost became extinct. Musk is a substance that keeps its scent intact for a very long time. The ancient peoples of Arabia mixed musk into the cement they used to build mosques. Its fragrance

fragrances. The enthusiasm for fragrances is part of every area of life. People knew the fragrances of the bazaar, of food, of the harem, of perfumes, of mosques, etc.

People in Eastern cultures loved heavy, sweet, and erotic fragrances. In most incense-burning mixtures, at least one substance has such a note: balsamic-sweet sandalwood, vanilla-sweet benzoin resin, spicy-warm cinnamon, velvety-heavy ambergris, and resinous-balsamic agar wood. Such sweet fragrances please the heart and, as people in Arabia tell us, offer us protection against the evil eye. The nomads of Morocco used benzoin resin because they believed that this fragrance was one of the best ways of finding favor with the unseen powers that could influence the life of human beings and to keep less benign beings at a safe has filled those spaces for thousands of years. In addition, the mosques are also sprayed with the wonderful aroma of rosewater, mixing fragrance and prayer in a very pleasant way. You can only obtain musk seeds and oil at a very high price, when you can find it at all. However, it is my opinion that we ought not to use them because by doing so, we are hastening the extinction of these animals. Since scientists believed that synthetically produced musk fragrance causes cancer, we ought to refrain from using that as well. We use no fragrances obtained from animals for healing purposes, in any case. The seeds of a particular kind of hibiscus, called "rose mallow" are a substitute for the real musk.

The Mysterious Fragrances of the Sufi

The Sufi poets Rumi, Hafis, and Saadi, of the mystical order of Islam, praised fragrances in wonderful ways in their verses and songs. The Sufi knew about the spiritual energy of pleasant aromas, incense, and oils that could aid their mystical experiences. They classified fragrances according to certain spiritual situations and developments. The Sufi symbol came from the world of fragrant plants. This symbol was the mystical rose, which they considered to be "the mother of fragrances." The "father of fragrances," on the other hand, was ambergris. This is a substance that could be a byproduct of a whale's metabolism, storax, or

the resin of a particular type of Scotch pine, *Pica succinfera*. The Sufi were very fond of this substance and used it fresh or in a fossilized state: "amber" deposits buried in the earth for millions of years. They burned ambergris in the form of small shavings. They had access to many different grades of ambergris, but the one from Afghanistan was the one they valued most highly. Incense burning with ambergris creates a warm, balsamic, sweet fragrance considered a healing remedy for all heart problems.

In his works *Canon Medicinae* and *Treatise About the South,* Avicenna (980–1037 A.D.), the great physician and mystic, mentioned many aromatic resins, such as frankincense, storax, galbanum, ambergris, asant, and myrrh, all noted for their healing. He also connected these fragrant substances to different situations of the human soul. He believed that the soul of a plant resides in its fragrance and that, in turn, the fragrance has a healing effect on the soul of a human being.

Effective Incense-Burning Substances from Arabia

The list of the incense-burning substances used in the East (Shakespeare called them "the pleasant fragrances of Arabia") is very long. To this day, they still use approximately 150 different fragrance substances from plants: rose, moschus, ambergris, frankincense, myrrh, Mecca balsam, cinnamon, sandalwood, benzoin, storax, coriander, lab-

danum, camphor, cinnamon, mastic, jasmine, asant, pine resin, saffron, mastic thistle, sandarac, fragrant musk, and spikenard. They were, and still are, part of countless recipes.

Rose

Rosa damascena Mill.

Arabia is the land of roses. The Crusaders brought the first cultivated rose to Europe. The Persian poet Saadi (1189–1291 A.D.) praised the rose, "the mother of fragrance," in his book *Gulistan* (Rose Garden). Shiraz, his home city, and Isfahan were the primary areas where fragrant roses grew and where the ancient Arabians produced the finest rosewater. Rose fragrance is most potent in rose oil and rosewater. It loses much of its aroma when you burn the petals. However, when you add it to a mixture in proper amounts and combine it with resins, the fragrance develops during incense burning. This gives the mixture a flowery, gentle, and sensuous nuance. As they knew in ancient Arabia, the rose has a strong effect on our emotions. People considered it to be the symbol of romantic longing. For that reason, they used it to create a sensuous, charming, or tempting mood. For the Sufi, however, the rose was also a symbol of love of God, the desire to be close to God, and to reach a mystical union with all that is godly. They would mix it with resin and use it during ceremonies. The mystical power of the rose is beautifully captured in the recipe *Rosa mystica.* Avicenna dedicated his life's work to the rose. We believe he

Rose

was the first to distill pure rose oil.

Dried rose leaves will give the fragrance of the heart to any mixture. The fragrance opens the heart and is helpful in letting go of painful emotional injuries and disappointments. On a sub-liminal level, it can strengthen the heart chakra. For incense-burning purposes, use the small flower bud of the Damascus rose. For incense burning, crush the petals of the flower carefully. Don't use the hard center rose hip.

Sandarac

Tetraclinis articulata (Vahl)
Mast. (Syn. Callitris quadrivalis)

Sandarac, also called avar tree, belongs to the Cupressaceae family and grows in Morocco, Algeria, Tunisia, southeast Spain, and also Malta. In these countries, the resin, also called san-darac, is valued for its incense-burning purposes and exported to other countries. Today, people in the West only use san-darac resin in raw form to make liquor. The resin used for this purpose usually comes from an Australian sandarac tree (*Cal-litris collumelaris*). The Aus-tralians also use this resin for incense burning. They obtain the resin by cutting into both the trunk of the tree and the branches. The liquidlike resin that seeps from the cuts hardens into small stalactites which are then scraped off the trunk. The color ranges from light lemon yellow to reddish to amber. They sell the colored resin in small sta-lactitelike drops in Asian mar-kets. When broken in half, the surface is shiny, like glass.

Sandarac gives off a warm balsamic, frankincenselike fra-grance. You can often find it in a mixture that contains coriander seeds, benzoin, and mastic. In Morocco and Algiers people consider it part of folk medicine. For example, it is a remedy mid-wives use if a birth becomes diffi-cult. It has a calming effect and reduces cramps. In North Africa, people mix sandarac with polei mint and burn the mixture when children have stomachaches. To this day, people in Arab coun-tries still use the smoke to treat colds and catarrh. People take the resin internally for round-worms and tapeworms. Its warm, balsamic fragrance works well in the evening because it relaxes, calms, and eases tension. The fragrance has a strong effect on the nervous system. It is helpful in cases of insomnia caused by tension and stress.

Sandarac originally came from Morocco. This sandarac is hard to find, but you can buy sandarac gum in the form of small pearls or powder. The san-darac sold on the market usually comes from the Australian san-darac, which belongs to the Cal-litri family. It is an acceptable substitute for Moroccan san-darac, but it does not have as strong an effect. In fact, it is also used as a glue for adhesive ban-dages. In Arabia, people also used sandarac to dilute or cam-ouflage the ambergris obtained from sperm whales. Sandarac gives off a frankincenselike, bal-samic, light, and fruity fragrance. It is very similar to high-quality copal resin. Burning sandarac produces clarifying, strengthening, and cleansing effects. It neutralizes illness-causing tension indoors and clears the air. Since this resin creates a great deal of smoke, people usually combine sandarac with other ingredients rather than using it by itself.

Ambergris

Picea succinfera, Ambra, Succinum

Ambergris is the product of a sperm whale's metabolism. It is part of the content of a whale's intestinal system and heals the wounds in the intestines created when the whale eats cuttlefish (*Elodone moschata*). Ambergris is excreted in lumps. Each lump weighs less than a gram. It floats to the surface and washes up on the beach as flotsam. Primarily, however, whalers harvest it from the intestines of whales they have killed. Ambergris has always been a very precious fragrance substance. It is black, gray, and white in color. Historically, only a few people could afford to purchase it. Ambergris has a warm, soft, animal-like, balsamic fragrance. Many people think it is one of the most sensuous and beguiling of all the fragrance substances. Today, we don't burn ambergris from sperm whales for healing purposes. Continued demand would only contribute to the decimation of the whale population.

The ambergris the Sufi liked so well, as described in the Old Testament, came from the amber Scotch pine, *Pinus succinifera Schub.*, whose resin and pulverized wood have an ambergris-like, warm, soft, honeylike fragrance. It is very rare in the West. In Arabian countries or Asia, however, it is available where spices are sold. The amber available in the West is often enriched with synthetic fragrances that try to imitate the fragrance of ambergris, but, when burned, the smoke is very damaging to your health. In India, ayurvedic medicine has a recipe called "Amber Dhoop." It contains delicately crushed herbs, ambergris resin, piment wood, sandalwood, storax, and sometimes musk and Indian rubber. You can use this mixture as a substitute for amber Scotch-pine resin. Used by itself or in combination with other incense-burning substances, such as sandalwood, cinnamon blossoms, and sandarac, it creates a very pleasant fragrance.

People recommend this resin as a remedy for all types of heart problems. Ambergris, "the father of fragrances," is helpful in cases of anxiety and a weak heart, sadness, and depression. Some people say that it is helpful in cases of mental illness. Its fragrance creates an atmosphere of comfort. In combination with sandalwood and cinnamon, ambergris creates a warm, erotic incense-burning substance. Even more· effective is the amber stone, *succinum*, the product of fossilized amber resin. Delicately grated or in powder form, it is believed to have strong healing properties when burned (see also chapter on *Greece*). It is available in chunks of amber.

Agar Wood

Aquillaria agallocha Roxb.

The extraordinary effect of the fragrance of agar wood is well known in the East. In his book *Gulistan*, the Persian poet Saadi (1189–1291) speaks about the special magic that the fragrance of agar wood produces. The wood, also used for incense burning, contains essential oils seldom found in the West. Even today, only the initiated, who have special knowledge of fragrances, know of it. People have jealously guarded the secret of Ud, the name given to agar wood in the East. People there consider Ud a mystery that accompanies and supports the soul to its highest possible development. This precious wood comes in pieces that are a little more than 1 in. (3 cm) long. Use only small shavings for incense burning. You can use it individually or in combination with other substances. Its indescribable fragrance needs to be experienced to understand how special and lively it is.

Sandalwood is the fragrance for those who are just beginning to experiment with incense burning. Agar wood is the treasure of the initiated. People often use it during important Islamic festivities, such as the

27th day of Ramadan, the feast celebrating the birth of the Prophet, or at the conclusion of the month of fasting. For these occasions, they combine the wood with other incense-burning substances. Moroccans burn a particularly good quality of Ud on the day they name a child. The Sufi burned the oil or the wood during exercises to deepen the initiation of the human soul into the depths of the mysteries. The exotic flavor of the fragrance was very valuable, and they added the wood to different incense-burning mixtures in the form of small slivers or powder. The fragrance of agar wood, jasmine, ambergris, rose, and musk were all part of the legend of *A Thousand and One Nights*. A perfume the ladies of the East often used is called *Naad*, a combination of musk, ambergris, and agar wood. How can anyone resist such a fragrance?

Saffron

Crocus sativus L.

The golden yellow or deep orange powder of the saffron plant is the product of the stigma from the flower of the lilac-colored crocus. The plant belongs to the family of the iris, Iridaceae. Saffron is one of the most expensive of all spices and fragrant substances. To produce about ⅓ oz.(10 gm), of saffron powder, you need 1,500 flower stigmas, collected by hand. The word "saffron" comes from the Persian word *caffer*. The stigma is sweet, warm, spicy, flowery, and comforting.

People use saffron as a spice or, because of its color, as a dye for many foods. They use the extremely expensive oil as a perfume. For incense-burning mixtures, you add only a few filaments. In Arabia, people added saffron powder to very special fragrant "pearls" made from incense-burning substances. Instead of burning these pearls, they used them along with real pearls and gold jewelry to make necklaces. As the body temperature rose, the necklace released a particularly beguiling fragrance. On very special occasions, they used these precious fragrant pearls for incense-burning purposes. The use of saffron pearls followed the Egyptian tradition of incense-burning pellets. The Persian poet Saadi speaks about the gracious use of fragrant incense-burning pellets:

It was while we were taking a bath that
My loved one, one day,
Handed a fragrant stone to me.
Is it from musk or
Ambergris, was my question?
It was this fragrance alone that so bewitched my soul . . .

In the Arabian tradition, saffron was a very strong magical substance that accompanied certain religious rites. People used it during birth, at weddings, and at a death. The nomads often gave saffron and frankincense to the bride before her wedding. They believed it would increase fertility. The combination of saffron, cloves, benzoin, ginger, and sandalwood was a mixture used for love rituals that would awaken a couple's affection for each another. Ayurvedic medicine also uses saffron for some incense-burning mixtures.

Cinnamon

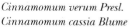

Cinnamomum verum Presl.
Cinnamomum cassia Blume

The cinnamon tree grew in Arabia during the reign of the queen of Sheba. Merchants exported the bark via the caravan route. However, Arabian merchants also obtained cinnamon and cassia from Ceylon and Indonesia and sold it in Israel, Greece, Rome, and other places. In order to prevent curious people from finding out the source of this lucrative product, merchants created horror stories about how to obtain this valuable fragrant bark. In Rome and Greece, they told people that the bark of the cinnamon could only

1. Golden frankincense
2. Cinnamon
3. Frankincense, first quality
4. Frankincense, cleansed
5. Strings of saffron
6. Scotch-pine amber
7. Myrrh
8. Agar wood
9. Asant powder
10. Sandarac
11. Rose buds

be obtained by shooting down the nests of the phoenix, high on steep cliffs, with bow and arrow. Another cinnamon plant, so they told, grew in swamps, guarded by winged serpents or bats. The brave customers in Rome and Athens found these stories astounding, and, thus, they were even more willing to pay a good price for it. Cinnamon is one of the most popular fragrances in the East. It gives many incense-burning recipes their sweetness. It symbolizes a fragrance that we in the West think is sweet and heavy. Cinnamon works well in recipes with sandalwood (see also chapters on *India, Egypt, Japan*).

Asant

Ferula assafoetida L.
Ferula narthex Boiss.

Asant

Asant, also called devil's dirt, belongs to the Apiaceae family and is closely related to lovage. It grows in Iran, Iraq, countries of the former Soviet Union, and Afghanistan. People in the Middle East, Egypt, Greece, and Rome burned it as incense. The plant has whitish umbelliferous flowers and feathery leaves, similar to carrot leaves. After five years, the plant is cut off close to the ground during the summer.

The resin is collected and dried. In the East, you can purchase the gum resin in large globules.

In Western shops that sell resin, asant is available as asafetida gum, either in powder form or in pieces. Both have a yellowish-brown color. The broken surface of the resin is first white and then red and brown. Because people in India still use it in recipes, you can buy it in specialty shops that carry Indian food items. In ancient times, people knew two different types of asant: one with a very pleasant scent and the other whose fragrance was anything but pleasant. The pleasant-smelling asant disappeared a long time ago. We only know about it from reports in literature. Therefore, we have to be satisfied with the asant that smells somewhat garlicky. This is the one that ancient people used for medicinal purposes, particularly as a tonic for nerves.

In the East, people who use asant in cooking praise it as an antiflatulent. In the West, we only use it in Worcestershire sauce. For medicinal purposes, people burned asant as a strong tonic for panic attacks, anxiety, and nervousness. The fragrance is able to relieve cramps. People believed it was a strong and effective remedy for the nerves. In ayurvedic and Tibetan medicine, asant is a remedy for psychosis as well as an aphrodisiac. Asant smells like a combination of onions and garlic. Not everyone likes its pungent aroma.

For incense burning, you should mix it with other substances that have similar characteristics. People in the East

believed that it was precisely because of its pungent aroma that asant would drive out evil spirits. Maybe the ghosts of yesteryear are today's neuroses and psychoses. During ancient times, these mental problems were difficult to explain rationally, and people feared they were caused by evil spirits. In Morocco, they still burn asant around people who seem to be possessed and around people with mental illnesses. The idea is that the illness-causing ghosts will then let go of their victims. Many people believe that asant is the best protection against psychic, illness-causing influences. The nomads recommended burning equal parts of asant and myrrh in cases of severe overstimulation or shock.

Recipes for Burning Incense from Arabia

Incense-burning vessel made of meerschaum

Flight of the Soul

Mastic	1 part
Sandarac	1 part
Frankincense	2 parts

Crush (don't pulverize) small pieces of the resin with a mortar and pestle. This combination has a clean and very gentle ethereal fragrance. It awakens in us the desire for a power greater than ourselves; it invites us to pray, meditate, and reflect. The mixture has a tremendous power to cleanse emotions. When emotions take over, this fragrance can help harmonize and soothe the soul.

Rosa Mystica

Frankincense	3 parts
Myrrh	2 parts
Storax	1 part
Sandarac	½ part
Labdanum	2 parts
Rose petals	½ part
Golden frankincense	

Crush the frankincense, myrrh, storax, and sandarac with a mortar and pestle. Scrape off the labdanum with the back of a knife. Crush the dried rose buds between the palms of your hands. Mix everything well. You might want to add a few pellets of golden frankincense to the mixture. These are available in shops that carry incense-burning substances. They will add brilliance to this rather dark mixture. The fragrance of the rose, the mystical flower of the Sufi, affects the subliminal energies of the heart. It leads to prayer and meditation that connect with the energies of love. Warm, deep, and velvety, this fragrance can open the soul and touch the heart.

Gulistan
The rose garden

Sandalwood	5 parts
Agar wood	1 part
Rose mallow seeds	½ part
Cloves	½ part
Cinnamon bark	1 part
Saffron	¼ part
Benzoin	1 part
Rose leaves	½ part

Pulverize the sandalwood with a mortar and pestle or buy it in powdered form. Also pulverize the agar wood, rose mallow seeds, cloves, cinnamon bark, saffron, and benzoin. Dry the rose leaves thoroughly, remove the stems, and add them to the mixture.

The mixture has a warm, sensuous fragrance that will lure you into a wonderful rose garden. Sensuous and tempting, it will charm your senses to relax, let go, dream, and be affectionate. Burning this mixture awakens your imagination and carries you on its wings into the land of fantasy.

Miniature of caravan of Arabian merchants, 13th century

131

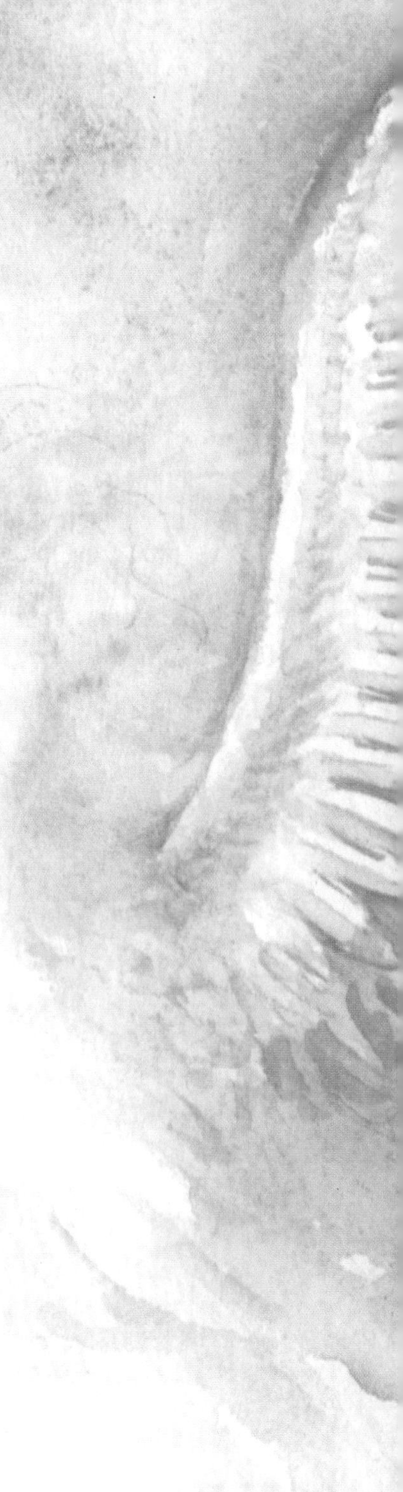

What is this, coming up from the desert,

Like a column of smoke,

Laden with myrrh, with frankincense

And with the perfume of every exotic dust?

You are a park that puts forth

pomegranates,

With all choice fruits;

Spikenard and saffron, calamus and

cinnamon,

Myrrh and aloes with all the fine spices.

You are a garden fountain, a well of water,

Flowing fresh from Lebanon.

Arise, north wind! Come, south wind!

Blow upon my garden,

That its perfume may spread abroad.

from: The Song of Songs 3:6 and 4:13–16

8 Israel

What the Three Kings Have Brought

She opened a small salve jar made from delicately grained marble. Surely it came from this faraway place called Egypt. Where might she have found it? A wonderful fragrance rose from the jar. Spicy, heavy, and mysterious. And immediately we knew: this is the fragrance of the oils of the Kings. From the jar emanated the rich fragrance of spikenard and the warm spicy aroma of balsam, and the most precious incense from the balsam of Gilead. Magdalene was given this precious fragrance, only used to anoint kings, from her father. He was the owner of the only balsam tree forest in Israel. He had died a few years ago. She poured some of the oil into her hands, bowed to Him, and anointed His feet.

The King's Love of Fragrances

When reading The Song of Songs, close your eyes, listen, and let yourself be touched by the affection, love, sensuality, and joy of these precious fragrances: warm and velvety cinnamon, frankincense, sweet saffron, sweet henna flowers, spicy calmus, warm and soft balsam, spicy and mysterious aloe. While you treasure these fra-

grances, feel a warm south wind gently caress your body and hear a spring murmuring gently in the grass.

Many poems speak about the sensuality and charm of the fragrances mentioned in the Bible. The Song of Songs in the Bible contains one of the most enchanting descriptions in world literature of pleasing aromas and their effects. Thanks to this "hymn to the fragrances," we have a fairly precise record of the spices and scents used by the

Israelites 1000 years B.C. Reading these poems is like an invitation to a walk through one of the most fragrant plant worlds in antiquity.

At the time of King Solomon, the author of The Song of Songs, the trade in fragrances and incense-burning substances was at its height. His kingdom was an important commerce center. Jerusalem was the city of perfumery. People who produced perfumes, salves, and incense-burning substances even had their own street. King Solomon himself seems to have been a great admirer of fragrances, and we are not too far off when we assume that he had a certain amount of experience with fragrant erotica. In addition to his very beautiful wife, he is said to have made countless other women quite happy.

Love, eroticism, and fragrance were closely intertwined during his time. People used fragrant symbolism to express love. At that time, ladies were not satisfied with using just a dab of perfume, as is the custom today. They rubbed fragrant oil over their entire bodies until they could not distinguish the scent of their skin from that of the fragrance. Even taking a bath would not remove the fragrance. For six long months, they would lubricate their body with myrrh and balsam oil. For another six months, they luxuriated in fragrant baths to which they added myrrh or labdanum. People connected sensuous pleasures and fragrances. But let's leave King Solomon to enjoy his incense-burning substances and look at the history of the Israelites' in-

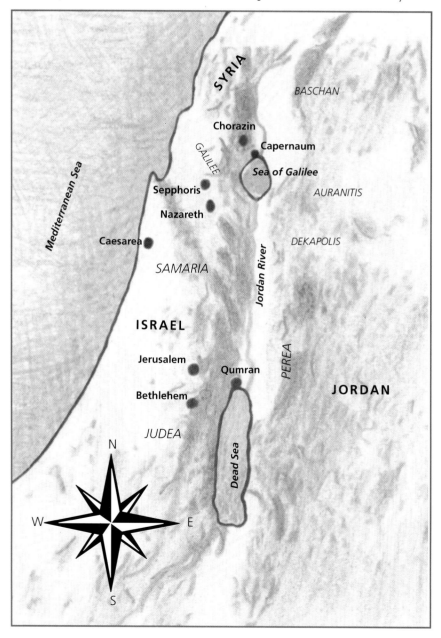

The ruins of Ma'rib

cense-burning tradition from its early beginnings.

Incense-Burning Recipes from God

The Israelites were strongly influenced by the traditions surrounding them. They were simple shepherds who knew very little about incense-burning substances, perfumes, and fragrant salves for sacred or worldly purposes. We know little about the incense-burning tradition of the early Hebrews. The first prophets spoke about many possibilities in which God would find favor with them. The use of fragrances, however, was not one of them. After Joseph's brothers sold him to spice and fragrance merchants, he sent different perfumes and incense-burning substances to Israel.

They were carrying spices, balsam, and myrrh and traveled to Egypt (Genesis 37:26).

However, during their prolonged captivity in Egypt, the Jews learned much about burning incense for sacred as well as for worldly purposes. At the end of the second century B.C., when they finally returned to their homeland, they began to share what they knew about the use of fragrant incense. Earlier, Moses announced that he had received a recipe for incense burning from God, the first biblical account concerning fragrances. God gave Moses precise quantities, including instructions on how to use the different ingredients. This took place in approximately 1500 B.C. The recipe was part of the Law of God in which He gave the order to burn incense as a sacrifice to Him and included a ban:

Whoever would burn incense for worldly reasons for himself must be banished and destroyed by his people.

You can find the recipe for the temple frankincense in Exodus 30:34–37. The Lord told Moses:

Take these aromatic substances: storax and onycha and galbanum, these and pure frankincense in equal parts; and blend them into incense . . . Grind some of it into fine dust and put this before the commandments in the meeting tent where I will meet you."

In addition, God told Moses what an incense-burning altar should look like:

For burning incense you shall make an altar of acacia wood, with a square surface, a cubit long, a cubit wide, and two cubits high, with horns that spring directly from it. Its grate on top, its walls and all four sides, and its horns you shall plate with pure gold. Put a gold molding around it." (Exodus 30: 1–3)

The altar that Moses built was

135

about 16 in. (40 cm) long, 16 in. (40 cm) wide, and 3¼ ft. (1 m) tall. The acacia wood was plated with gold.

About Incense-Burning Sacrifices

In the book of Exodus, we find the first explanation of the sacredness of sacrificial incense burning and the instructions given by God to Moses. The ascending smoke is "the image of the breath and the name of the Lord." In this sense, incense burning had become a means of communication with God. It was also a message to the heavens. The ancient Hebrews considered these incense-burning sacrifices sacred. The fragrance of Temple frankincense and the sacred oils, whose recipes God also gave to Moses, represented the presence of God and a guarantee of the connection between God and the people.

The Kabbalah explains the mysticism of the four substances that make up the sacred incense-burning mixture used in the Temple. The substances stand for the four elements: water, earth, air, and fire. To Christians, they symbolize the four parts of prayer: petition, intercession, glorification, and thanks. Balsam, myrrh, galbanum, and frankincense represent our inner feelings of humility, faith, love, and hope. They find union in the ascending, fragrant smoke. The high priest would burn incense on the altar in the morning and in the evening as part of the sacred ceremonies. However, over time, incense was burned for purposes other than sacred ones. But in the early days of Christianity, the so-called "sacred smoke" was not used during certain periods at sacred ceremonies.

For 200 years, Christians considered incense burning to be a heathen tradition and banned it from churches. During the reign of Constantine the Great (280–377 A.D.), the awareness of the divine nature of sacred fragrances won out, and frankincense was again part of every worship. It became an enduring component of traditional ceremonies in Roman and Greek churches. The enthusiastic use of frankincense, however, turned into sheer exploitation, and this fragrant resin became rather rare. Pope Pius V allowed the use of Peru balsam for incense burning as a substitute for frankincense. However, with that exception, the Catholic churches continue to use frankincense, even today. The incense-burning vessel, carried in pendulous fashion in the aisle of a church, releases a smoke familiar to almost all of us.

This vessel was not developed until the ninth century. Prior to that, the priests burned aromatic substances in open vessels. The incense-burning vessels carried through the church during worship have developed over centuries into truly artistic objects. Those from the Italian and Spanish Gothic style are particularly

Hebrew incense-burning altar

136

beautiful. In these, angels are depicted as controlling the chains of the incense vessels, just as they were seen in the figurines displayed in churches, as well as in the paintings. For instance, in the cathedral in Freiburg, Germany, an angel stands in a lead-glass window alcove, industriously swinging the frankincense vessel back and forth.

The containers used to store the precious frankincense were also made of precious materials. In that sense, the containers expressed the high value, material and mystical, of frankincense. People have found small, golden frankincense vessels in the treasure chambers of cathedrals that have stored frankincense since the late Middle Ages. Golden spoons have been found that the priest would use to sprinkle the frankincense on the glowing charcoal. The fact that many acolytes fainted when frankincense was used too enthusiastically leads to the conclusion that this resin contains psychoactive substances. Like marijuana, frankincense contains tetrahydrocannabinol, which expands awareness. If you burn too much frankincense, slight changes in consciousness may occur.

About the Fragrance of Princely Clothing

Let us return to the Hebrews. After the priests abolished the severe law about the use of incense, they allowed people to indulge in the pleasure of fragrances again. Other incense-burning substances found their way into worship as well as into households. Women had to adhere to very specific cleansing rituals, which included the use of fragrances and incense-burning substances. For instance, they loved to use fragrances on their clothing and blankets. They placed fragrant plants and resins between layers of clothing and stored them in chests. They suspended clothing above an incense vessel so the rising smoke would carry the fragrances into the fabric. King David had his royal clothing treated in this manner in order to tempt the daughters of neighboring kings.

With myrrh and aloe and cassia your robes are fragrant (Psalm 45:9).

In addition to essential oils and incense substances used for sacrifices, such as frankincense, storax, galbanum, and myrrh (stakte), God mentions four additional fragrant substances used in recipes for sacred salves: balsam, cinnamon, spice reed, and cinnamon clove. Together, they make up the eight pleasing fragrances of Moses. The practice of incense burning and the use of salves for sacred and also worldly purposes gained more and more favor.

Perfume and incense gladden the heart (Proverbs 27: 9).

Other fragrances the Israelites used for incense burning included: aloe wood, mastic, myrtle, labdanum, spikenard, cedar, sandalwood, and opoponax.

The Saint of Fragrances

The biblical spikenard is connected to a female figure who intentionally used the spikenard plant as a symbol for esteem and mercy. The oil Mary Magdalene used to anoint the feet of Jesus contained spikenard, much to the consternation of the priests, since at that time this substance was very expensive. Mary Magdalene's father was an incense merchant and had given her three small marble flasks of this precious "Oil of the Kings." Mary Magdalene became the saint of fragrances. During the Middle Ages, she was the patroness of perfumery in all of Europe. The value placed on these oils at that time is obvious when we look at the gifts that the Three Kings carried: frankincense, myrrh, and gold. The Wise Men from the East brought three of the most precious gifts of their time, and two of them were incense-burning resins.

They were overjoyed at seeing the star and on entering the house found the child with Mary, his mother. They prostrated themselves and did him homage. Then they opened their coffers and presented him with gifts of gold, frankincense, and myrrh. (Matthew 2:10–11)

Let's follow the Three Kings on their journey into the fragrant land of the Hebrews, where we will get to know the incense-burning substances in more detail.

Effective Incense-Burning Substances of the Bible

The Eight Pleasing Fragrances of Moses

Cassia

Cinnamomum cassia Flower

Cassia, also called Chinese cinnamon, was one of the ingredients used in the sacred oils. It was also used as a perfume.

You love justice and hate wickedness; therefore God, your God, has anointed you with the oil of gladness above your fellow kings. With myrrh and aloes and cassia your robes are made fragrant . . . (Psalm 45: 8–9).

Sometimes cassia was part of the sacred incense-burning mixtures used in the Temple. Cassia reached Israel from East Asia along the merchants' route. People used the dried bark and dried flower buds for incense-burning mixtures. Cinnamon and cassia work well in incense mixtures designed for Christmas and in mixtures that should have a sensuous flavor. Today, Cassia is grown in Indonesia, Vietnam, and Japan (see also chapters on *India* and *Japan*).

Frankincense

Boswellia sacra cartary Birdw.

People considered this resin, also called *levonah,* to be one of the treasures of the Temple of the Israelites (Nehemiah 13:5). It was part of the popular Temple incense-burning mixture of Moses, but people also burned it by itself. The Bible mentions frankincense 22 times. Up until the days of Solomon, people only used frankincense for religious purposes. According to a legend, God permitted Adam to take frankincense with him when He drove Adam from Paradise.

The Phoenicians brought frankincense to Israel via the spice route through southern Arabia. We believe that the Three Kings brought the frankincense with them from Yemen as a precious gift for Jesus. To this day, the Roman Catholic Church still uses frankincense, also called olibanum, as an incense-burning substance during ceremonies and worship services (see also chapters on *Arabia* and *Egypt*).

Balsam

Commiphora gileadensis (L) Engl.
Commiphora opobalsamum (L.) Engl.

Balsam, obtained from a tree, and also called Mecca or Balsam of Gilead, belongs to the same family as the frankincense and myrrh trees, the Burseracae. This tree or shrub thrives in the hot desert. It sheds its pinnate, deciduous leaves during the dry periods. The small pitted fruits contain a yellow, fragrant seed that people boiled and then pressed into a waxlike substance for incense burning. At the time of the harvest, they cut the bark of the tree. The tree produced a light yellow to greenish, honey-like liquid that takes on a red or reddish brown coloring during the drying process. In biblical times, the balsam tree grew mainly in the forests of Gilead and in the mountains around Mecca, which gave it the name Mecca balsam.

The resin with the best quality came from the area around Jericho and the village of Ein Gedi. The king maintained a monopoly of the balsam trees. This tree was one of the most important and valued commodities for commerce. In biblical times, people paid double the weight of its resin in silver. In addition to the resin, the wood was traded as balsam wood and the fruits as balsam seeds.

The fragrance of balsam seems to have enchanted people in ancient times. Pliny wrote that its fragrance surpassed all others. Balsam has a lemony, gentle, herblike, velvety, warm, and rosemarylike fragrance. Mary Magdalene's father owned a balsam forest, and he was under orders from the king to produce a consecrated oil. Both the oil used for consecration and the frankincense used in the Temple contained balsam. Judea cleverly kept a monopoly of the balsam trees for a long time. They exported balsam throughout antiquity. Egyptians used balsam for sacred purposes, for embalming, and for producing some of the most precious perfumed salves. Balsam arrived in Europe during the Crusades. There, too, it was one of the most precious and rare incense-burning substances. But somewhere along the line, the West lost the fragrant trail of this aroma. Today, it is almost unknown. It is almost impossible to find pure balsam.

Myrrh

Commiphora abyssinica (Berg) Engl.
The Bible mentions myrrh just as often as frankincense, but it seems that the Hebrews preferred the fragrance of frankincense. During Solomon's time (960 B.C.), both myrrh and frankincense were used exclusively for rituals. Myrrh was also an ingredient in the sacred in-

Balsam tree

cense-burning mixture used in the Temple. In these recipes, it is called *stakte*. The part of myrrh used in this recipe is fresh bark, which is harvested, boiled in water, and then pressed. During antiquity, *stakte* was even more valuable than myrrh resin.

According to Pliny, the price of *stakte* was much higher than that of myrrh. In that sense, the gift of the Wise Men from the East was particularly precious,

since they brought *stakte*, not myrrh to Jesus. At that time, people used myrrh resin to make sacred oil. It was also one of the most valued beauty creams used by Hebrew women. Jesus received myrrh at his birth and on the day of his death. He accepted the myrrh handed to him before he was crucified. In early history, the custom was to give myrrh wine to a condemned man before he was executed, as a

Myrrh

kind of anesthesia. The extensive cleansing rituals that Hebrew women performed stipulated the generous use of myrrh. The myrrh sold by resin merchants was myrrh gum and originated mainly in Somalia (see also chapters on *Arabia* and *Egypt*).

Cinnamon

Cinnamomum zeylanicum Breyn.

The bark of the cinnamon was also part of the sacred oil. The Hebrews used it as an incense-burning substance, for perfume, to scatter indoors, as an aphrodisiac, and as a spice. They imported it from faraway places

(see also chapters on *India, Japan, Egypt*).

Spikenard

Nardostachys Jatamansi (All) D.C.

Spikenard belongs to the Valerianaceae family. The part of the plant used most often is the aromatic root. The fragrance is earthy and musky. Sometimes, it reminds us of a goat, and, in fact, Pliny called the spikenard

root "little goat." The plant grows in the Himalayan Mountains at elevations of 10,000–16,500 ft. (3,000–5,000 m). During ancient times, people thought spikenard root was the tail of an animal because it is covered with curly root hairs that give this elongated root a tail-like appearance. In Israel, people used spikenard in incense burning and for anointment. Sometimes, they added the root to the sacred frankincense mixtures used in the Temple. The Song of Songs mentions it three times.

> *For the king's banquet my spikenard gives forth its fragrance.* (Song of Songs 1:2)

Spikenard was one of the most precious fragrance substances. People believed it was the fragrance of love, but they also thought the plant had strong mystical powers. They used is as a sacred oil for the anointment of kings and the dead. It had particular meaning for Mary Magdalene.

> *Mary brought a pound of costly perfume made from genuine aromatic spikenard with which she anointed Jesus's feet. Then she dried his feet with her hair and the house was filled with the fragrance of the anointment.* (John 12:3)

The mysterious and tangy fragrance of spikenard has a strong effect on the nervous system. Depending on how you add spikenard to incense-burning substances, the plant's fragrance promotes a very specific effect. Since ancient times, people have used spikenard as a strong sedative for the treatment of the nervous system. Spikenard has a balancing and deeply calming effect on all types of restlessness, feelings of fear, and insomnia due to nervousness and stress.

When burned, it has a grounding effect and works well in cases of nervousness and stress due to mental exertion. For incense-burning purposes, finely grate the root and place it on top of burning charcoal or into an incense-burning vessel. You should burn spikenard together with other herbs and resins since its aroma, when used individually, is very strong and sharp. Because spikenard was a very rare and precious incense-burning substance, plants with similar fragrances were often used to replace it, for example, camel grass, *Cymbopogon schoeanthus (L)*, which grew wild in the region where the Hebrews lived. Here, too, they used the roots in a dried and grated form.

Agar Wood
Aquillaria agallocha Roxb.

The Bible often mentions the agar wood tree. Unfortunately, translators often mistakenly call it aloe, a plant that belongs to a different family. We often have difficulty trying to determine

when the text means aloe and when it means agar wood. Agarwood trees grow in northern India. This fragrant wood is one of the most precious incense-burning substances of antiquity. Kings perfumed their clothing and beards as well as their indoor quarters with it (see also chapters on *Japan* and *Arabia*).

Aloe
Aloe ferox Miller
Aloe barbadensis Miller

Aloe is a plant with thick, sword-shaped leaves, similar to the leaves of the agave. It belongs to the Asphodelaceae family, although in the past, people thought it was part of the lily family. The edges of the leaves are serrated. The stem of the flower, which can grow up to 2 ft. (60 cm) tall, has tube-shaped orange-yellow flowers. The thick liquid from inside the leaves turns into dark brown, square, resinous gumlike pieces when dried. Today, the aloe commonly used comes from South Africa. It is called cap aloe and now grows in many countries around the world. Originally, aloe came from southwestern Arabia. The Phoenician and Greek merchants distributed it widely. Since antiquity, people have used the juice fresh or thickened as a laxative or for intestinal cleansing. You thicken it by boiling it over an open fire for four

Aloe

1. Aloe
2. Spikenard
3. Cinnamon blossoms
4. Frankincense, purified
5. Galbanum
6. Agar wood
7. Frankincense
8. Myrrh
9. Golden frankincense
10. Frankincense

hours. To this day, people consider it an important element in their medicine cabinet. What is less well known is that aloe is one of the classic incense-burning substances. The peoples of Mesopotamia, Egypt, and Greece valued it highly and used it for healing purposes, embalming, and incense burning. The Hebrews considered aloe to be a sacred incense-burning substance and also used it for embalming.

"Nikodemus, the man who had first come to Jesus at night, likewise came, bringing a mixture of myrrh and aloe..." (John 19:39)

When burned as an incense, aloe develops a fruity, sweet, heavy, and warm fragrance. It reminds one of ripe plums or black raspberries. Small blisters will open when you expose aloe to heat, and the blisters will expel puffs of smoke. Sometimes, we use aloe in combination with other ingredients to give the mixture a warm, pleasant background. Aloe is relaxing, calming, and comforting.

Galbanum

Ferula galbaniflua Boiss.
Ferula gummosa Boiss.

Galbanum, an oleo-gum resin, comes from the fennel-like umbelliferous plants that grow wild in Iran and Lebanon. Two different types of galbanum are available. People select the soft, Levantine, whose color is anywhere from yellowish to olive brown primarily for its fragrance. Manufacturers use it in great amounts for perfumes. The second type of galbanum resin, Persian, is solid. People value it for its great healing properties. Galbanum has a green, mossy, woody, balsamic, resinous fragrance that is similar to musk. The fragrance is highly complex. You can produce galbanum resinoid by cleaning raw galbanum resin in a solvent. The solid mass produced by this process is then used for incense burning.

Galbanum was a highly valued medicine used to calm a patient who was experiencing severe nervous states or anxiety attacks, particularly in cases of agoraphobia. It calms and relaxes in times of confusion and tension. Galbanum-gum resin was also part of the sacred incense-burning mixture used in temples. In ancient Mesopotamia, people frequently used galbanum for incense burning, and it is likely that the Israelites learned about its use during their imprisonment in Babylon. Merchants brought galbanum from Babylon to Israel. The Bible mentions galbanum twice. While frankincense could only be used for sacred purposes, galbanum and myrrh were often added to other mixtures for household use (see also chapter on *Mesopotamia*).

Recipe for Incense Burning from the Holy Land
Incense from the Three Holy Kings

Frankincense	3 parts
Myrrh	2 parts
Benzoin	1 part
Mastic	1 part
Cinnamon flowers	½ part

Crush the resin with a mortar and pestle. Crush the cinnamon bark or cinnamon flowers (*Flores cassiae*) separately and then add them to the resin, possibly adding a small amount of golden frankincense—"gold-plated" frankincense seeds. This gives the seeds a brilliant luster and is very decorative in any incense-burning mixture. The Catholic Church reserves golden frankincense for very specific events. The fragrance is full-bodied, warm, comforting, strengthening, and uplifting. It is a gift for the body, mind, and soul. This incense-burning mixture is particularly effective for emotional rejuvenation when you feel washed out and lacking energy.

The Queen of Sheba visiting King Solomon

Guardian Angel
for Simocho

Frankincense	1 part
Mastic	2 parts
Sandarac	1 part
Dammar	1 part

Use a mortar and pestle to crush the resin into small pieces, but do not pulverize it. Add this in small pinches to the charcoal. This produces a delicate, ethereal mixture. The fragrance surrounds you in a protective aura. People believe that this sublime fragrance connects them to the helpful energies of the angels. The fragrance gently supports prayer, meditation, and reflection. It strengthens the soul, neutralizes negative energies, and creates a clean atmosphere.

The Kingdom of Angels

Mastic	2 parts
Iris root	½ part
Myrtle leaves	½ part
Dammar	1 part
Sandarac	2 parts

Crush the resin in a mortar and pestle, but do not pulverize it. Grate or crush the iris root. Crush the myrtle leaves in your hands and mix all the ingredients well.

This is a fragrance full of gentleness and light. It gives wings to the soul so that we may fly to the kingdom of angels. The mixture makes us aware of angels, opens spiritual energies, and supports healing activities.

King David's Temptation

Myrrh	4 parts
Agar wood	½ part
Cinnamon bark	1 part
Sandalwood	1 part

Crush agar wood with a mortar and pestle. Do the same with the myrrh. Add pulverized cinnamon and pulverized sandalwood to both ingredients. Place a pinch at a time on hot charcoal.

King David used this mixture to seduce and flatter the ladies. He suspended his royal clothing in the smoke, and the fragrance filled his bedroom. The mixture has a velvety-warm fragrance with a touch of seduction, ideal for tender hours!

Busame—
The Secret Garden

Myrrh	1 part
Cinnamon bark	1 part
Spikenard	1 part
Sandalwood	2 parts
Mastic	1 part
Rose petals (dried)	a few

Finely grate the spikenard root. Crush the myrrh and mastic with a mortar and pestle. Crush the sandalwood and cinnamon and add them to the other ingredients. Add a few dried rose petals. This recipe creates a warm, deep fragrance with a fine scent of sandalwood that is an invitation to retire to a mysterious garden for dreaming and deep relaxation. It is very harmonizing, calming, and relaxing when you are stressed or restless. It is also useful in cases of insomnia.

Incense for the Temple

Storax	1 part
Myrrh	2 parts
Frankincense	2 parts
Galbanum	1 part

Finely crush solid pieces of resin and knead them into the softer ingredients. Shape this into pellets the size of peas. This Hebrew mixture symbolizes the four elements. It produces a balsamic, dignified, and powerful fragrance. It works well for prayer, petition, and meditation.

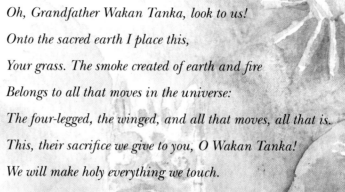

Oh, Grandfather Wakan Tanka, look to us!

Onto the sacred earth I place this,

Your grass. The smoke created of earth and fire

Belongs to all that moves in the universe:

The four-legged, the winged, and all that moves, all that is.

This, their sacrifice we give to you, O Wakan Tanka!

We will make holy everything we touch.

Incense-burning ceremony for vision search,

from Dennis and Barbara Tedlock, *The Edge of the Deep Canyon*

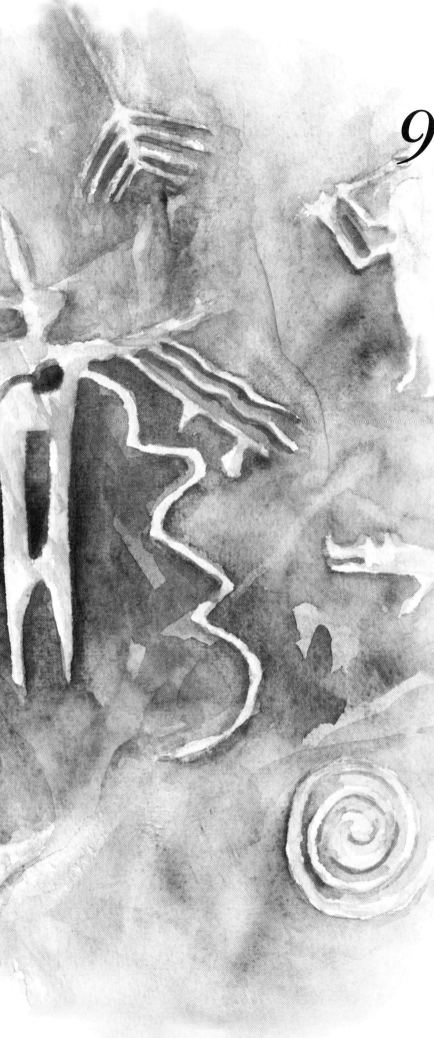

9 AMERICA

THE PLANTS OF POWER

I am looking down. Below is the earth, just awakening and gently illuminated by a silver streak on the horizon, announcing dawn. Four nights and four days I kept watch, prayed, and sang songs. I have looked deeply within myself and searched, being awake and aware of what is around me and above. I searched for my vision. Searched for something that would reveal the meaning of my life. The night had been difficult. Fear had attacked me like a pack of hungry wolves. I almost gave up. But then I remembered the small green medicine bag my grandfather had given me and which I had placed on a piece of bark. It was made from green deer leather and decorated with pearls. With hands outstretched I searched for it in the dark across the rocky ground. And there it was; I opened it. The bag was filled with fragrant sacred herbs. My grandfather had impressed on me the importance of using this mixture only in an extreme emergency—when I needed help from my angel. I placed a handful of the herbal mixture on a hot stone in the campfire. A warm, power-ful fragrance surrounded me. It calmed my fears. My mind followed the smoke upwards, and then it seemed as if a wall of clouds was opening up, and I could see everything clearly in front of me. I saw myself, my journey, and my task for this, my life. I thank Wakan Tanka for this vision, for this light, for these herbs of power.

North America

About the Balance of Earth

To this day, the Native American tribes of the American continent have retained a knowledge that tells us about Father Earth and Mother Earth. It tells us that all who are alive are brothers and sisters. Everything lives in an unimpeachable balance of which the *elnog*, the human being, is a very important element. Respect, responsibility, and high regard for the earth, the plants, the animals, and other people are natural consequences of the Native American belief system. The white settlers who claimed the land were amused by the Native American' religious attachment to nature. To the settlers, considering plants and animals to be their brothers and sisters was a sure sign that the Native Americans were heathens. The settlers considered the Native American culture primitive, without a written language worth mentioning, without art and architecture, and, therefore, not worthy of any further consideration.

But now the white man has come up against the limits of Western civilization in a sense, against the limits of what Mother Earth can bear. The tremendous accomplishments of Western civilization have expanded so far that they have become destructive. The water of the earth is polluted, the air is lifeless, and an expanding hole in the ozone allows deadly, cancer-causing rays to penetrate the atmosphere. Only recently have scientists recognized that the earth is an organism that needs to be handled with care, as the Native Americans understood centuries ago. The earth is an entity that nurtures its inhabitants, but it needs attention and respect. Amazingly enough, today's modern scientific methods and ancient Native American spiritual wisdom are coming closer every day. In 1855 in Washington, DC, Chief Seattle said in a speech that we are, after all, brothers and sisters. For these siblings, so unlike each other, to join together might be just what we need to rescue us from the approaching collapse of the whole earth. Only through attention and respect toward Mother Earth and all her inhabitants can we learn to live with nature in a nondestructive way.

Spiritual Companion

Using Native American plants for incense burning can open us up to a deeper and more respectful way to communicate with plants. Today, our contact with medicinal plants is usually limited to book knowledge, a collection of facts about substances contained in plants, and the effects of those substances. This does not allow for the spirit of the plant, its very essence, to reach us. With a more intuitive knowledge, we can better understand that a medicinal plant can be the carrier of energy, healing, and wisdom.

Plants can teach us what we

Pacific Ocean

New York

San Francisco

UNITED STATES

Los Angeles

Atlantic Ocean

N

Gulf of Mexico

MEXICO

W   E

Mexico City

S

burn incense to support healing ceremonies and to activate the potential for self-healing. In addition, incense burning can be a part of ceremonies of initiation, transformation, departure, and death. Incense burning often accompanied sacred spiritual dances. Native Americans often burned incense during council meetings and when giving a person a name. They even cleansed their horses with incense burning whenever they prepared for a long journey. Burning incense connects people to sacred energies and symbolizes opening up to the cosmos and to that which is godly.

Native American incense-burning plants are particularly tough, powerful plants that thrive under very difficult conditions—plants similar to those that grow at high elevations in the Himalayas. The plants collect the energy surrounding them and pass it on when they are used for incense burning. At the same time, they create and strengthen a connection between earth and heaven. The expanse of the horizon, the endlessness of the Native American landscape, are essential parts of the spicy, aromatic fragrance of the plants, and open new horizons for us. From the very beginning, Native Americans used pottery bowls, iron pans, and hot stones, or brilliant blue shells. They would fill half the shell with sand as a safe base for the glowing charcoal. They burned the dried herbs on the charcoal. To keep the charcoal glowing and spread the smoke, Native Americans used particularly beautiful large

would be unable to find in books. As has been the case in every traditional culture, plants reveal their knowledge through incense burning. When we burn herbs as incense, they transfer their energy to us. Traditional Native American incense-burning plants are powerful gifts from Mother Earth that can accompany human beings on their search for their origins in heaven. The rising smoke takes our thoughts to Wakan Tanka, the creator of all things. In order to walk this earth properly and peacefully, we need to make use of plants that can support us on our spiritual journey. They can strengthen us, remove our fear, neutralize negative influences, cleanse our mind and the atmosphere around us, and support our search for a vision of the meaning of life.

In the Native American tradition, to live in harmony and beauty with all things that the Creator has given us is to be a good and happy person. Plants can fulfill our aspirations. Fragrant, sacred smoke can be helpful to us as we discover our life's journey and the tasks ahead. We

feathers, often decorated with pearls, to fan the fire. Feathers from different birds symbolized power and energies or wisdom and knowledge. A similarly symbolic use of feathers exists in the Tibetan culture.

The Sacred Pipe

The pipe ritual is a specialized kind of incense-burning tradition developed by the Native Americans. In this ritual, the incense-burning herbs were smoked in sacred pipes. The pipe symbolized the earth with a feminine element (the head of the pipe) and a male element (the stem of the pipe). With the burning tobacco and the rising smoke, the elements of heaven and the creator became visible. The ceremony connected earth and humans with heaven. The rising smoke was the messenger, carrying the thoughts and desires of those seeking advice from the Creator. In this ceremony, the

pipe was first offered toward the sky in six different directions. Next, the pipe was lowered to touch the ground and then

Ceremonial teepee

raised up to the sky. Only then could the ceremonial smoking begin, accompanied by songs and prayers.

Native Americans used tobacco, or a mixture called *Kin-*

nick Kinnick, for this smoking ceremony. In addition to tobacco, the traditional mixture contained other plants, such as mullein, yerba santa, red willow, sweet grass, bear's grape, and osha root, as well as passion flowers, sassafras bark, birch bark, and piment. Tobacco grows wild in North and South America. People felt it was a holy plant with sacred meaning because they believed it connected them to the gods. But tobacco was also thought of as a medicinal plant, used to treat toothaches, malaria, and many other conditions. White settlers in North America adapted the use of tobacco as a healing plant. But because tobacco was a pleasurable substance, its use became more and more a matter of habit. Thus, this powerful plant lost its healing energy and was no longer thought of as medicinal. It even became hazardous to the health of those who smoked it for pleasure.

Ceremonial pipe

Native American Cleansing Ceremonies

Native American incense ceremony

A simple incense-burning ceremony was very beneficial at the beginning of a gathering, seminar, or discussion and for ceremonies, sweat-lodge rituals, inner cleansing, and focusing with people gathered in a circle. Native Americans lit incense-burning herbs in an incense bowl or shell. The facilitator or leader of the ceremony then walked clockwise around the circle. Sitting or standing in front of each person, he offered the burning herbs for cleansing, gently fanning the smoke with a feather. The partic-

ipants used both hands to draw the smoke to the heart, above the head and arms, and then towards the ground, imagining throughout the ritual that the smoke from the burning herbs was cleansing and strengthening. At the conclusion, the leader placed the bowl outside on the ground until the herbs and the charcoal were completely burned and the fire was out. They offered the smoke and the subliminal energies that surrounded the people present as a gift to the space. Simple songs or prayers supported this ceremony.

Effective Incense-Burning Substances of Native Americans

Sage, White Sage

Salvia apiana

White sage is one of the most common incense-burning plants used by Native Americans. North America is home to many different types of sage used differently by tribes in different regions. Sage was used for incense burning as well as for many varied medicinal purposes. The Navajos crunched the leaves to treat burn wounds. Many tribes burned sage to treat rheumatism. They also used it for hot compresses. Native American tribes from the desert region used sage tea to replace the fluids lost due to perspiration. Sage reduces perspiration and thus keeps the liquid in the body. Supposedly, this is one of the reasons the Apaches could survive in the desert for such a long time during a war.

One of the most popular types of sage for incense burning is the so-called "white sage," *Doh-loo-na*. White sage grows in the coastal regions in southern California between Santa Barbara and Baja California. This powerful plant has leaves with a whitish, hairy covering that give the plant its name. Its blue labiate flowers are a beautiful contrast to the silvery white leaves and stems. Native Americans thought it was an effective atmosphere-cleansing plant and used it during healing rituals, sweat lodge ceremonies, and ritual feasts. But they also used sage to cleanse indoor spaces and objects. When burned, sage has a fresh, herbal fragrance. It refreshes the mind and enhances memory. Burning white sage supports the path to wisdom and mental clarity. But you can substitute other types for white sage. Whatever sage you use must be completely dry because damp sage has a musty scent. Sage is easy to cultivate in a flowerpot or in the garden. Nurseries offer different kinds of sage. All of these work well for incense burning, such as:

Garden Sage

Salvia officinalis L.

This type of sage originally came from the Mediterranean. It is not winter hardy, and in rough climates must be brought inside. Garden sage develops a sweet, herbal, typical sage fragrance when burned.

Incense Sage

Salvia repens var. repens

This sage comes from Africa. It produces an abundance of particularly beautiful blue flowers. In South Africa, people burn the leaves for ceremonial purposes. Incense sage produces a strong, resinous aroma. The plant is available in nurseries and is easy to cultivate.

Russian Sage

Perovskia abrotanoides Karel
Perovskia atriplicifolia Benth.

Botanically speaking, this plant is not a sage, but people use it as such because it contains very similar substances. In Russia, people have used this sage for incense burning and as an herbal tobacco for a long time. It has a very intense, fruity, herbal fragrance and works very well as an addition to incense-burning mixtures. The plant is also available in nurseries and easy to cultivate. You should harvest it on a warm summer's day. Place the leaves on a piece of cloth to dry or tie them together in small bundles and suspend them in the air.

Traditionally, Native Americans used sage together with the tips of juniper and sweet grass. Incense burning with sage works particularly well for cleansing indoor spaces and objects and to accompany healing ceremonies. In Europe during the Middle Ages, people also used sage to cleanse the air in a sickroom. In many countries, people routinely burn sage for medicinal purposes because it creates an atmosphere of wellness and stimulates healing. Native Americans knew that sage was a plant that would bring harmony to arguments, dispel hate, and reduce dissatisfaction. They employed its disinfecting and lung-strengthening energy to heal chronic bronchitis.

Juniper (Hoo-Na)

Juniperus monosperma Sarg.

For Native Americans, juniper was one of the plants used most often for incense-burning. They used the evergreen tips of twigs. Juniper creates a sweet, warm fragrance. It strengthens, heals, accentuates, and cleanses. The cedar tips that are part of Native American incense-burning mixtures are in reality tips from the juniper plant. Native Americans still burn juniper frequently to welcome guests and to support peyote ceremonies. They also still burn it to cleanse horses and automobiles. Burning juniper is particularly suited to accompanying prayer and sacred songs. The fragrance is dignified and carries all things to the Creator. People also place it on hot stones during sweat lodge ceremonies. The juniper of the high desert in New Mexico, Arizona, and Utah has a particularly strong, warm aromatic note. It has always been prized by Native Americans. Its fragrance expands the mind, creates and expands internal space, and clarifies. This type of juniper is effective for any type of incense burning.

Native Americans also use the dried needles or wood of the frankincense cedar, *Calocedrus decurrens*, which belongs to the cypress family. This tree, which grows primarily in the Sierra Nevada, in Baja California, and northern Oregon, is about 100 ft. (30 m) tall. People consider it a sacred, powerful tree that can recharge the energies of indoor and outdoor spaces. You can usually purchase it in shops that carry incense substances. It is sold as Indian cedar tips.

Juniper tree in Canyon Chelly

Sweet Grass

Hierochloe odorata (L.) Wahlenb.

Sweet grass, also called Seneca grass, has a vanillalike fragrance. It belongs to the Pocaceae family of sweet grasses, a large family that has approximately 9,000 different species. Many members of this family, such as palmaros grass, citronella grass, vetiver,

and ginger grass, are high in essential fragrant oils and provide a very aromatic smoke when burned. Sweet grass grows in the large expanse of the American prairie, in Canada, and even in Europe (see chapter on *Northern Europe*). Sweet grass loves damp soil. The lower ends of the long stems are a reddish hue. Sweet grass from America and Europe is available in nurseries and is easy to cultivate in pots or the garden. Native Americans dry and braid these long grasses. When they burn them as incense, they light one end and gently blow out the flame, allowing the grass to continue to smolder, slowly releasing its fragrance. While this is one way to use dried sweet grass, you can also crush it and add it to other incense-burning mixtures.

Sweet grass produces a pleasantly light fragrance that is much like freshly mowed grass and woodruff. It cleanses the atmosphere and is also used during sweat lodge and similar cleansing ceremonies. Native Americans also use sweet grass in tobacco mixtures for sacred pipe-smoking ceremonies, adding it to the bark of the willow tree. According to Native American tradition, "Kind and helpful ghosts love the fragrance of sweet grass." Burning sweet grass attracts positive energies. The sweet and pleasant fragrance is valued during ceremonies to heal, to create a positive connection between student and teacher, to cleanse a space, and to search for vision. Traditionally, Native Americans would first use sage to cleanse a space of the evil ghosts

that caused illnesses. Next, they burned sweet grass to create a positive atmosphere and to attract helpful ghosts.

Sweet grass is a fragrance for the soul. It creates a clean, pleasant atmosphere, allowing relaxation, helping to find serenity, lightness, and healing. During a ceremony, it connects those around the fire with the positive energies of plants. Incense burning with sweet grass can help the people within a group become better attuned to one another. What would it be like if a conference, for instance, opened with an incense-burning ceremony that used sweet grass?

Desert Mugwort

Artemisia tridentata Nutt.

A species of mugwort that grows in the American Southwest is often mistakenly called desert sage. The plant loves dry, sandy soil. The coyote, a sacred animal according to Native Americans who often carved its likeness in totem poles, lives in the high desert between the silver-colored desert sage. The coyote stands for wisdom, cunning, and energy. It

is able to survive in even the most difficult situations. Native

Americans consider the desert mugwort the plant of the coyote, who, according to native mythology, used this plant to soothe water demons. During very specific, sacred ceremonies, for instance the Sun Dance, dancers wear desert mugwort on their clothing, masks, ankles, and wrists.

Native Americans believed that desert mugwort protected against the influence of illness-causing ghosts and negative energies. Its energy cleansed body and spirit. They used it to remove negative influences from rooms, buildings, and outdoor spaces. They covered the floor of the sweat lodge with desert mugwort, filling the lodge with its fragrance during the ceremony. They also used it to cleanse ceremonial objects, such as sacred pipes, medicine bags, prayer arrows, and shields, by suspending them above the smoke. They tied the plant together into sticks, about 4 in. (10 cm) long and 1 in. (3 cm) around, dried them, and used them for incense burning. They used desert mugwort alone as well as in mixtures.

During times of exhaustion and weakness, the fragrance of this plant provides new energy and helps rediscover our own energy reserves. In these hectic times, where we so often go beyond our limits, focus too much on the outside world, and over-exert ourselves, burning this ancient, powerful plant can help us rediscover our own boundaries and limitations.

Mountain Balm (Yerba Santa)

Eriodictyon californicum Benth.

Yerba Santa grows in the dry climate of the mountain regions in Arizona, New Mexico, California, and Mexico. These regions gave the plant its name. It is a

tough shrub, 3¼ ft. (1 m) high, with dark green, oval leaves that have a hairy, whitish covering. At the end of the branches grow six to 10 whitish to blue flowers. The leaves and stems excrete a gum-like liquid when they are exposed to strong sunlight. This substance has a very strong aromatic fragrance. The name "Yerba Santa" indicates that it was considered a sacred plant of energy. It is traditionally kept in medicine bags. As the name implies, people believe it has strong healing powers. But people also used it for many other purposes.

Native Americans believe that this plant neutralizes negative influences and illness-causing energies. Its fragrance creates an atmosphere of healing, which is why they burn the sacred balm during healing ceremonies and in sickrooms. According to Native American tradition, it re-duces weakness, fear, emotional injuries, and helps transform these into strengths and trust. It supports the process of inner growth and neutralizes the atmosphere created by arguments, fear, and aggression, allowing healing energies to return. Mountain balm can be helpful in correcting inappropriate behavior that has led to illnesses. Today, people also use this plant in flower therapy, which is very popular in California, to increase self-regard and begin a process of growth and development.

In Native American medicine, mountain balm was a preferred remedy for all illnesses of the respiratory system. It was used in the form of tea, as compresses, and for incense burning. People believe this herb is particularly helpful for chronic bronchitis, hay fever, asthma, lung infections, and tuberculosis. But they also consider it an important remedy for treating rheumatism and paralysis. It is helpful for all degenerative illnesses. Spanish monks gave this plant the name Yerba Santa. The Native Americans had made them aware of the plant's important medicinal effects.

When burned, mountain balm creates a warm, spicy fragrance. When you burn it by itself, use it in small amounts. The best way to use it is in a mixture with other plants.

Recipes for Native American Incense-Burning Substances

Healing (Na-Ho-Chldzl)

White sage	2 parts
Sweet grass	1 part
Mountain balm	1 part

When white sage is not available, you can substitute common garden sage, *Salvia officinalis*. Cut sweet grass into fine pieces and crush the mountain balm into small pieces. This mixture is useful for incense burning in sickrooms, for healing ceremonies, and for creating an atmosphere of healing for emotional injuries and grief. It is also beneficial when people get together after they have had disagreements or arguments. You can use it during seminars and the like. Literally translated, the Navajo word for cleansing, *Be-Hozho-Na Ho Glachl*, means "something that will return us to the original state of beauty and harmony."

Power and Clarity (Be-Ah-Dzill)

Juniper tips	10 parts
Sweet grass	2 parts
Juniper berries	1 part
White sage	1 part
Desert mugwort	1 part

Juniper tips (*Juniperus monosperma*) are, as we mentioned earlier, often mistakenly called cedar tips. Cut the sweet grass, desert mugwort, and white sage into small pieces. This mixture has a warm, woody, herbal fragrance. It strengthens and expands the mind and creates an atmosphere of clarity that helps us rediscover our own inner strength and supports the search for serenity. It is useful for many different purposes: for rituals, for cleansing outdoor spaces, objects, and indoor spaces. People also use it to welcome guests and to say good-bye. You can use it for personal incense-burning rituals meant to increase focus and to remove confusion during times of severe emotional upset.

Cleansing (Be-Hozho-Na Ho Glachl)

Juniper tips	4 parts
White sage	2 parts
Sweet grass	2 parts

Crush and mix all the ingredients. This incense mixture works well to cleanse the atmosphere where therapeutic work is done and in waiting rooms. People also use it in areas where either illness, fear, or arguments have left negative energies behind. It helps produce reconciliation and clarification after arguments. It clears a confused life situation, cleanses objects, and helps heal.

Entranceway, Pueblo ceremonial room

Oraibi

White sage	1 part
Desert mugwort	1 part
Boldo leaves	1 part
Juniper tips	3 parts

Dry all the ingredients, crush them, and mix them well. This mixture has a spicy, fresh, and powerful fragrance. People use it during ceremonies that open the spirit and give the gifts of freedom and esteem. Boldo leaves are available where herbs are sold. The rest of the ingredients are available wherever incense-burning substances are sold. Oraibi is one of three Hopi villages and the oldest continually occupied village in North America. The effect of this incense-burning mixture corresponds to the power and mysticism of its location.

Hopi

White sage	1 part
Juniper tips	1 part
Desert mugwort	1 part
Copal (white or gold)	2 parts

Crush the herbs in the palm of your hand. Crush the copal with a mortar and pestle. Then, mix all the ingredients well. This is a highly effective incense-burning mixture that creates an atmosphere of healing, power, and stability. It works well during ceremonies conducted for healing purposes and for prayers and meditation. People also burn it after a sweat lodge ceremony. This mixture cleanses internally, stabilizes, and supports clarity.

1. White sage
2. Desert mugwort
3. Juniper berries
4. Yerba Santa (mountain balm)
5. Juniper tips
6. Sweet grass

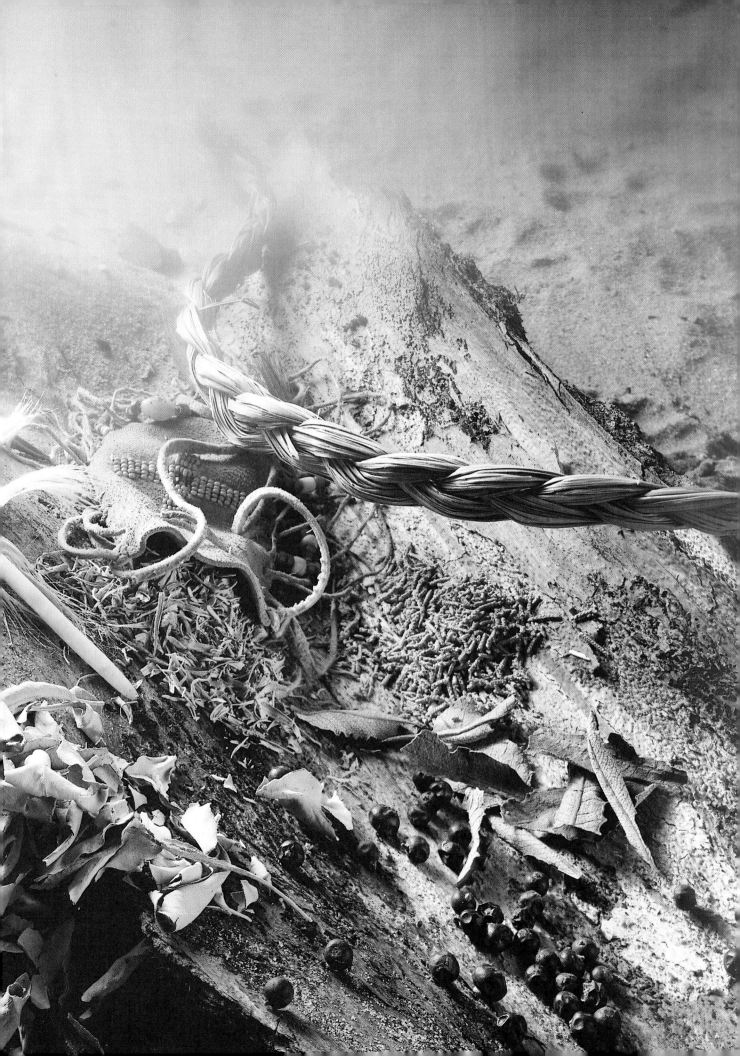

South America

In the Kingdom of the Sun and the Jaguar

The very advanced civilizations of the Aztecs, Incas, and Mayans flourished in Central and South America. The highlands of Mexico, the South American Andes, and the high plains of Guatemala were the home of people from highly developed cultures that had their golden age between the third and the 16th centuries. Medicine and pharmacology had reached a very high level of development.

In their greed for gold, the Spanish *conquistadores* decimated the whole culture. Fortunately, a few remnants still give witness to the incredible knowledge of these cultures. One of these remnants is the record made by a Spanish physician, Hernández. In 1510, the king sent Hernández to the New World to research the wealth of medical knowledge known to exist in ancient Mexico. Hernández was amazed by how much these "primitive heathens" knew—far more than people in Europe. Botanists in the New World had identified over 4,000 healing plants and had listed their applications. In addition to the work left by Hernández, we also have the so-called "Book of Wisdom" of the Mayans, the *Popol Vuh*, which gives us insight into their use of plant substances.

In the ancient cultures of Mexico and Peru, burning incense was part of medicine. They also burned incense during rituals dedicated to the gods and during complicated magical ceremonies. Native people would burn incense in honor of the arrival of the European *conquistador*, not realizing that it would

not prevent the Europeans from raping the country. The preparation of certain incense-burning mixtures for sacred purposes was solely the province of the priesthood. The recipes, it was said, came directly from the gods. The priests received the recipes after consuming plants that created hallucinations. The sacred Teonanacatl mushroom enabled them to enter into a dialogue with the gods. They connected everything with the divine. Fragrances represented color, sounds, constellations in the sky, and stones. A prescription for a sick person was designed according to his horoscope and a very complicated calendar system.

Fragrant plants played a particularly important role in their medicine. They believed that fragrant plants were endowed with great powers, that these plants could have very strong emotional effects, and that they could even cleanse a person of his sins. The forests of Central and South America have an inexhaustible reservoir of healing and incense-burning plants.

Tribes that still live in these regions use plants for healing and for magic purposes. Many of these plants are unknown in the West, so in this chapter, I will limit myself to those incense-burning plants that are available to us.

The Gift of the Jaguars

One of the most important incense-burning substances of the ancient American cultures was the resin from the copal tree. The holy book of the Mayans says that the divine god of the earth extracted copal resin from the tree of life and gave it to humans as a gift. That made the Mayan copal a heavenly, sacred resin embodying the presence of the divine.

Depending on the type, a copal tree delivered three different types of resin: black, golden, and white, also called Copal Negro, Copal Oro, and Copal Bianco. For the "frankincense-of-the-gods" mixture, they mixed all three together and sacrificed

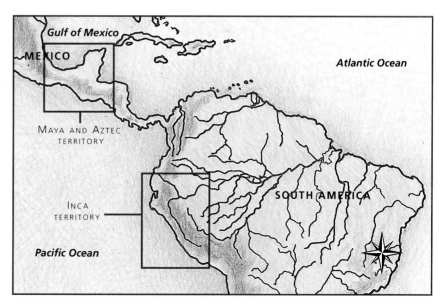

Steam bath of the Aztecs

the mixture to the gods. They bound three bundles together and burned them as a sacrifice, turning towards the east and the rising sun. The Incas assigned copal resin to the sun. They considered it an incense-burning substance for the god of the sun. They placed copal incense on golden plates and burned it four times a day as a sacrifice. People considered copal incense to be the fruit of the gods. They burned aromatic herb mixtures inside the house in beautifully decorated terra-cotta containers placed on small altars of ceramic, bronze, or stone that usually stood on three legs. Sometimes they decorated these sacrificial plates with animals, such as jaguars, hummingbirds, and serpents.

Each pre-Columbian culture created its own design. Their incense-burning mixtures usually had a warm, sunny fragrance, as if they were prescriptions designed by the god of the sun. The sun, whose power the jaguar symbolized, seems to have been captured in the incense-burning substances of the Mayans, Aztecs, and Incas. According to Mayan mythology, the *Popol Vuh*, the three different copals were given to them by three different jaguars.

Jaguar vessel

Mixtam copal is the copal that the jaguar Quitze has brought,
Caniztan copal is the copal that brought the night,
Golden copal was brought by the jaguar Mahucutah.
Each one had his own copal which they burned as they turned in the direction of the sun.
They howled sweetly as they shook the burning copal, the copal that is so precious.

They used other mixtures to induce sleep, and they burned plants to create hallucinations. They stuffed incense herbs into pillows to stimulate dreams that would bring healing and harmony. They believed, as the ancient Greeks did, that incense burning could stimulate prophetic dreams. Plants with specific cleansing properties were assigned to the goddess of the moon, Tlazolteotl. She was also called "the one who devours impurities." She would swallow the emotional impurities of human beings and spit them back out again, cleansed in the form of health and vitality. They believed that the goddess of the moon invented sweat lodges and saunas to cleanse the body and the soul. Instead of using branches and animal skins to construct sweat lodges, as was the custom of northern Native Americans, Mexican and Peruvian sweat lodges were built with volcanic rock heated from the outside. For the Aztecs, a steam bath early in the morning was part of their daily routine. For that reason, each house had its own sweat lodge. The Aztecs boiled plants with cleansing properties inside so that the rising fragrance could increase the effect of the sweat lodge.

Effective Incense-Burning Substances of the Mayans, Aztecs, and Incas

Copal

Protium copal
Bureseru microphylla

The three civilizations called the copal tree *Copalquahuitl,* which is why we call it copal today. Originally, the copal tree grew in Mexico. Today, however, it also grows in western Africa, India, Madagascar, Mozambique, Zanzibar, Manila, and Congo. Several different trees provide copal, including the resin of the Australian kauri spruce, *Agathis australis hort. ex Lindl,* an evergreen tree that grows up to 130 ft. (40 m) tall. East Indian copal comes from the *Canarium bengalese,* which also produces fossil resin, and is sometimes also available. The resin of the dammar tree, *Agathis alba,* is sold as Manila copal. Authentic copal, the type used in pre-Columbian cultures, comes from trees in Central and South America.

The copal resin considered most precious and valuable comes from trees that were hit by lightning. Ancient peoples considered this a gift from the "god of lightning," who passed his power on to the tree through lightning. They sacrificed this resin to the god of the sun during very specific ritual feasts. The Mayans considered copal resin so sacred that once they placed it on the altar, they could only touch it with very special wooden instruments. Some tribes still practice this ancient tradition of incense burning today. Ancient tribes burned copal during ceremonies involving initiation or consecration. Today, some tribes practice ceremonies of prophecy in which they throw corals, crystals, and corn seeds in the fire as an oracle while copal is burning. In ancient times, burning copal accompanied all official activities having to do with the gods.

In Central America, copal resin comes in three different varieties: yellow-white, transparent, and black. Transparent copal has a fruity, lemony, light, bright, frankincenselike fragrance, which is like a touch of tenderness. It is spiritually cleansing and aids in mental and spiritual work. White copal is harvested in liquid form and placed on leaves to dry. Black copal has a powerful, mysterious, heavy, balsamic, mystical fragrance. It is much more expensive than white because people feel it is a better quality. Night copal, as it is also called, carries the secret energies of the night. It is grounding and connects to the deeper layers of the soul. It is also calming and can be helpful in recognizing contradictions within, letting you find the darker side of the soul. Gold copal, which is amber in color, has a gentle, soft, and warming fragrance. It opens the soul. It stimulates imagination and intuition and can support creativity and inspiration. Gold copal supports imaging and visualization for therapeutic purposes. Mayans burned it at sunrise to honor the sun.

All three types have a very strong healing power. You can use each copal resin individually or you can mix them together. Experiment to find which one of these wonderful resins speaks to you. Each one strongly affects emotions. The raw resin has almost no aroma. It only develops an aroma when you heat it. The copal resin available today comes from Central and South America, Manila, and Congo.

Peruvian Balsam (Naba)

Myorxylon balsamum (L) Harms var. pereirae

Peruvian balsam grows in the northern regions of Central and South America, not just in Peru. It grows chiefly in the tropical forests of Guatemala, Honduras, Costa Rica, El Salvador, and Nicaragua. The tree reaches heights of 60–65 ft. (18–20 m). The Mayans burned its resin for medicinal purposes. Naba, as they named the tree, served as a remedy for kidney and bladder illnesses, irregular menstruation, and colds. Knocking on the tree stimulates balsam production. The natives peeled off the outer bark later and soaked up the dark brown syruplike liquid with

Peru balsam

rags. They boiled the rags in water to release the resin. Peruvian balsam is not stringy and won't dry out. It has a very pleasant vanilla and cocoa flavor.

Synthetic Peruvian balsam, *Balsamum perurianum arteficiale*, is also available. It contains resins, balsam, and synthetic ester. You should not use this balsam for incense burning. Pay attention when you buy Peruvian balsam. For a long time, Europeans have used balsam as part of natural healing. Peruvian balsam also has a very long tradition as an incense-burning substance. In 1521, the pope gave permission to substitute Mecca balsam for Peruvian balsam, for incense burning and for sacred oils used in anointments.

When using Peruvian balsam for incense-burning purposes, knead it with the other dry substances into a usable dough. It has a warm, vanillalike fragrance. Peruvian balsam was also part of the so-called "incense-burning ceremony for luck" because people believed it attracted wealth and happiness and protected against emotional excesses. It supported creative imagination and dream work.

Tolu Balsam

Myroxylon balsamum (L) Harms var. balsamum

Tolu balsam trees grow in the northern part of South America, primarily in Colombia. Experts say that the best tolu trees grow in the lower delta of the Magdalena River near the city of Santiago de Tolú. This tree, like the Peruvian balsam tree, belongs to the Fabaceae family. The tree has a straight trunk and will grow as tall as 40 ft. (12 m). It has deciduous leaves and small white flowers. All parts of the tree have an aromatic fragrance. The balsam discharges from V-shaped cuts in the bark and is collected in calabash containers.

Tolu balsam is soft, can be kneaded, and contains crystals. The liquid hardens over time, and the resin becomes dark brown or reddish brown. Tolu balsam is a traditional remedy even in European medicine. In 1882, it was officially listed and available in apothecaries as a remedy for coughs and colds because of its mucus-dissolving and antiseptic properties. In addition, people also treated headaches, gout, and stomach problems with this balsam. The fragrance of vanilla, cinnamon, and freshly mowed grass is due to vanillin, cinnamon acid, and coumarin. A balsamic, warm base surrounds these individual fragrances.

People have used tolu balsam as an incense-burning substance for a long time. They consider its fragrance to be healing and comforting in cases of emotional wounds. It accompanies meditation and ceremonies that promote inner healing and coming to terms with emotional injuries and conflict because it is calming, relaxing, and harmonizing. When burned in the evening, it works well to calm racing thoughts and prepare for a refreshing sleep. Tolu is able to blend the individual substances in a mixture harmonically and can soften tangy fragrances.

Copaiba Balsam

Copaifera reticulata Ducke
Copaifera guyanensis Benth.

The copaiba tree grows in South America, primarily in Venezuela, Brazil, and Guatemala. It belongs to the Fabaceae (Leguminosae) family. This variety has extremely powerful resin channels. People valued copaiba balsam as a remedy for venereal diseases and for problems involving the mucous membranes. Until recently, people used this balsam to make tracing paper and varnishes for painting porcelains. Some trees can produce up to 13 gallons (50 l) of balsam. The balsam comes in a thick liquid that varies from clear to yellowish to yellow-brown. Copaiba balsam has a balsamic, woody, spicy fragrance similar to patchouli. You can also add this balsam to other dry or pulverized incense-burning substances and form the mixture into small pellets.

Oracle Sage (Pipiltzintzintli)

Salvia divinorum

Oracle sage, the sacred plant of the Aztecs, has an almost unpronounceable name. It belongs to the family of the labiates, like its relative, the sage. You cannot grow this plant from seed, which leads us to assume that the way it was cultivated a long time ago created very distinct characteristics. To this day, the Mexican Oaxacans, descendants of the Aztecs, cultivate this plant in forests whose locations they keep secret. It is still used today to promote visions; for instance, people believe that burning the leaves allows the Virgin Mary to appear during Annunciation.

The Western world had no knowledge of this plant until the 1960s, when an American ethnobotanist discovered it. With the permission of an Oaxacan priest, he brought some plants to California for cultivation. Now, you can also buy oracle sage in European nurseries. This plant needs a soil rich in humus. It also re-

quires high humidity to thrive. The plant is not winter hardy. Aztec mythology tells us that this plant was a gift from the gods to make it possible for humans to make contact with them. The Aztecs believed that it promoted human awareness of spiritual and cosmic energies. It is one of the many sacred, mysterious plants of the world, and we should use it with gratitude and respect.

Dream Herb (Zacatechichi)

Calea zacatechichi

The dream herb, the mystical plant of the Maya, is still used as a plant for fortune-telling. The Mayans believed that it made it possible for people to receive advice and remedies in dreams. As was the case in ancient Greece, people were searching their dreams for answers to the important questions of life and for healing remedies. Scientists have discovered that Zacatechichi actually strengthens dream phases during sleep. In that sense, this ancient, sacred Mayan plant may become an aid in dream analysis and dream research. If you use your dreams as a gate to the unconscious, you may want to experiment with this plant someday. Use one of the dream mixtures and burn it in the evening before you retire. Consciously

1. Benzoin
2. Tolu
3. Tonka beans
4. White copal
5. Dark copal
6. Gold copal

concentrate on dreaming and make notes when you wake up. Use the notes for reflection, searching, creative work, or simply as an adventure.

Zacatechichi is a shrub that grows up to 5 ft. (1.5 m) tall. It is easy to cultivate from seed in pots; however, because it is not winter hardy, bring it indoors for the winter. In Mexico, it thrives at higher elevations in the rain forest, where it grows between Scotch pines and oak trees.

Boldo

Peumus boldus Mol.

The small, evergreen boldo tree can grow up to 20 ft. (6 m) in the Andes in Chile. The natives consider it a very important healing remedy for parasitic infections, diarrhea, bladder infections, altitude sickness, problems involving the uterus, and more. It is also an accepted remedy in European medicine, used particularly for liver illnesses. Ancient people burned boldo leaves mixed with the resin of copal, pine, or Scotch pine. They believed it was helpful for respiratory illnesses and nervous insomnia. The smoke of the boldo plant is calming, spiritually cleansing, harmonizing, and is helpful for nervousness and sleep disorders. The fragrance of the aromatic leaves is very similar to mint, camphor, laurel, and grape.

Tonka Bean

Dipteryx odorata Willd.

The elongated, dark brown tonka bean is the seed of the tonka tree, which grows up to 65–80 ft. (20–25 m) tall and belongs to the Leguminosae (Fabaceae) family. It grows in Venezuela, Guyana, Brazil, and Nigeria. The fragrance of the tonka bean is reminiscent of a freshly cut mountain meadow at the height of the summer. Coumarin gives it a sweet, herblike fragrance. Finely grind the tonka bean and add it to mixtures in small amounts. It lightens the mood and is emotionally warming and harmonizing.

Boldo

Recipes of South American Incense-Burning Mixtures

Golden Jaguar (Mahucutah)

Gold copal	1 part
Sage	1 part

Copal should have a golden to amberlike coloring. Crush it with a mortar and pestle into small pieces; don't pulverize it. Use oracle sage or North American white sage, *Salvia apiana* (see also chapter on *North America*). Crush dried sage in the palm of your hands and mix it in equal parts with copal. The mixture is cleansing and a good preparation for meditation and reflection. It calms restlessness and is helpful in situations that need clarification. It frees you from everyday troubles.

Jaguar of the Night (Caniztan)

Gold copal	3 parts
Dark copal	1 part
Myrrh	1 part
Tolu	½ part
Vanilla powder (not synthetic)	¼ part

Grind the resins with a mortar and pestle and add the vanilla. Jaguar of the Night carries you into the exotic sensuality of a warm tropical evening. Its velvety, flattering fragrance strokes the senses and the soul. It allows imagination to play and invites dreams. It is an incense-burning recipe for the evening and the night. Its fragrance is very calming and works particularly well in cases of severe stress. Only burn it in small amounts, a pinch at a time.

Goddess of the Moon

Oracle sage (*Pipiltzintzintli*)	1 part
Copal, gold or white	4 parts
Boldo leaves	1 part
Benzoin	1 part

Crush the resins into fine pieces with a mortar and pestle. Crush the dried leaves in the palm of your hands and mix all well. This is a mixture with a fine, ethereal, herblike fragrance. It encourages intuition and sharpens the senses. People believe that it creates true dreams and is helpful in discerning the future. It supports healing and works well during divination, for instance, I Ching, Tarot, and Rune laying, etc.

Aztec incense-burning bowl

Frankincense of the Gods

Black copal	1 part
Gold copal	1 part
White copal	1 part
Golden frankincense	½ part

Crush (but don't pulverize) all three copal resins with a mortar and pestle and add the golden frankincense. This mixture has a balsamic, resinous, dignified fragrance. It is an enormously effective incense-burning recipe that connects us to divine inspiration. It works well for ceremonies, prayers, and healing rituals.

Dream Colibri

Dream herb (*Zacatechichi*)	1 part
White copal	3 parts
Black copal	1 part

With a mortar and pestle, crush the resins into small pieces the size of seeds. Crush the dried herb between the palms of your hands. Mix everything together well. This mixture can clarify dreams and help you remember and understand them. Burn the incense before you go to bed but before you actually get into bed. Air out the room well and lie down, concentrating on the idea that your dreams will be crystal clear. Have a note pad and pencil handy on your nightstand and write down your dreams when you wake up. The next day, take time to think about and re-experience your dreams.

The perfume asked the flower:

Tell me why I exist.

Don't be discouraged, my friend,

In the completeness of the dawn of the morning,

Your life will be united with everything that is alive,

And you will know, finally, your purpose.

Rabindranath Tagore

10 INDIA

MOTHER OF FRAGRANCES

India is an ocean of fragrances. Waves of pleasant fragrances emanate from flowers, trees, incense-burning substances, such as perfume, fragrant powder, sacrifices, and incense sticks. Sometimes they are heavily sweet and often almost unbearable in the face of the suffering on the streets. When I reach India by plane, the fragrances of India, the mother of all fragrances, greet me at the airport. Pleasant warm spices mix with the sweet aroma of incense-burning sticks and the fragrance of dry earth. Then, on the way into the city, the diesel fumes of crowded streets mix with the sensuous breath of jasmine flowers that grow alongside the road. I close my eyes. Mother India, I feel the embrace of your warm, sensuous fragrance.

From the Abundance of the Fragrant Flora

No land on earth possesses such an immense amount of fragrant flora as India. The "Mother of Fragrances" stretches from the highest elevation of the Himalayan Mountains down to Cape Comorin on the Indian Ocean. Each of the many different climate zones produces its own plants with their own gifts of fragrant flowers, balsamic woods, and aromatic resins. No wonder

India developed the whole culture of fragrance to its highest level and for centuries its fragrances were part of religious life. The people of India used fragrances for incense burning, for medicinal purposes, to prepare medicines, and for perfumes and beauty products.

The Indian tradition of fragrances has influenced the entire Asian region. Life in India is often accompanied by fragrances that are always available. In India, you can purchase a great variety of fragrant substances from a merchant called a *gandhika*. Mountains of fragrant substances, often in open sacks, huge wooden crates, and bags made of newspaper, offer sandalwood shavings, fragrant resins, vetiver roots, and incense sticks. Every street in every city has its own peculiar fragrance. Sometimes every corner of every house has its own fragrance. Incense sticks and incense-burning substances burn in countless temples in the villages and cities. Traveling through the country, you are awash in a constantly changing wave of fragrances. Rudyard Kipling, the famous English writer who traveled throughout India and described it beautifully in his novels, insisted that he was able to recognize each region in India by its specific aroma.

But we will confine our visit to those fragrances used for incense burning and leave aside the endless variety of fragrant plants that are specifically used for perfumes. For incense burning, people in India use simple brass and stoneware, as well as artistically created incense-burning pans in the shapes of animals. These are usually made of brass or bronze and hang from the ceiling on very delicate chains.

The religious practices of Hinduism are closely connected to fragrant substances. Ancient people thought that fragrances were helpful in bringing divine inspiration. They burned fragrant sacrifices for the many different gods and goddesses in temples, as well as on altars in the house. For instance, the religious honor

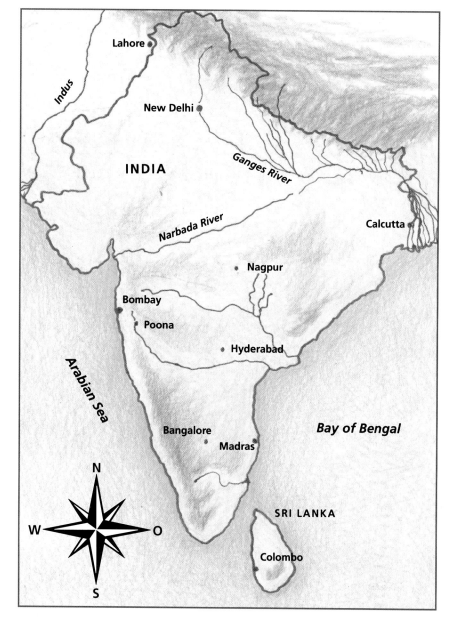

Incense burning in the temple

the god Shiva every four hours with fragrances. During the ritual of the Holy Fire, called *Agni Hota*, they ritually light a fire every evening and every morning, and burn fragrant substances on dried cow manure, the commonly used heating material. In *Sakuntala*, a poem by Kalidasa (fifth century A.D.), we find a fragrant incense-burning sacrifice:

> *Sacred fires on consecrated ground, nourished by wood, blaze in the hearth around the altar. May they, together with the holy sacrifice of fragrance, erase my sins and cleanse you!*

From the "Instruction in the Art of Love"

People used fragrances as sacrifices to the gods. They also used them to please their own senses. According to the principles of Hinduism, a prerequisite for a life lived in harmony, corresponding to the divine principle, is a life with a fulfilling and well-balanced love life. The use of pleasant fragrances supports this life. The people of ancient India used fragrant oils for massages and scented baths to please the senses. They believed that using plants such as sandalwood, aloe, and benzoin for incense burning increased sensual attraction. The poet Kalidasa wrote the following about the pleasures of the senses:

> *Beautiful ladies, preparing themselves for the feast of pleasures, cleanse themselves with the yellow powder of sandal, clear and pure, freshen their breath with pleasant aromas, and suspend their dark hair in the smoke of burning aloe. aloe.*

The *Kama Sutra*, the "Instruction in the Art of Love," written in the fourth century A.D., describes the daily morning ritual of Hindus who are members of a higher caste. They nourish their bodies with a fragrant cream, caress their lips with wax and plant

Gita Govinda, Radha and Krishna

juice, brush their teeth, attach a flower to their clothing, and inhale a very gentle fragrance.

The *Kama Sutra* considers the artful handling of fragrances as one of the 64 arts that ladies and gentlemen of the cultured class needed to exercise well. They burned incense in the form of mixtures, powders, as *Dhoop* (herbs and resins combined into a pliable substance), and incense sticks, called *Agarbatti*. All of these were frequently used in India, creating a lifestyle drenched in fragrances. Indians pulverized parts of plants, such as sandalwood, aloe, benzoin resins, spikenard roots, patchouli leaves, and vetiver roots, and mixed them with a bonding substance such as gum arabic. They added saltpeter, with or without pulverized charcoal, to guarantee that the mixture burned well; then, they formed long cones 4–12 in. (10–30 cm) long and allowed them to dry. You can find fragrant incense sticks almost anywhere in India: on altars, in taxicabs, buses, at the vegetable stand, and in households, where people burn them as a sacrifice. They fill the air with sweet fragrances. Unfortunately, today, manufacturers add a great deal of synthetic fragrances, often imported from the West. Pure, natural incense sticks are very difficult to find.

The Most Beautiful Gift from India

First follow me to one of the holiest places in India, to Benares (Varanasi), where the mighty and sacred Ganges River, originating in the Himalayas, is the longed-for destination of every Hindu believer. Since Hindus believe that everything in life moves in circles, it is not important if we join the celebration of birth or observe a burial ceremony. For the Hindus, both are the beginning of a new life. Along the Ganges are burial sites where, after the bodies are burned, the ashes are given to the river. Here we might experience one of the most important fragrance substances of India: sandalwood. When a family cremates a wealthy Hindu, they often add large chunks of precious sandalwood to the fire. Sandalwood, they feel, supports the person's journey to a more magnificent life. Describing the many different ways in which people on the Indian subcontinent use sandalwood would fill an entire book, because it is almost inseparably connected to the Indian way of life. Its fragrance accompanies every stage in life. It is a fragrant gift for the journey into the next life as well as an erotically stimulating fragrance for sensual pleasures. According to Kalidasa,

> *During the summer months the ladies of the court,*
> *rub oil of sandalwood on their breasts,*
> *oil of jasmine in their hair and,*
> *that prepares them for love making.*

Fragrant sandalwood is one of the most beautiful gifts India has given to the world. Wherever people inhale it, they have a sense of being enriched, of well-being, of the fullness of life. Warm, soft, gentle, balsamic, sandalwood caresses the senses. It is a fragrance for lovers and a gift that promises wonderful dreams. In India, they use sandalwood for body powder, oils, perfumes, incense sticks, and, of course, also for incense burning. This has been the custom for centuries. *Chandan*, as sandalwood is also called, is mentioned in the *Nirukta*, the oldest Vedic

commentary (fifth century A.D.) as well as in Sanskrit writings, such as the *Ramayana* and *Mahabharata*. People were making sandalwood oil as early as the sixth century B.C. European tastes came relatively late to the pleasures of the precious sandalwood. It didn't appear in Italian apothecaries until the 15th century. Let's give in, then, to the pleasures of this wonderful Eastern aroma, allowing our souls to be inundated by it. Burning just one small piece of this precious wood gives us an immediate sense of the balsamic fragrance.

Healing With Sandalwood

People in India, the homeland of sandalwood, believe it has great radiance and protective energies. Very early on, people in India observed that termites,

Sandalwood twig

which destroy so much of the precious wood that grows in India, never attack sandalwood. For that reason, they considered it a symbol of vitality.

Ayurvedic medicine, considered the science of longevity, used this wood as a remedy and termed it bitter, cooling, relaxing, and contracting. Ancient people used it to treat bladder and kidney infections, problems of the respiratory tract, and many other illnesses. They used the pulverized wood for compresses for inflammations and skin problems. A paste produced from powdered wood and rosewater is used as a remedy for scorpion bites, inflammations, hemorrhaging, eczema, and other skin diseases. The sandalwood fragrance is used as a remedy for headaches and as a highly effective antibacterial substance when disseminated in living spaces. Here, sandalwood was mixed in powdered form with clarified butter, formed into small pellets, and burned on hot charcoal.

Tibetan medicine, which has been strongly influenced by Ayurveda, uses the fragrance of sandalwood to ease emotional weariness stemming from too much mental work and intellec-

tual exertion. The fragrance of sandalwood creates an atmosphere of calm and supports the search for inner peace, reflection, and balance. Today, this fragrance works particularly well for people who suffer from stress and a hectic lifestyle. Sandalwood fragrance will slow you down without making you sleepy. It penetrates deeply into your emotional world, soothing, calming, and relaxing. Because it dissolves tension, it aids you in rediscovering deeply buried inner strengths. The fragrance of burning sandalwood is an invitation to the imagination to go on a wonderful and rejuvenating journey. You may use sandalwood in the form of wood chips, shavings, or powder. For a mixture, powder is best.

Botanical Research into the Forest of Sandalwood

Let us now take a closer look at this magical, fragrant tree, *Santalum album*. Don't be disappointed to hear that this plant is a semi-parasite that receives part of its nutrients by withdrawing them from other trees. Because it has green leaves, the tree is capable of photosynthesis, but it needs additional nutritional substances, such as nitrogen and phosphorus that it sucks out of the roots of other trees. Sandalwood trees love all types of bamboo, palm, teak, guava, and clove trees as hosts. The sandalwood tree can grow up to 33 ft. (10 m) tall and can have a diameter of up to 7 ft. (2 m). Its evergreen leaves are elongated, lanceolate, and opposite each other on soft branches. The small flowers, arranged in panicles, have no fragrance.

The essential oil of sandalwood, the fragrant substance of the tree, only develops in trees that are more than 25 years old. You can harvest if from trees that are between 30 and 60 years old. The true sandalwood tree, *Santalum album*, grows in India, primarily in eastern India in the regions around Mysore and Karnataka, where the best aroma develops. Transplanted into different soil in different regions, the tree loses its very specific fragrance. The present yield of Indian sandalwood, which is the property of the government, amounts to about 1,000 tons per year. The wood is auctioned off to merchants in India. The Indian government is trying to prevent the exploitation of this precious wood; however, illegal harvesting and smuggling of sandalwood has not stopped.

Another tree, the *Anyris balsamifera L.* from the West Indies, is also sold as sandalwood. It grows in Venezuela, Jamaica, and Haiti. However, this tree belongs to a different family and species (Rutaceae, rue plant). It is sold at a considerably lower price because the quality of the fragrance is far below that of the Indian sandalwood tree. People use the red sandalwood tree, *Santalum rubrum*, mainly for medicinal purposes for internal use, although it does add a beautiful visual element to any incense-burning mixture.

The antelope-colored true sandalwood provides the base for Indian incense-burning mixtures and incense sticks. Depending on the recipe, people use it by itself or they add it to other incense-burning substances. Sandalwood is very compatible and works with almost any fragrance. Other incense-burning substances that are typical of India are: benzoin, common myrrh, spikenard, costus, patchouli, galangal, agar wood, cardamom, vetiver, clove, copaiba, dammar, cinnamon, elemi, tree moss, saffron, calmus, tulsi, nutmeg, inulin, terminalia, and rose mallow.

Effective Indian Incense-Burning Substances

Elemi

Canarium luzonicum (Miqu) A. Gray
The elemi tree belongs the Burseraceae family. It grows in the tropical regions of Asia. Growers in the Philippines cultivate most of it. The resin available on the market usually comes in a thick liquid. The process of extraction produces a more solid resinoid. To harvest the resin, you make incisions on the bark 50–100 ft. (15–30 m) above the ground. When you burn elemi, it provides a lemony, woody fragrance

Sandalwood tree

Elemi

with a hint of fennel, frankincense, and grass. It has clarifying, cleansing, and energizing properties, and it stimulates mental ability. Elemi works well for meditation and yoga exercises in the morning. It creates a spirit of new beginnings and hopefulness and relieves depression. Traditionally, people use elemi with substances that are refreshing and cleansing, such as mastic, lemongrass, and sweet grass.

Common Myrrh

Commiphora mukul (Hook ex Stocks)
Boswellia serrata Roxb.

The resin of this Indian frankincense tree is called Indian frankincense or Indian *Bdellium* (in Sanskrit called *Guggulu* and in Hindi called *Guggu*). The people in ancient India used it the way people in Arabia used frankincense. Common myrrh grows in middle and central India, mainly in Rajasthan and Gujrat. Very powerful thorns cover this small tree, which is gnarled and looks much like the frankincense tree in Arabia.

The resin, harvested by making incisions in the bark, comes mainly from trees that grow in the wild. In India, people burn the gum resin of the common myrrh tree for sacred offerings in temples and in the house. It is also a well-known remedy in Ayurvedic medicine and highly valued for its reducing and antiseptic energies. According to Ayurvedic teachings, common myrrh increases *pitta*, or energy. In Arabic countries, they use common myrrh as a tonic for stomach tension. They also use it as a remedy for rheumatism in the form of a salve to massage into the affected areas or for incense burning. In addition, it is a diuretic and is helpful in dissolving thick mucus in the respiratory tract. It is also a remedy for treating colds.

Ayurvedic medicine uses common myrrh to strengthen the uterus and calm nerves. Ayurvedic doctors also prescribe it for sciatica and arthritic pain. They use a salve made with common myrrh to treat the area around bone fractures, swollen glands, and skin ulcers. In India, people believe it is the best remedy for detoxifying tissue and helping with weight loss. Common myrrh is also taken orally. It is usually combined with other plants and prescribed in tablet form (*Naraka guggulu* and *Triphala guggulu*). Ayurvedic medicine uses a prescription that contains common myrrh as a very effective treatment for psoriasis (*Guggulu tiktaka ghrta*). In India, common myrrh is offered as an Ayurvedic medicine called *Sallakie*, used with great success to treat inflammatory arthritis.

Few people in the West are aware of the many benefits of common myrrh, despite the fact that scientific research has shown that it reduces pain, has calming properties, and quickly reduces muscle cramps. Common myrrh has a milky white-to-golden coloring. Its fragrance is simultaneously sweet, balsamic, herblike, and resinous with a slightly vanillalike tone. Use it for incense burning individually or in mixtures. Burn it on charcoal or on the metal sieve that covers the opening of incense-burning urns. Burning common myrrh is helpful for chronic colds and lung problems. For these purposes, mix it with dried sage and use it as an overall strengthening substance for the respiratory tract, particularly for heavy smokers. It also improves the air, particularly in city apartments and houses. Burning common myrrh strengthens the immune system. It cleanses the body and works well during a detoxification and weight-loss program.

In India people believe the fragrance reduces appetite. According to Ayurvedic medicine, common myrrh rejuvenates and emotionally revitalizes. It creates a feeling of emotional well-being. Used during prayer and meditation, it cleanses the aura and dissolves disturbing influences. This makes common myrrh very useful for treating severe stress and nervous insomnia. Burn common myrrh in the evening, allowing enough time to relax before retiring. In India, people often mix common myrrh with benzoin resin.

Benzoin

Benzoe Siam-Styrax tonkinensis Craib.
Benzoe Sumatra-Styrax benzoin Dryand.

Benzoin is a resin, or gum, produced by the benzoin tree. It belongs to the Stryraceae family. For incense burning, people usually use resinoid, which is more solid. You obtain the resin through an extraction process that uses alcohol or other solutions: 6½ lb. (3 kg) of resin produces 2¼ lb. (1 kg) of benzoin resinoid. The fragrance of benzoin is highly valued in India because it is soft, sensuous, and warm. It mixes well with other ingredients, gives them fragrance, and, together with sandalwood, makes one of the most typical incense-burning mixtures of Asia. Benzoin trees grow in India, Sumatra, Java, Thailand, and Cambodia. In India, people have long used it as a remedy for respiratory and skin diseases. They believe the smoke to be particularly helpful for dry cough. Benzoin is the equivalent of frankincense in the temple. It is burned in front of statues and paintings that depict the divine entities that symbolize Brahma, Vishnu, and Shiva. (See also chapter on *Egypt*.)

Dammar

Canarium strictum
Canarium prostratum Schiffn.
Shorea wiesneri Schiffn.

The dammar tree grows in India and Southeast Asia, where you can find whole forests of it. It belongs to the Dipterocarpaceae family. Different qualities of dammar resin are available. Sometimes you have difficulty determining the exact quality because dammar is often a collective term used for different resins from Southeast Asia. The resin

comes to the market in pieces that are transparent and shaped like stalactites, usually with a yellowish or reddish tint. But it can also be transparent and colorless. A dusty film covers the surface of the resin. In Malaysia, dammar means "light." The resin has powerfully refractive qualities. In Germany, the name for dammar resin is cat-eye resin, alluding to this characteristic. Burning dammar lifts the spirit and brings light to the darkness of the soul. It is particularly useful when sadness, melancholy, and depression strike. People believe that dammar can make you clairvoyant and that it supports attempts to contact the angels. Dammar's fragrance is lemony, transparent, and delicately ethereal.

Ceylon Cinnamon

Cinnamomum zeylanicum Blume.

This tree is 66 ft. (20 m) tall and originates, as the name implies, in Ceylon, today's Sri Lanka. People cultivate it on almost all of India's shores. It belongs to the family of the laurel and, like the laurel, is an evergreen tree. Its elongated, dark green, stiff leaves show distinct leaf veins. The cream-colored flowers are arranged in panicles but do not have a particularly delicate fragrance. The flowers produce dark brown berries.

Cultivated cinnamon trees are deliberately kept short, no taller than 6–10 ft. (2–3 m). The bark is peeled off by hand but only harvested every one to two years. The beautiful fragrance is in the bark, which is rolled up and sold in the form of cinnamon sticks. The pleasant fragrance of the bark is from the essential oil, which has a high content of cinnamaldehyde. Almost everyone can identify the fragrance of cinnamon, and almost everyone considers it pleasant. Warm, soft, sensuous, and sweet, it creates a sense of well-being and physical and emotional comfort. Ayurvedic medicine uses the bark of the cinnamon tree (in Sanskrit called *Tamalapatra* and in Hindi, *Dalchini*) as a remedy for stomach and intestinal problems and nausea with vomiting. People also use it as an antiseptic. The ability to relieve tension makes it an ideal remedy for headaches, stomach cramps, and tongue paralysis. In powdered form, cinnamon bark is a favorite addition to incense sticks and incense-burning mixtures in India. The fragrance is relaxing, calming, and, when mixed with other ingredients, sensuously stimulating. (See also chapters on *Egypt* and *Japan*.)

Dragon's Blood

Daemenorops draco B.L.
Dracaena draco L.

The dragon's blood palm grows in the marshy regions of Southeast Asia, as well as on Java, Borneo, Sumatra, and the Moluccan islands. It belongs to the Palmae family. The fruit is covered with scales. The resin seeps out between them and is collected, cleansed, and melted. The resulting substance comes to the market in the form of pellets or sticks. Dragon's blood, *Sanguis draconis*, is a deep red, shiny mass. People in India have used this mysterious incense-burning substance as part of their rituals for a long time, particularly ones that neutralize negative energies. They believe that it protects, and they use it for sacrifices. People usually burn dragon's blood together with other substances, since it creates a very strong black smoke when burned by itself. Dragon's blood is cleansing, like frankincense. For that reason, people add it in small amounts to the classic frankincense mixture used in churches. The resin develops an herbal, spicy, sometimes charred fragrance.

Patchouli

1. Dragon's blood
2. Vetiver
3. Sandalwood powder
4. Elemi
5. Sandalwood
6. Benzoin
7. Dammar
8. Common myrrh
9. Patchouli leaves

Patchouli

Pogostemon cablin Benth.
Pogostemon heyneanus Benth.

Patchouli is closely related to the mint plant and has similar leaves. Both belong to the Lamiaceae family. Patchouli grows to be about 3 ft. (1 m) tall. As far as its fragrance is concerned, opinions differ widely. People either love it or they turn their noses up in dislike. In India, the powdered form is a popular ingredient in incense sticks. It goes particularly well with common myrrh, vetiver, and sandalwood. People add small amounts of patchouli leaves to Asian incense-burning mixtures. Patchouli has a very intense, deep, woody fragrance. During the 1960s, it was very popular in the West. In India, people use it on valuable clothing and carpets to repel moths.

Vetiver

Vetiveria zizanioides (L.) Nash

Vetiver grass belongs to the family of the sweet grasses, Gramineae. People in Asia plant it to protect against erosion. Its strong, widely branched roots hold the soil together even when rains turn into floods. For incense-burning purposes, people use the dried and pulverized root in incense sticks. When added to a mixture in small amounts, it produces an earthy, sweet, heavy, erotic fragrance that is particularly popular in Asia.

Vetiver

Recipes for Indian Incense-Burning Mixtures

Meditation in the Morning

Dammar	3 parts
Mastic	3 parts
Camphor	1 part
Elemi	1 part
Lemongrass	1 part

Crush the resins with a mortar and pestle. Add the elemi and camphor and mix everything well. Elemi is a viscous mass you can disperse evenly through the incense-burning mixture with a mortar and pestle. Add the dried lemongrass or sweet grass cut into small pieces. This recipe works well for meditation, prayer, and yoga exercises in the morning. The fragrance opens awareness and has cleansing and clarifying properties. It is helpful for maintaining inner balance throughout the day. Burn it in small amounts on charcoal.

Meditation in the Evening

Common myrrh	2 parts
Benzoin Siam	1 part
Sandalwood powder	2 parts

Crush common myrrh and benzoin almost into powdered form. You can use frankincense instead of common myrrh. Mix all the ingredients together and sprinkle on charcoal, but use no more than you can hold on the tip of a knife. The mixture has a warm, gentle fragrance. It balances and calms. At the same time, it increases awareness. The fragrance gently leads you to your center.

Ganges, Varanasi

Shakti

Common myrrh	4 parts
Patchouli	1 part
Sandalwood powder	3 parts
Costus root	1 part
Clove	1 part
Benzoin	1 part
Coriander	1 part
Rose mallow seeds	½ part

Crush the common myrrh resin and rose mallow seeds. You may substitute frankincense for common myrrh resin if you have to. Grate the costus root or pulverize pieces of the root with a mortar and pestle. Crush the clove, benzoin, and coriander. Mix everything together well. This mixture has a sweet, heavy fragrance that touches the senses and opens the heart. It supports meditation and love. Enjoy it alone or with someone else. This feminine fragrance stimulates creativity and imagination and can be an inspiration when working on music. Enjoy this exotic mixture with beautiful music in the background.

Shiva

Sandalwood powder	5 parts
Common myrrh	2 parts
Clove	1 part
Dragon's blood	½ part
Costus root	1 part

Crush the common myrrh resin, grate the dry costus root or use it already cut, and pulverize the cloves. If you have dragon's blood pieces, crush them also. Mix everything well. This is an incense-burning mixture with an herblike, resinous fragrance. It provides energy, strength, and vitality. It helps you assert yourself. During the incense-burning process, imagine how your emotional, physical and mental energies are growing. It is a fragrance for rejuvenation.

Burning Incense

A gentle column of frankincense is rising:
Transparently shimmering like crystal,
Airy blue like the distant horizon,
Vibrating like a note played on a violin.

A gentle veil descends from the dark ceiling,
Into the quiet space:
Toning down the warm glow of the candle,
Cooling the glowing color of the flowers,
Shrouding the golden head of the Buddha
In the distance.

But three monks, sitting, immersed in thought,
In the late hour stillness of the room:
They never see the splendor of the flowers,
They do not hear the crackle of the candle's flame,
No more can they feel the beat of the heart.

Buddha's golden countenance itself
Is erased from their soul:
They only see the column of frankincense,
They only sense the crystal-like clarity,
They only hear the vibrating sound,
Imagining the faraway horizon.

Lama Anagarika Govinda

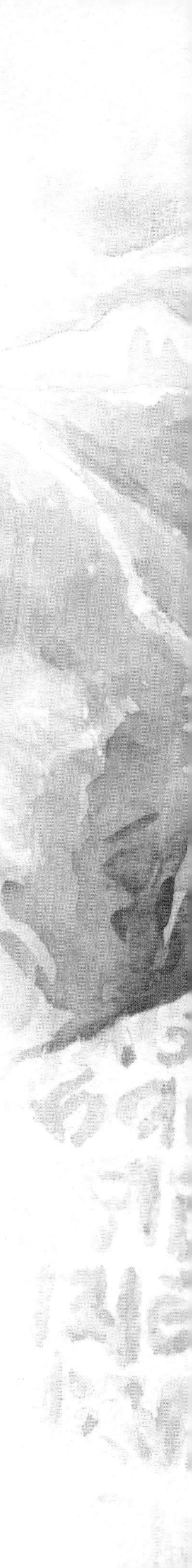

11 THE HIMALAYAS

PLEASANT FRAGRANCES FROM SHANGRI-LA

High above the shimmering wall of the rocks, prayer flags flutter in the wind. The great expanse of the deep blue sky stretches above the endless mountains of the Himalayas. A gentle humming noise in the ears made the hiker aware of the extreme elevation of this place. It is here that thousands of years ago a famous female hermit spent time in a small cave at the foot of the rock wall, meditating. How did she ever get up there? The narrow trail, winding along the rim of steep cliffs, seems almost insurmountable. What would he find up there? Now, on the side of the rock, he could see a gentle column of smoke rising straight to the sky. Hours later, he was sitting at a small fire in the cave above. He made it. Was it the warm, trusting fragrance of the fire, nurtured by herbs, that guided him? Or was it the magic of the great teacher still very much present in this faraway place? The shepherd, who had started a sacrificial fire, who had been waiting for him, threw another handful of herbs into the small fire and smiled. They could not converse with words, but together they looked at the smoke rising and followed its gentle, fragrant strands as it ascended to the heavens.

About the Fragrance of the Hidden Valleys

The highest mountain range in the world is 1,550 miles (2,500 km) long and shaped like a bow. It was created when the Eurasian continent collided with the Indian subcontinent. The collision lifted the Himalayan mountains above the plains, creating the "Roof of the World." Before the collision, an earthquake had lifted the ocean floor 13,000 ft. (4,000 m). This area became the Tibetan Highland. Here, in our search for incense-burning plants we are literally walking on the ocean floor.

The Himalayan Mountains form a barrier between two completely different climatic zones, giving different regions different climates. Each individual region in turn developed a specific flora. This is why the Himalayas are blessed with so many different species of plants. The southern slopes with their moisture-drenched clouds from the lowlands are drenched by monsoon rains. Ferns grow in evergreen forests; scarlet-red flowers blos-

Brahmaputra Valley, central Tibet

som on tall rhododendron trees; moss covers the branches; lichen hang from trees. In the semi-shade, aromatic plants such as ginger, galangal, dream moss, costus, and ginger lilies flourish. Beautiful orchids nourish themselves in the humid air. We find a variety of juicy, aromatic, medicinal plants that can also be used for incense burning. The majestic Himalayan cedar, *Cedrus deodora*, whose resin, needles, and bark we use for incense burning, flourishes on the slopes of the southern mountains. Branches

look like blue-green umbrellas above the floor of the forest, and soft, long needles grow on gracefully bent branches. Many people feel the Himalayan cedar forests are the most beautiful evergreen forests in the world.

Almost every valley of the Himalayan mountains has its own microclimate and grows its own particular plants. This is the result of the differences between the dry north and the humid southern slopes and between the eastern and western climate variations, where, for instance, some areas have a deep snow cover in the valleys and a flora of tropical plants, including bananas and mangoes, on the slopes.

The north slope of the Himalayas is bare, cold, and dry. At higher elevations, where the ground is rocky and barren because it was once the floor of the ocean, you'll find powerful, arid, but vigorous plants growing. Mugwort, dwarf juniper, thistles, and miniature violets nestle close to the ground to avoid the cold winds. They, too, produce

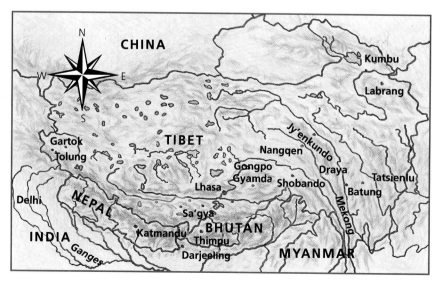

medicinal and incense-burning substances. The fragrance of these plants usually creates a feeling of expanse and clarity because they carry within them the energy of the region where these robust plants grow.

The legend of Shangri-La, the hidden mysterious valley, is alive in all the Himalayas. According to the legend, this is the place where the last wise people lived in secrecy, safeguarding intellectual treasures. This is where a kingdom is hidden, where the future of the earth is created, and where magical plants grow. It is the paradise of the mountains. Many people have searched for Shangri-La.

The Lawudo Valley, located at the foot of Mount Everest, is one of the magic valleys connected to incense burning. A trail, starting in Solo-Khumbu, leads higher and higher through a small valley until a canyon opens up and you see the Lawudo: elevation 4,500 ft. (1,350 m). Katmandu is 14 days away by foot. The valley is sacred, and the clear air carries particularly beautiful spiritual vibrations. This special setting has attracted hermits for a long time. They believe that at this elevation you can meditate in the caves and complete your spiritual journey.

To this day, hermits use the caves in this high valley. Sherpas, the Tibetan people, collect specific herbs for the Lawudo incense-burning mixture there because the valley carries the sacred, cleansing, and clarifying spirit of the region. They use this incense-burning mixture for very specific mental illnesses and severe psychic disturbances. They believe the mixture balances and harmonizes in times of severe stress, depression, restlessness, and insomnia. The Sherpas consider it a reliable aid for mastering difficult transitions during intellectual development. Its fragrance can neutralize illness-causing energies. Using it daily is supposed to help stabilize the psyche and improve the sense of inner balance.

The Seat of the Gods

For its inhabitants, as well as for the people in neighboring countries, the Himalayan mountains are the seat of the gods, a sacred mountain range where the snow-covered peaks and eternal ice are the majestic throne of the gods. The infinite expanse, the majestic world of the mountains, the thin and unbelievably clear air make the inhabitants of the Himalayas particularly sensitive to cosmic energies. Life there flourishes in graceful spirituality. In our search for the history of incense burning, we will finally witness an unbroken tradition of the "message to the heavens." The indigenous Buddhists of Tibet use incense burning for spiritual sacrifices and for their meditation practices. In convents and cloisters, they use fragrances for very specific purposes, guiding the individual states of meditation. They have studied the effects of fragrances extensively and use incense-burning fragrances as a guide for the soul's journey to enlightenment and as a connection to the highest level of wisdom.

They believe that everyday life is inseparably connected to the spiritual, and this is how they use incense burning. Each household burns incense daily to honor Buddha and patron saints, to remain healthy, and to send petitions to the gods. Mantra and prayers support incense-burning ceremonies. In the morning, they burn incense outdoors in stoves made of stone, using large branches of juniper, cedar, and sage. Tibetan cloisters burn rolled incense sticks. The incense sticks

Elderly man burning incense in Bhutan

provide a characteristic fragrance that is warming, strengthening, and harmonizing.

The aroma is certainly very useful and pleasing during the bitter cold winters of the Tibetan highlands, where monks often live in unheated cloisters.

Incense burning in the morning

The people of this region believe the smoke from the incense-burning plants is sacred. It protects them from dark forces that can penetrate the atmosphere and bring illness and bad luck. No home, even the poorest hut, is without an altar, a place of honor for the divine, where the inhabitants burn incense daily in front of the house altar. Here, of course, they don't use the large juniper branches or incense-burning mixtures intended for outdoors. Rather, if they can afford it, they use small amounts of more delicate incense-burning substances. People also try not to create too much smoke when burning incense inside. In front of the altar, they keep a vessel filled with sand, inserting incense sticks into the sand. When they use incense in powdered form, they break off a piece from an incense stick, light it, and sprinkle powder on it. People use ancient recipes to create incense-burning powders. Some of the ingredients include sandal-wood, myrrh, agar wood, juniper wood, rhododendron, and cedar tips.

Psychosomatic Incense-Burning Medicine

The basic theory of Tibetan medicine is that illnesses occur because of a disturbed and pathological attitude of the human spirit. The three poisons of the spirit—greed, hate, and ignorance—form the root of every illness. When the spirit is depressed, fear, exhaustion, and restlessness will cause illnesses, such as inflammations, tumors, and cancer. Tibetan medicine studies the connection between the mind and the body and uses it to determine the type of therapy the patient needs. In the West, science has just recently acknowledged this connection. In Tibetan medicine, burning incense has played a major role in influencing the disturbed human psyche and any resulting imbalance. A very specific incense-burning mixture exists for every type of disturbance of the human psyche. The treatment requires the patient to cover his head with a cloth, bend over the

incense-burning vessel, and inhale the smoke. In the evening, before retiring, the patient does not cover his head.

The people of Tibet use some generally effective incense mixtures for psychic instability. These include the Lawudo mixture and others that can be purchased in Katmandu from Tibetan physicians. The mixtures contain the following: dark, light, and reddish aloe wood; common myrrh; frankincense; nutmeg; raisins; juniper; three different types of myrobalan resin; sal resin; and Chinese larkspur. Mixtures made according to very complicated guidelines often contain up to 30 different powders. People use them as incense-burning substances or as incense sticks. The Tibetan incense-burning mixtures work well for relaxation and for regaining balance after severe nervous exertion and for treating insomnia, general tension, and emotional instability.

If a psychic situation is so severe that the patient has developed a psychosis, Tibetan medicine prescribes a strong incense-burning substance, such as inulin or nutmeg, to be burned as incense or massaged into the skin. However, the correct use of Tibetan incense-burning medicine

for advanced illnesses or psychoses requires a very detailed knowledge of Tibetan medicine. Under no circumstances should you attempt to treat these conditions. Prayers and mantras usually accompany the making of incense-burning mixtures and

incense sticks. People believe that the positive energy of a mantra transfers to the incense-burning substances. When you burn the mixture, the people who are present receive the positive energy.

In addition to plants and minerals, the mixtures contain other substances that have a strong symbolic or magical meaning.

For instance, sometimes peacock feathers are added. This bird is a symbol of strong transforming energies. People believe that the poisonous substances the peacock eats create the beautiful colors of his tail feathers. Owl and crow feathers are cut into small pieces and also added. We can trace back to ancient shamanic traditions the concept of adding energy-filled substances to incense-burning mixtures.

The incense sticks from Tibet exported to the West are usually produced by Tibetans in Nepal, Darjeeling, and Sikkim. They are the only naturally pure incense sticks. The recipes date back to an ancient incense-burning tradition.

A specialty of Tibetan incense-burning medicine is the addition of pulverized precious stones, such as lapis lazuli, ruby, turquoise, and others. Tibetans have very distinct stone medications with detailed instructions on how much of each ingredient to use.

Effective Incense-Burning Substances of the Himalayan Region

The following incense-burning substances are specific to Tibetan medicine: red and white sandalwood, juniper, rhododendron, hedychium, costus, spikenard, saffron, musk, ambergris, nutmeg, clove, agar wood, asant, pepper, fern herb, myrobalan, common myrrh, galangal, ginger lily, nagarmotha, mountain alant, pomegranate, cardamom, cinnamon, terminalia (arjuna), sughanda cocola, camphor, tamala, and tagar.

From the wealth of existing incense-burning substances, let's discuss the most important ones and those available in the West.

Arjuna

Arjuna (Arura)

Terminalia chebula Retz.
Terminalia arjuna (Roxb.) Wight u. Arn.
Emblica officinalis Gaertn.

Arjuna is one of the best-known medicinal plants used for incense burning in Tibet. It belongs to the Combretaceae family. People believe that this deciduous tree, used in many medicinal incense-burning recipes, heals over 400 illnesses. People burn the pulverized fruit to treat asthma, but they also add the pulverized bark to mixtures. They believe that incense burning with arjuna heals illnesses caused when energy is blocked in the body. When burned, arjuna has a gentle, woody, warm fragrance.

Rhododendron

Rhododendron anthopogon D. Don

Approximately 200 different species of rhododendron grow on the slopes of the Himalayas. All belong to the Ericaceae family. Some are as tall as trees and look like Christmas trees with brilliant red flowers; others are low-growing and hide under masses of snow in winter. One of them is highly valued as an incense-burning plant. The fragrant dwarf rhododendron, a low-growing small shrub, has leathery egg-shaped leaves. Picked and dried, the leaves have a soft, sweet, fruity, warm fragrance. Together with mountain juniper, they are part of the famous Lawudo incense-burning mixture. Tibetan medicine uses rhododendron to stimulate the heart and circulatory system. On a psychological level, it conveys a sense of trust and removes fear and apprehension. People use it for emotional instability and physical weakness. You can use the small leaves individually or add them to a mixture. They work particularly well with juniper berries and cedar tips. Since rhododendron stimulates the activity of the heart, you should not use it in cases of high blood pressure.

Himalayan Cedar

Cedrus deodora G. Don

The Himalayan cedar belongs to the family of the Scotch pines, the Pinaceae. People in the Himalayan region use the wood, needles, and resin for incense burning. The resin of this majestic tree produces a very specific and characteristically warm, balsamic fragrance. People believe the fragrance strengthens, improves energy, brings good luck, and protects. Himalayan cedar

has a stronger psychological effect than that of Atlas cedar.

Costus

Sassurea lappa C.B. Clarke

Costus

The wild costus root, a plant that belongs to the Asteraceae (Compositae) family, grows in the valleys of Kashmir at elevations up to 13,200 ft. (4,000 m). It is similar to a type of European thistle and has dark lilac-colored flowers. The plant grows up to 13 ft. (4 m) tall. Since ancient times, people have considered the root to be a powerful remedy for cramps, asthma, rheumatism,

and chronic skin problems. In antiquity, merchants sold costus from Kashmir to Greece and Rome. Costus has a green, violet-like, somewhat earthy, furry, and animalistic fragrance when it is burned. People in Arabic countries added costus root to sensuous incense-burning mixtures because they valued it as an aphrodisiac. In India's Ayurvedic medicine, it is a love potion. People in Asia consider its fragrance very sensuous. The Japanese add finely grated costus root to incense sticks and incense pellets. Japan imports huge amounts of

189

1. Juniper needles
2. Galangal root
3. Arjuna
4. Costus root
5. Lawudo mixture
6. Rhododendron leaves
7. Himalayan cedar
8. Tibetan incense sticks

this root from the Himalayan region. When used in incense burning, they believe it is emotionally elaxing and, at the same time, rejuvenating and revitalizing. Tibetan medicine uses it in cases of emotional weaknesses.

Juniper

*Juniperus wallichiana Hook
Juniperus recurva Buch.*

Approximately 40 different species of juniper grow in the Northern Hemisphere. In the Himalayan region, they grow at elevations up to 20,000 ft. (6,000 m). In Tibetan medicine, people use juniper to prevent and treat cancer. Throughout the Himalayan region, people consider the juniper to be a sacred tree burned for rituals during many ceremonies. For incense-burning purposes, people use the needles, tips of the twigs, or the resin. *Dhupi,* as incense burning is called in the Himalayas, is used for cleansing during rituals, during prayers, for the daily incense-burning ceremonies in the morning, and to increase mental attentiveness. Juniper is part of the famous Lawudo mixture.

Ginger Lily

Hedychium spicatum Buch. Ham

Ginger lilies grow in the foothills of the Himalayas at elevations up to 10,000 ft. (3,000 m). They belong to the large and varied

Zingiberaceae family. Approximately 38 species of this family grow in the Himalayan region. Ginger lilies are particularly abundant in Nepal. During July and August they produce delicately scented white flowers. The root is a prized incense-burning substance sold as *Kapu-Kachali.* When burned, it creates a light, violetlike, camphor fragrance. Ginger lily is part of the *Abir* mixture, a colorful, fragrant powder used in India for religious ceremonies, particularly during the Holy Feast. It is also used in traditional Indian incense sticks. When burned, the fragrance of the ginger lily is an antidepressant and nerve tonic.

Galangal

Galangal

Alpinia officinarum Hance
Alpinia galanga Willd.

Galangal, a ginger plant of the Zingiberaceae family, grows wild in the forests of the southern Himalayas. Its reedlike leaves grow up to 6½ ft. (2 m), and the rhizomes grow to 3¼ ft. (1 m). Throughout antiquity, merchants exported galangal to Egypt, Mesopotamia, Greece, and Rome. During the Middle Ages, people considered it a very important medicine. In her book *Natural Science,* written 800 years ago, the abbess Hildegard von Bingen mentions galangal as a remedy for many illnesses, including paralysis, disorders of the pancreas, breast, and heart, and as a remedy for backaches.

> *Whoever is suffering from troubles of the heart, or where the heart is not working properly, may take a sufficient amount of galangal, and he will feel better.*

Tibetan medicine and Ayurvedic medicine use galangal for rheumatism, bronchitis, and tuberculosis. Burning galangal strengthens and stimulates the flow of energy throughout the body. It energizes in times of exhaustion and despondency. It has a gingerlike, peppery, wild, slightly camphorlike fragrance and is usually used in combination with other plants.

Recipes for Incense-Burning Mixtures from the Himalayas

Lawudo

Himalayan rhododendron leaves	3 parts
Juniper tips	2 parts
Juniper berries	¼ part

Rhododendron is sometimes available in shops that sell incense-burning substances. Juniper tips may be those from North America used in Native American incense-burning recipes. Juniper berries are easy to find. Mix all the dry ingredients together well. The mixture has a tangy, balsamlike fragrance. It creates an atmosphere of expanse and clarity. It harmonizes, stabilizes, calms turbulent emotions, and works well during meditation and prayer.

Shangri-La

Juniper tips	1 part
Arjuna	½ part
Rhododendron leaves	3 parts

Grate the fruit of the arjuna. If Himalayan juniper is not available, you may substitute North American juniper. Crush all three substances between the palms of your hands. The result is a healing mixture that stabilizes emotional energy channels. It is helpful in cases of mental and emotional disturbances because it reestablishes balance. For severe emotional instability and stress, healing ceremonies, and cleansing rituals, burn this mixture in the evening before retiring.

Kailash

Galangal	1 part
Common myrrh	1 part
Sandalwood powder	2 parts
Cinnamon bark	½ part
Camphor	¼ part

This balsamlike, spicy mixture stimulates inner strength. It is revitalizing on every level and is helpful in times of exhaustion, overwork, and to combat feelings of powerlessness. It is ideal for dealing with burnout. Crush the galangal root and cinnamon bark. Crush the common myrrh. Pulverize the sandalwood if it is not in powdered form. Make sure to use real camphor. Mix all the ingredients well. Use this mixture only in small amounts and burn it on charcoal.

…Under the wonderful glow of a slightly clouded moon,
The rain just stopped—the wind moved gently,
Dispersing the beautiful fragrance of flowers.
Throughout the palace, this fragrance was joined by
The unbelievably delicate fragrance of incense burning,
Creating a mood of enchantment .

from *The Tale of Genji,*

an ancient Japanese love story, written by

Murasaki Shikibu, a lady-in-waiting

12 JAPAN

LISTENING TO THE FRAGRANCES

The sun was high in the sky. It was noon. But the canopy of leaves in the ancient forest at the foot of the Himalayan mountains allowed only a few of the sun's rays to reach the ground. A diffuse light surrounded us, interwoven by the outline of the leaves. I inhaled the fragrance of the vegetation deeply: the scent of moss, ferns, tree bark. The ground beneath my feet became softer, and, with each step, we sank ankle-deep into the marshy soil. Sampo led the way, clearing the trail ahead with his machete. He sensed that I was almost at the end of my energy. Mosquitoes had bitten my face. Perspiration from every pore attracted them. Humid, warm heat paralyzed every step. "This must be the place," he said finally. We could see that somebody had dug in the soil. Using a small spade Sampo had carried in his knapsack, he began to remove moss and ferns from the humid soil. Then he held it in his hands, showing it to me with pride. It was a piece of dark brown wood, still musty and covered with moss. But it was as precious as gold. The mysterious agar wood. It carries within it the fragrance of a thousand worlds.

Escaping Ignorance

As is the case in Egypt and Arabia, the fragrance culture in Japan is closely connected to the history of a beautiful woman. In this case, she did not venture on an expedition to Punt, the land of fragrances, like the pharaoh princess Hatshepsut, nor did she join a frankincense caravan through the deserts, like the Queen of Sheba. Instead, Murasaki Shikibu, a lady-in-waiting, wrote a novel about love and fragrances in ancient Japan. In the book, which is almost 1,800 pages long, a lady-in-waiting to Empress Kyotos gives us a glimpse of a fragrance tradition that was the most highly developed and most exquisite in the world. Before aristocrats in ancient Japan could enjoy their royal fragrances and, as they referred to it, "listen" to them, they needed to import the aromatic woods that were not native to the country.

In Japan the tradition of using fragrances did not start at the elegant court of the empress but with Zen Buddhists, who did not stimulate the senses but refined and tamed them. The tradition of incense burning came to Japan from China via Korea with the teachings of Buddha in the middle of the sixth century. The

The Daibutsu Buddha

monk Bodhidharma is said to have imported Buddhism to Japan. In pictures, he always had his eyes wide open to show that he was completely awake, clear, and attentive. Buddhism teaches, "Ignorance is the root of all suffering." Ignorance creates hate, greed, jealousy, and discord among people. The way out of ignorance is by becoming attentive through mental discipline and devotion to spiritual awareness. Positive characteristics in a human being should be strengthened so a person's own Buddha nature can come to the fore.

Originating in India, the motherland of fragrances, Buddhism always involved incense burning to support people on their journey to perfection. Buddhists used incense burning to stimulate meditation and to enhance deep breathing. For the different stages of spiritual development, they designated specific fragrances. The fragrant smoke rising to the heavens was a symbol of unity with a god and of

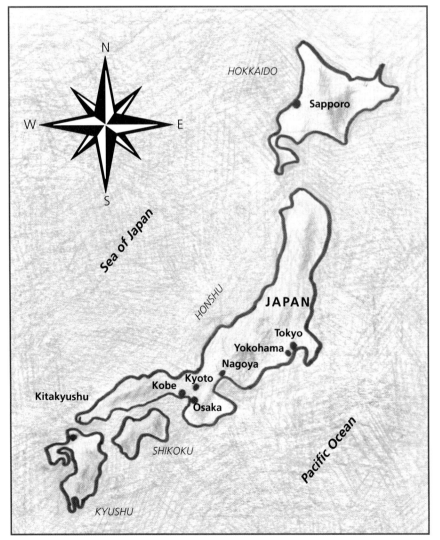

the fleeting nature of all phenomena.

Burning incense is a guide during times of inner cleansing and attentive stillness. In this way, the fragrance of carefully chosen incense-burning substances can be helpful "to flee ignorance and cleanse the soul." Keen observers researched the effects fragrances had on the human spirit and made use of what they learned. Incense-burning substances could be helpful in reclaiming the spirit and creating a cated fragrance culture that was unique in all the world. A Zen priest in the 16th century summarized the manifold virtues of incense burning, called the *Koh*, which we still possess.

Originally, Japanese Zen Buddhists used five to seven different incense-burning substances. These included agar wood, sandalwood, cinnamon, cloves, camphor, ginger, and ambergris. They placed the mixture on burning charcoal in incense-burning vessels. The art of creating in-

The Fragrance of the Prince

Japanese Zen Buddhists as well as Shintoists had a high regard for incense burning. Their regard carried over to the Emperor's court. Aristocrats found so much pleasure with these precious incense-burning fragrances, they not only used them for sacred purposes, the *Sonae-Koh*, they also began to use them to enlighten everyday life. The so-called *sora-daki*, or "useless incense burning,"

The 10 Virtues of the Koh

1. *Incense burning opens us to the transcendental.*

2. *Incense burning cleanses our spirit.*

3. *Incense burning cleanses and clarifies our spirit of worldly blindness.*

4. *Incense burning makes us attentive.*

5. *Incense burning is a friend and companion in times of loneliness.*

6. *Incense burning brings peace and reflection during a hectic day.*

7. *Incense burning never loses its value, even if used often.*

8. *Even with a small amount of incense, we will experience satisfaction.*

9. *Incense-burning substances never lose their effectiveness, even when stored over a long period.*

10. *Even if used daily, incense burning never does harm.*

peaceful mood.

In China, Buddhism was part of an existing, highly developed tradition of fragrance use. This union of Buddhism and incense burning reached Japan during the middle of the sixth century. The Japanese people had a deep connection with nature and an interest in spiritualizing the experience of fragrances. After the arrival of Buddhism, they proceeded to cultivate a sophisti- cense sticks was not known until the 16th century, when it arrived from China. Now they pulverized, moistened, and formed substances into small sticks. Over time, this tradition and art became much more refined in Japan. Japanese incense sticks are considered some of the purest and finest in the world. People in Japan refer to smelling incense sticks as "listening to their fragrance." as it was called disparagingly, began to spread throughout the land. Japanese incense-burning tradition reached its first high point during the Heian era (700–1150 A.D.). The enthusiasm for these precious incense-burning fragrances gave the world its first love story. We will begin our journey through the Japanese incense tradition with this love story, written by the beautiful and highly educated

Lady Murasaki.

This story, written in the 11th century, is *The Tale of Genji*. We

read about great passions for music, poetry, love, and the fragrances that were popular at the time. Fragrances weave like a gentle breath through the pages of the book. We hear about clothes suspended in fragrant smoke; about beautifully flowing hair drenched in precious fragrance; and about the inside of kimono sleeves, which held tempting fragrances. Prince Genji was a lover no lady could resist. His passion leads him to many delicate love adventures. Each movement the prince makes is accompanied by a breath of the fragrance he wears on his clothing, deeply impressing the hearts of the ladies surrounding him.

It was during this time that the art of preparing incense mixture developed in Japan. Noble aris-tocrats took part in a competition in which the most precious mixture won a prize. The competitions, called *Ko-awase*, were conducted playfully and are described in detail in the Genji story. Each participant was given several substances, such as agar wood, sandalwood, cloves, musk, saffron, etc. From these they created their own recipes, which were then judged. Participants often chose substances and fragrances with a seasonal theme in mind. This is a tradition in Japan. They also had to find an appropriate and pretty name for the mixture.

People mixed incense-burning substances, crushed them with a mortar and pestle, and then combined them with substances such as plum jam or honey. They placed the mixture in a stoneware container and buried it in the ground, allowing it to ferment and mature. They formed the dough into small pellets and used the pellets for incense burning. To this day, Japanese companies, such as Sho-yeido in Kyoto, still produce fragrant pellets from these ancient recipes.

Listening to the Seasons of the Year

Japanese people love fragrances. They are very much aware of how fragrances change with the seasons. As far back as Prince Genji's time, they assigned subdued, gentle, elegant fragrances to winter. These were as delicate and regal as snowflakes in a pine forest. For spring, they chose intense, fresh fragrances that would create a happy mood. For summer, they loved sweet, enticing fragrances. For fall, they decided on delicately herbal and fruity fragrances. The simple awareness of the specific fragrances of the season can increase attentiveness, awareness, and perception. Becoming aware of the fragrances that match the rhythm of the year can be a source of inner wealth and quiet peace. It can help us find inner harmony and be in tune with the seasons and nature. The conscious perception and pleasure of incense burning that carries the fragrance of the season opens the senses to the fragrances of nature.

Life today in cities has seriously diminished this kind of awareness. Unpleasant odors are

increasingly a fact of life there. The smell of exhaust fumes has numbed our senses. And as if that weren't bad enough, we use artificial fragrances, some even in our food, to pretend we live a life surrounded by health and nature. Burning incense and using the fragrances of the season can help us regenerate our sense of smell and open us again to the intrinsic fragrances of the earth. Create a mixture using substances that have fragrances of the season. Let the smoke rise, close your eyes, and let your imagination paint the pictures of a season. What does spring smell like? What does the fragrance of

Cherry blossoms

fall touch in us? Where did you spend the most beautiful winter?

The Journey of the Fragrance

The highest level of sophistication and awareness of fragrance in Japan is evident in *Ko-doh*, the "journey of the fragrance." *Ko* means fragrance; *doh* means the way. It was developed during the Ashikaga era (1350 to 1500 A.D.). The Shogun Ashikaga Yoshimasa demanded that all incense-burning fragrances be classified. He established rules that regulated the use of incense-burning sub-

stances. The Ko-doh ceremony, the way of "listening to a fragrance," was born at this time. As was true with archery competitions, tea ceremonies, and the Ikebana, the Ko-doh ceremony served to raise the human spirit to higher levels.

Experiencing a fragrance consciously during Ko-doh can expand the soul, strengthen spiritual energy, and stimulate creativity. Participants were asked to give absolute concentration, similar to that exercised in Zen Buddhist meditation. At the same time, they learned how to give in to the play of the emotions aroused by the fragrances and to observe and enjoy them. Ko-doh is the art of allowing the fragrance emanating from a small incense-burning bowl to create a whole internal landscape. Experiencing the fragrances in a Ko-doh ceremony stretches the participant from metaphysics and transcendence all the way to the simple, sensuous enjoyment of a fragrance. Highest concentration and playful attention alternate with one another. During a Ko-doh ceremony, fragrances are brought into a certain context and often connected to literature and po-

Japanese illustration of the Prince Genji stories

etry. It might sound simple, but it is actually a very difficult undertaking. The sense of smell is located in the limbic system of the brain. This is also the center of the emotions. Words, classifications, and terms develop in a different area of the brain. To connect both parts, to be able to differentiate between a great number of similar fragrances for instance, to name them, and to connect them with literature and poetry opens up an entirely new world.

A Ko-doh ceremony is highly regulated. In the beginning, the master will announce the rules, to eliminate the need for conversation or questions during the ceremony. The whole ceremony takes about an hour. It is held in a sparsely furnished space to avoid any distractions. Participants are not to eat any foods that have strong odors, such as garlic, onions, or leeks. Perfumes, strongly scented aftershave lotions, and hair sprays are also to be avoided to minimize distractions from the actual Ko-doh fragrance.

A traditional ceremony usually has eight to 10 guests and is overseen by a Ko-doh master and an assistant. The guest of honor sits to the left of the master, the assistant to the right. The master prepares the incense-burning substances. These include valuable aromatic wood shavings the size of half a grain of rice. The incense-burning bowl, the size of a teacup, holds rice-straw ash and, according to specific instructions, has the shape of a small volcano with an indentation at the top. The master makes the indentation with a spatula, one of the seven different pieces that are part of the Ko-doh silverware. He places a piece of burning charcoal inside the indentation of the ash volcano. With a pair of pliers, he puts a small, square, mica plate on the ash without touching the charcoal. The master then places the aromatic wood on the mica plate, where the heat of the glowing charcoal slowly releases the aroma. The master passes the incense-burning bowl clockwise from participant to participant. Each person places it on the floor in front of him before passing it on to his neighbor. The participant reaches for the bowl with his right hand, raises it chest high, and holds the bowl with his index finger and thumb around the rim, creating a slight cover. Next, the person lifts the incense bowl to the nose and carefully inhales the fragrance deeply. The participant "listens" to the fragrance and makes a note of what he "hears."

Experienced Ko-doh students practice *nana soken*, a breathing technique of seven breaths. But it is possible to experience the fragrance without this breathing technique. However, it is important that you turn your head away when you exhale. If you don't, the ashes will blow in your face and possibly in your eyes. The usual practice is to inhale and exhale two or three times and then pass the bowl to your neighbor. After passing the bowl, participants reach for the pencil and paper in front of them and, depending on the game, make notes. The assistant collects all of the notes. After one round, the master changes the substance by removing the mica plate with a pair of silver tongs. At the end of the ceremony, he removes the charcoal with metal sticks and submerges it in a bowl of water. The ashes can be reused.

Fragrant Pellets

Before the introduction of Ko-doh ceremonies, people used incense-burning mixtures called *shokoh*, made by Buddhist monks. As told in *The Tale of Genji*, the aristocracy had raised the art of incense-burning mixtures to a high level. People owned their very personal fragrance mixture, which remained a well-kept secret. The incense-burning mixture used to scent living quarters, clothing, and hair always corresponded to the emotional state of the aristocrat. The mixtures had beautiful names, usually borrowed from Japanese literature. Incense-burning mixtures were often made with dried herbs, in the form of incense sticks, cones, or pellets.

One famous type of Japanese

incense pellet, *nerikoh*, contains a variety of substances in powder form. These are made into a dough using hot water. Adding Japanese sweet pea or mountain chestnut honey is supposed to prevent the incense-burning pellets from becoming moldy. Plum jam is used as a base for the dough. The sticky bark of the Japanese *tabuko* tree provides a neutral binding substance for incense. The finished product is placed in a ceramic container, closed tightly, and then buried in humid soil, just as was the custom during the time of Prince Genji. The dough may take up to three years to mature and ferment. A similar method, known to European alchemists, is sometimes still used in popular medicine. (Remnants of this type of underground fermentation preparation are used to make a particularly effective cough syrup.) After the maturing process, the dough is unearthed and shaped into *nerikoh* pellets by hand. The pellets often contain 20 fragrant substances. We'll only list the most important here. These substances can be used individually as well as in mixtures. Let yourself be inspired by the individual substances and create your very own fragrance, just as the ancient Japanese aristocracy did. Try to discover which fragrances touch your soul. Find a poetic name that expresses or mirrors its effect.

Simple Games of Ko-Doh

What follows are a few examples of Ko-doh ceremonies, traditional as well as modern, for Western connoisseurs. Ko-doh is undergoing a renaissance in Japan, but people prefer to use it in a much looser, uninhibited fashion, adapting it to the present. It has become a very relaxing way to compensate for the stress-filled, performance-oriented way of life in Japan. Ever since I received my first Ko-doh kit and was introduced to the ceremony, I have used it frequently within the quiet of my own four walls. Later on, I introduced it to friends, and they began to join me. It is a beautiful way of getting together in the evening, perhaps after a shared meal or a meeting, to enjoy these fragrances. It most certainly is an enriching experience that you can enjoy with your friends. Someday, you might try such a ceremony. Thoughtfully experiencing fragrances is a wonderful way to relax. I have also introduced this ceremony during my seminars, and time and again, my students have confirmed my belief about how enriching, centering, and balancing this experience can be.

In Japan, people mainly use aromatic wood for their Ko-doh ceremonies. I have experimented with other fragrant substances from the many that exist in other cultures. The following are among those that are particularly useful for creating a deep inspirational experience: Labdanum (see also chapter on *Crete*) opens up a whole internal picture book and can truly enrich a Ko-doh ceremony. However, you need to burn it on charcoal or on an incense-burning stove; otherwise, the mica plate becomes clogged. Sandarac, a resin (see also chapter on *Arabia*), must also be burned on charcoal or a stove. Its fragrance can create a beautiful and delicate experience. When you have become more familiar with these ceremonies, try to experiment with

Koh-doh ceremony

201

different fragrances. Each fragrance holds its own secret world, story, and experiences. Each is just waiting to be set free, like the genie in the bottle. In the beginning, you don't need special Ko-doh utensils to enjoy the fragrance of this incense-burning ceremony. To start, all you really need are an incense-burning bowl, sand, a pair of tweezers to hold the charcoal, incense-burning charcoal, and some incense-burning substances

The Tameshi Game

For a simple Ko-doh ceremony, it is customary to first pass the fragrances around so everybody can "listen" and recognize them. You should recognize the first three items in sequence. Different qualities of individual incense-burning woods have similar fragrances and require your attention when they are introduced. Shave small pieces from each of the aromatic woods and

aside. Now the guest of honor determines the sequence in which the aromatic wood will be burned and passed around. In this way, even the master cannot know the sequence. The vessel is passed around the circle. Participants place their individual envelopes on top of each other in sequence or place them on a skewer that is part of the Ko-doh set. At the end of the game, the master opens the envelopes and identifies the proper sequence.

Preparing the Incense-Burning Vessel

- Fill the vessel with ash.
- Ignite the charcoal and bring it to a glow.

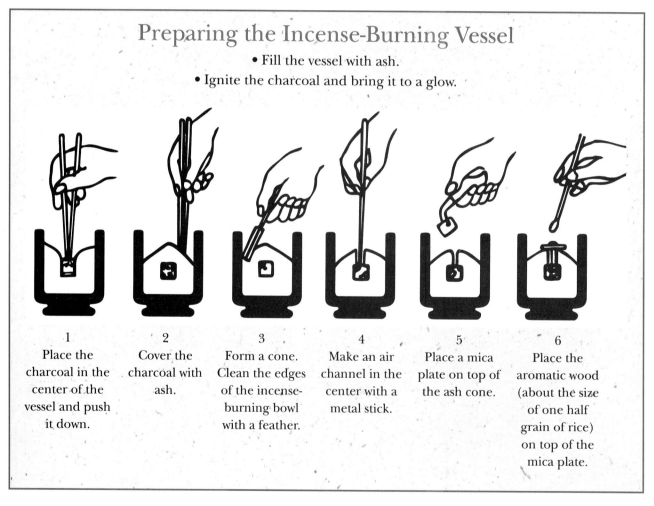

1	2	3	4	5	6
Place the charcoal in the center of the vessel and push it down.	Cover the charcoal with ash.	Form a cone. Clean the edges of the incense-burning bowl with a feather.	Make an air channel in the center with a metal stick.	Place a mica plate on top of the ash cone.	Place the aromatic wood (about the size of one half grain of rice) on top of the mica plate.

(possibly three different types of Japanese fragrant woods, including agar wood and sandalwood). Should you develop a liking for Ko-doh, you can purchase the appropriate utensils over time.

place each in a paper envelope. Mix the nine envelopes. One of the participants selects three envelopes. In Japan, the guest of honor usually performs this task. Put the remaining envelopes

Morning Fog and Fall Winds

For more advanced players, use 10 different varieties of aromatic woods, including the first three fragrances (*tameshi*) and one additional "host fragrance." The Genjiko game, which is played by truly experienced Ko-doh players, consists of five parts, each of which consists of five different incense-burning substances. For the Kumikoh game, the players

give the fragrances names taken from Japanese literature or ones that are appropriate to a certain poem. For instance, name them from a certain passage from a play, and call them morning fog, fall wind, or bamboo river. Players frequently connect the names to the fragrances of the season. In the Kumikoh game, participants "take a walk" through nature on the wings of the fragrances of a season. The wings might take you to faraway lands, to explore a poem, to experience moods or events emotion-

ally. Since no one wins or loses in this game, the host usually gives each participant a gift at the end of the game. At the very least, each participant has been enriched by new experiences and emotions.

The master introduces two of the fragrances first. Each participant begins to "listen" to the fragrance as the master passes the incense-burning vessel around the circle. Then, the master chooses three envelopes and passes each around the circle. The participants "listen" and then write down the proper sequence.

Playing With the Beauty of Nature

Three Beautiful Landscapes, or *Sankei-koh*, is a well-known Koh-doh game. It is based on the three most popular natural vacation spots in Japan. The first is Matsushima, a collection of 260 small islands with a forest of piñon trees. The second is Aura-nohashidate, a white, narrow sandbar that is 1¾ miles (3 km) long on which a row of Scotch pines grow. The third is Itsuku-shima, where a large wooden gate greets the traveler who approaches the island by boat. For this game, the participants imagine that they are visiting these three islands. One of the fragrances offered represents the boat and the journey itself. The master selects one aromatic fragrance for each place and introduces them to the guests in the incense-burning vessel. While the vessel is circulating, the participants "listen" to the fragrances

and imagine traveling to these beautiful places. The fragrances create a sense of fog rising out of the water, paint the silhouettes of the bizarrely shaped Scotch pines, and make the splashing waters audible. Now, the master shuffles, draws the envelopes, and passes the three fragrances around the circle. He then asks the guests to write their decisions on a piece of paper. At the conclusion, he announces the original sequence.

You can easily play this game by choosing places that are familiar to your guests. You can also limit the theme to a common natural experience, such as a trip in the mountains in the winter, strolling through a sunny meadow, walking in the rain in the fall, etc. Choose fragrances that closely represent the respective places and the effects they create.

A Journey with Friends

This is a Ko-doh game I created. It is meant for beautiful hours spent with friends or as a way to break the ice at the beginning of a seminar. Fragrances elicit secret pictures, stories, and events. They stimulate imagination and carry us to faraway lands. They are like a gift after a day's work, allowing us to take a break, relax, and simply be. The leader determines the theme. This could be a temple in the jungle, a search for signs of spring, a magic ring, hiking through the forest, etc.

Prepare three different fragrances and place them in small envelopes. Mix the envelopes and allow a guest to draw one envelope. Open the envelope and pass the first fragrance around. While the incense-burning bowl travels around the circle, each participant writes the beginning of a story on a piece of paper that he folds into three equal parts. The participants must not write more than what fits on the first third of the page. After they finish writing, they fold their paper and place it in a basket standing in the middle of the circle. Mix the papers and pass the basket around. Allow each guest to pull one piece of paper, open it, and read it. Now, pass another fragrance around. Inspired by this fragrance, participants continue the story that someone else started. Again, they use only one third of the paper. They fold the paper and place it back in the basket. The leader mixes the papers, and each guest draws a paper. The third fragrance represents the end of the story. After all the papers are back in the basket, mix them and ask each guest to pull one and read aloud the story on that paper. You might want to serve a special tea and play gentle music in the background during the game.

Effective Incense-Burning Substances From Japan

Agar Wood

Aquillaria agallocha Roxb.

According to legend, a large piece of agar wood washed up on the shores of the island of Awaji during the seventh century A.D. The wood was buried, and, over time, it developed a beautiful

Prince Genji

aroma. Prince Shotoku presented this wood to the Emperor, who was so taken by the fragrance that, from then on, he imported this aromatic wood from China or Korea. This agar wood, *jinkoh*, still plays an important part in Japanese Ko-doh ceremonies. But the Japanese also used it in incense sticks and pellets, as well as in incense sachets and similar objects. For Ko-doh ceremonies, people in Japan usually use agar wood, which comes in many different qualities, and sandalwood. They use both individually, with nothing

Itsukushima shrine near Hiroshima

added. In the West, agar wood is almost unknown. If you ask people in Japan about the origin of the tree, they will usually tell you that the exact origin is still a secret. If we trace the fragrance to its homeland, we will find ourselves in the rain forests of Assam, Bhutan, Cambodia, Vietnam, and Indonesia.

The agar tree belongs to the Thymelaceae family. Its branches are, like the outstretched wings of an eagle. The Japanese only use agar wood for incense burning when it has been infected by fungus (*Aspergillus sp.* and *Fusarium sp.*). This resin produces the fragrant substance. The more resin the wood contains, the more aromatic the fragrance, and the heavier it becomes. Truly good agar wood will not float, which is why the Japanese call it, *jinkoh*, the sinking wood. However, many other factors determine the fragrance of the wood. The location, the microclimate, and the condition of the soil can all play a role. The fragrance of the wood is different from that of the branches or the roots. When an old tree is uprooted, by lightning, mud slides, etc., plants and leaves will eventually cover it. This starts the fermentation process. Sometimes a piece of wood is covered by plants or water for hundreds of years. The pressure compresses the resin and makes it compact. People in Japan consider these old and partially fossilized pieces the purest incense-burning wood. Such pieces are very expensive. Prolonged exposure to soil or water causes decay, but the aromatic resin pieces

Agar wood

are indestructible and remain behind. Agar wood has a balsamic, ambergris, woody, deep fragrance. To experience the many nuances of this unique incense-burning substance is like a journey on the road to spiritual perfection. In its original state, the wood is light gray. It becomes darker when exposed to fungus and the fermentation process. Unfortunately, in Asia people use dyes to treat less valuable wood to make it look like agar wood. If you are really interested in the best quality of this precious and mysterious wood, buy shavings from a traditional incense-burning manufacturer in Japan. The quality of the fragrance is divided into six categories. The names of the categories are traditional groups or communities in Japanese society:

Kyara

A dignified, gentle fragrance with a slightly bitter tone. It smells like an elegant and graceful aristocrat.

Rakoku

A tangy, biting fragrance that reminds one of sandalwood. It is generally somewhat bitter and smells like a warrior.

Manaka

A bright, tempting fragrance; changeable, like the emotions of a beautiful woman.

Agar wood tree trunk

Manabau

Its fragrance is usually sweet, but sometimes rough and boorish like a farmer. Sticky remnants of oil left on a mica plate are similar to the Manabau fragrance.

Sumotara

This has a sour fragrance at the beginning and the end. It is easily mistaken for Kyara. Sometimes the fragrance has a somewhat offensive and uncouth background. It has the scent of a servant who pretends to be an aristocrat.

Sasora

A cool and somewhat sour fragrance. Good-quality Sasora can be mistaken for Kyara, particularly at the beginning, when the wood just begins to heat up. Sometimes it is light and gentle, almost unnoticeable. It reminds one of the fragrance of a monk.

Burn agar wood on mica plates in tiny splinters. "Listen" to the fragrance and the story that the wood tells about mysterious forests. The fragrance of agar wood is deeply relaxing and balancing. In 1993, Japanese scientists studied its effects and determined that it is a strong sedative and extends sleep periods. When you burn agar wood in the evening, the fragrance is deeply relaxing.

Sandalwood

Santalum album L.
You can find a more detailed discussion of this aromatic wood in the chapter on India. In Japan, people use a particularly delicate quality that is sold in small square slabs, packed beautifully. You cut small splinters from these slabs and place them on a mica plate for burning. A warm, sweet fragrance soon spreads through the room. The fra-

grance is relaxing and harmonizing. It strokes the soul and senses. Although the Japanese don't use sandalwood for Kodoh ceremonies, they enjoy it by itself in the evening alone or in a group. The substance far outweighs the simple fragrance of the essential oil of sandalwood.

Japanese Anise (Steranis)

Illicium anisatum L.
(I. religiosum Sieb et Zucc.)
Japanese anise trees grow in China and Vietnam and belong to the family of the magnolia plants, Illiciaceae. In Japan, it is honored as a sacred tree. It grows to a height of 65 ft. (20 m), and its yellow flowers are similar to narcissus flowers, shaped like

an eight-pointed star. For incense-burning purposes, you crush the dried stars. When burned, their fragrance is similar to that of anise. Added to a mixture in small amounts, it provides a warm, sweet anise fragrance. People use the pulverized, fragrant bark of this tree, called s*hikimi* (Buddha tree), for incense-burning purposes and as a body powder. People believe the fragrance creates a dignified atmosphere in temples.

Cinnamon

Cinnamomum verum Presl.
Cinnamomum Loureirii Nees
Cinnamomum cassia Blume

The peeled bark of the cinnamon tree, which belongs to the laurel plant family, Lauraceae, is added to different incense-burning mixtures in powdered form. It gives these mixtures a typical warm, sweet, cinnamon fragrance. The Japanese use Chinese and Ceylonese cinnamon, as well as the

Japanese cinnamon tree

fragrance from the native laurel tree, which also has a slight cinnamonlike scent. The Japanese cinnamon tree, *Cinnamomum camphora var. glaucescens,* produces cinnamonlike fragrant substances that have a slight camphorlike undertone. If you want to make your own Japanese incense-burning mixtures, you can simply use powdered cinnamon from the kitchen. Better yet, use a piece of freshly crushed bark. For incense burning, the Japanese use the branches, bark, leaves, and dried flower buds of the cassia cinnamon tree, an evergreen plant that grows all over Southeast Asia. Everything smells sweet, warm, and has the typical cinnamon aroma. Its effects are warming, relaxing, and calming. In general, cinnamon fragrance opens the heart and works well in sensuous incense-burning mixtures. Incense burning with cinnamon and cinnamon sticks is very pop-

ular in Asia because, in addition to the effects we've already discussed, it keeps insects at bay.

Cloves

Syzigium aromaticum (L.)
Merr. et L.M. Perry

Cloves, one of the most well known of all spices, belong to the family of the myrtle plants, the Myrtaceae. With few exceptions, we only use the pulverized dried flower buds for incense-burning purposes. These have a spicy, warm fragrance. Cloves increase the fragrance of incense-burning mixtures and energize them. They stimulate creativity and intuition. In Asia, people believe that cloves free us from negative thoughts. Mixed with other substances, they can have aphrodisiac effects. Like cinnamon, cloves are very popular in Asia as incense sticks because they also repel insects.

1. Incense-burning utensils
2. Cinnamon
3. Night-leaf mixture
4. Rose mallow seeds
5. Agar wood in three qualities
6. Sandalwood
7. Cloves
8. Japanese anise
9. Camphor
10. Dried prunes
11. Charcoal
12. Envelopes for Shoyeido incense-burning

Borneo Camphor

Dryobalanops aromatica Gaertn.

The Borneo camphor tree, in Japan called the *hon-sho*, has a particularly mild and pleasant fragrance when compared to other camphor trees. Camphor is a pure white crystal, and, in most cases, it is synthetic. Therefore, beware when buying camphor. Always request natural camphor, specifically *Camiphorica Japonica vera Pulv D (+)*. The addition of the plus sign means that this camphor turns polarized light to the right. Camphor trees develop into magnificent giants. The ancient Chinese honored them as holy trees. The sacred camphor tree at the Hachiman shrine in the Kagoshima district is 1,200 years old. During the time of Marco Polo, people paid for camphor in gold. The tree excretes fragrant camphor naturally through cracks in the trunk. The excretion increases when you heat the wood. Camphor added to an incense-burning mixture provides a fresh note. It is clarifying, refreshing, revitalizing, and helpful for maintaining concentration. It also strengthens awareness and reduces sexual urges.

Musk (Ambergris)

Japanese incense-burning mixtures may contain three animal substances:

Musk is the sexual gland of the musk deer, which is now on the endangered species list because it is in danger of extinction. Nevertheless, the illegal trade is flourishing, and the Japanese use about 80 percent of the world's musk production. Musk is very expensive. In my opinion, we should not buy or use this fragrant substance because it hastens the animal's extinction; the species could permanently disappear from the earth. Instead of the musk obtained from the deer, you can substitute rose mallow seeds from a hibiscus-type plant, *Hibiscus albelmoschus L.* They have a sweet, flowery, heavy fragrance that is reminiscent of musk.

Ambergris is the product of the secretion of the sperm whale (see also chapter on *Arabia*) and of the finely crushed shell of a scented mussel (*Potamides micropterus, Eburna japonica*). The dried and crushed resin of the shell is an incense-burning substance. In the past, the fragrance of these ocean shells was very popular in Europe and Asia. People considered it to be a strong aphrodisiac. Today, we only use

it to produce Japanese incense-burning mixtures. I've listed incense-burning substances derived from animals only for the sake of completeness. I do not use them myself because of their endangered status. However, these three fragrant substances have been much in demand in China, and their use in Japan stemmed from there.

Additional fragrant substances used in Japan are: myrrh, frankincense, vetiver, benzoin, cloves, the bark of the Scotch pine, Hinoki tree, ginger, spikenard, and costus.

Recipes for Japanese Incense-Burning Mixtures

Fleeing from Ignorance

Frankincense	2 parts
Sandalwood	1 part
Agar wood	1 part
Clove	1 part
Cinnamon	1 part

Agar wood is now available in the West in the form of small shavings. Although it is not the best quality, it will do for mixtures. Crush the frankincense resin, cloves, cinnamon bark, and agar wood individually into a rough powder in a stone mortar. Mix well and add the sandalwood powder. Add a pinch to the charcoal or burn it on an incense-burning stove. The fragrance of this mixture is warm, soft, and deeply relaxing. It stimulates reflection and awareness, aids meditation and prayers, and spreads an atmosphere of silent devotion.

The Morning of Happiness
Spring

Frankincense	2 parts
Camphor	1 part
Cloves	1 part
White pine needles	½ part
Juniper tips	½ part

Use a good-quality frankincense, if possible. Pulverize the frankincense and cloves individually. Crush the dried white pine needles and tips from the juniper bush (see also *Juniperus monosperma* in chapter on *North America*) together. Mix all the ingredients well and use a pinch at a time on charcoal or an incense-burning stove. The mixture has a fresh, woody fragrance and creates a happy and light atmosphere. It provides energy and works against depression and tiredness. It stimulates creativity and creative work in the morning.

Blue Dragonfly on a Lotus Leaf
Summer

Sandalwood	6 parts
Myrrh	2 parts
Cinnamon	1 part
Cinnamon flowers	1 part
Cloves	2 parts
Lavender flowers	½ part

Crush the sandalwood, myrrh, and cloves. Mix all the ingredients well. Use a pinch at a time on charcoal or an incense-burning stove. This is an exquisite mixture with a warm, sunny, sweet, bewitching fragrance that touches the heart. It is meant for sensuous and erotic hours. It increases the joys of summer and warms the heart. It is a fragrant journey through the countryside to a secret paramour at the edge of a pond on a summer afternoon. It works well as an accompaniment for massages. It is helpful for creative work and for emotional regeneration.

Night Leaves
Fall

Labdanum	1 part
Storax	½ part
Sandalwood	½ part
Frankincense	½ part
Cinnamon flowers	½ part
Soft, dried prune (unsulfured)	½ to 1 part

Pulverize the frankincense, cinnamon flower, and sandalwood individually. Then, mix well. If you have storax in dry flakes, crush it like the labdanum. Mix all the dry ingredients and work the moist substance well until it has the consistency of wax. Form small pellets, about the size of a pea. Allow the mixture to rest for at least one week in a closed ceramic container. Use one pellet at a time on glowing charcoal with a layer of sand underneath. Cover lightly with sand and burn next to or directly on the hot charcoal. The pellet will burn more slowly this way. The fragrance is warm and soft, and it is drenched with the scent of fall. It stimulates imagination and creativity, allowing you to experience the energy and fullness of fall.

First Snowflakes in a Scotch Pine Forest
Winter

Agar wood	2 parts
Frankincense	2 parts
Cinnamon flower	½ part
Sandarac	1 part
Camphor	½ part
Myrrh	1 part

Crush agar wood, frankincense (use a very good quality), and cinnamon flowers. Also crush the sandarac resin and myrrh. Mix all the ingredients together well and use a pinch at a time on charcoal or an incense-burning stove. This exquisite mixture has a delicate, noble fragrance. It reminds you of the first snowflakes in an ancient Scotch pine forest, tumbling gently from the sky. It is a fragrance for meditation, for quiet company, for reflection and thinking, and for inner balance. It brings comfort when you are low, and it is helpful in solving problems.

The Breath of the Soul

Sandalwood	2 parts
Rose mallow seeds	½ part
Japanese anise	1 part
Cinnamon flower	1 part
Benzoin resin	1 part

Pulverize all the ingredients individually and mix well. The rose mallow seeds come from the hibiscus plant and are a good substitute for musk obtained from animals. This is a mixture that floats in the air gently, delicately, and sensuously. It is for deep relaxation, for reflection, to accompany music or painting, and for sensuous get-togethers, so you can "listen" to your soul!

CLASSIFICATION OF INCENSE PLANTS

Common Name	Species	Botanical Name
A		
agar wood, aquillaria wood	*Aquillaria agallocha* Roxb.	Thymelaeaceae
aloe	*Aloe ferox* Miller	Asphodelaceae
aloe, Barbados	*Aloe barbadensis* Miller	
angelica	*Angelica archangelica* L.	Apiaceae
anise	*Pimpinella aniseum* L.	Apiaceae
anise	*Illicium anisatum* L (O. religiosum Sieb & Zucc.)	Illiciaceae
arjuna	*Terminalia arjuna* (Roxb.) Wight &. Arn.	Combretaceae
arjuna	*Terminalia chebula* (Gaertner) Retz.	Combretaceae
asafetida	*Ferula assafoetida* L.	Apiaceae
asant	*Ferula narthex* Boiss.	Apiaceae
ash, European	*Fraxinus excelsior* L.	Oleaceae
B		
balsam torchwood	*Amyris balsamifera* L.	Rutaceae
balsam	*Balsamodendron gileadenisi* Knth.	Burseraceae
balsam	*Balsamodendron meccaensis* Gled.	Burseraceae
balsam	*Bulnesia sarmienti* Lorentz ex Griseb.	Zygophyllaceae
balsam	*Commiphora kataf* Engl.	Fabaceae
balsam, copaiba	*Copaifera guyanensis* Benth.	Fabaceae
balsam, copaiba	*Copaifera reticula* Ducke	Fabaceae
balsam, Mecca	*Commiphora opobalsamum* (L.) Engler	Fabaceae
balsam, Peruvian; tolu balsam	*Myroxylon balsamum var. pereirae* (Royle) Harms	Fabaceae
bean, tonka	*Dipteryx odorata* (Aublet) Willd.	Fabaceae
benzoin	*Benzoin Siam-Styrax tonkinensis* (Pierre) Craib ex Hartwich	Styracaceae
benzoin	*Benzoin Sumatra-Styrax benzoin* Dryander	Styracaceae
black elder, European	*Sambucus nigra* L.	Caprifoliaceae
boldo	*Peumus boldus* Molina	Monimiaceae
C		
calmus	*Acorus calamus* L	Araceae
camphor tree	*Cinnamomum camphora* (L.) J. Presl	Lauraceae
camphor, Borneo	*Dryobalanops aromatica* Gaertner f.	Dipterocarpaceae
cardamom	*Elettaria cardamomum* (L.) Maton	Zingiberaceae
cassia	*Cinnamomum cassia* Nees ex Blume (syn *Cinnamomum aromaticum)*	Nees Lauraceae
cedar, Atlantic	*Cedrus atlantica* Manet	Pinaceae
cedar, Himalayan	*Cedrus deodora* G. Dan	Pinaceae
cedar, incense	*Calocedrus decurrens* (Torr.) Florin	Cupressaceae
cedar, of Lebanon	*Cedrus libani* A Rich.	Pinaceae
cedar, red	*Juniperus virginiana* L.	Cupressaceae
chamomille	*Chamomilla recutita* (L.) Rauschert	Asteraceae
cinnamon	*Cinnamomum zeylanicum* Blume (syn. *Cinnamomum verum* J. Presl)	Lauraceae

clove	*Syzygium aromaticum* (L.) Merr. & Perry	Myrtaceae
copal	*Bursera microphylla*	Burseraceae
copal	*Protium copal*	Burseraceae
coriander	*Coriandrum savitum* L.	Apiaceae
costus	*Saussurea lappa* C.B. Clarke	Asteraceae
cypress	*Cupressus sempervirens* L.	Cupressaceae

D

dammar	*Canarium prostratum* Schiffn.	
dammar	*Canarium strictum* Roxb.	Dipterocarpaceae
dammar	*Shorea wiesneri* Schiffn.	
dog's mercury	*Mercurialis perennis* L	Euphorbiacae
dragon's blood	*Daemenorops draco* Bl.	Palmae
dream herb	*Calea zacatechichi*	Asteraceae

E

elemi	*Canarium luzonicum* (Miqu) A. Gray	Burseraceae
eucalyptus	*Eucalyptus citriodora* Hook.	Myrtaceae
eucalyptus	*Eucalyptus globulus* Labill.	Myrtaceae
euphorbia	*Emblica officinalis* Gaertn.	Euphorbiaceae

F

Fennel	*Ferula kokanika* Reg. ex Schmalh.	Imbelliferae
Fir, balsam	*Abies balsamea* (L.) Mill.	Pinaceae
fir, silver	*Abies alba* Miller	Pinaceae
fir, white	*Abies cilcica* (Ant. et Kotschy) Carr.	Pinaceae
frankincense	*Boswellia carteri* Birdw.	Burseraceae
frankincense, Indian	*Boswellia serrata* Roxb. ex Colebr.	Burseraceae

G

galangal	*Alpinia galanga* Willd.	Zingiberaceae
galangal	*Alpinia officinarum* Hance	Zingiberaceae
galbanum	*Ferula galbaniflua* Boiss. Buhse	Apiaceae
galbanum	*Ferula gummosa* Boiss.	Apiaceae
galbanum	*Ferula rubi caulis* Bois	Apiaceae
grass, cocoa	*Cyperus longus* L	Cyperaceae
grass, cocoa	*Cyperus rotundus* L.	Cyperaceae
grass, fragrant; sweet grass	*Hierochloe odorata* (L.) Wahlenb.	Poaceae
gromwell	*Lithospermum arvense* L. (also know as *Buglossoides arvensis* (L.) I.M. Johnston)	Boraginaceae

H

harmal peganum	*Peganum harmala* L.	Zygophyllaceae
henna	*Lawsonia inermis* L.	Lythraceae
herb bennet	*Geum urbanum* L.	Rosaceae
hop, common	*Humulus lupulus* L.	Cannabaceae
hyssop	*Hyssopus officinalis* L.	Lamiaceae

I

inula	*Inula helenium* L.	Asteraceae
iris	*Iris cretica*	Iridaceae
iris, German (var. orris)	*Iris germanica ver florentina* Dykes	Iridaceae

J

jimsonweed	*Datura stramonium* L.	Solanaceae
juniper	*Juniperus drupacea* Labill.	Cupressaceae

juniper	*Juniperus monosperma* (Engelm.) Sarg.	Cupressaceae
juniper	*Juniperus occidentalis* Hook.	Cupressaceae
juniper	*Juniperus oxycedrus* L.	Cupressaceae
juniper	*Junniperus phoenicea* L.	Cupressaceae
juniper, common	*Juniperus communis* L.	Cupressaceae

L

labdanum	*Cistus creticus* (L.) Heyw.	Cistaceae
labdanum	*Cistus ladanifer* L.	Cistaceae
Larch, European	*Larix decidua* P. Mill.	Pinaceae
laurel	*Laurus nobilis* L.	Lauraceae
lavender, English	*Lavandula angustifolia* P. Mill.	Lamiaceae
lavender, French	*Lavandula stoechas* L.	Lamiaceae
ledum	*Ledum palustre* L.	Ericacea
lemongrass	*Cymbopogon citratus* (DC. ex Nees) Stapf	Poaceae
lemongrass, East Indian	*Cymbopogon flexuosus* W.Wats	Poaceae
lily, ginger	*Hedychium spicatium* Buch. Ham	Zingiberaceae

M

mallow, rose	*Hibiscus abelmoschus* L.	Malvaceae
	(syn *Abelmoschus moschatus* Medik.)	
marjoram	*Origanum majorana* L.	Lamiaceae
marjoram, hop	*Origanum dictamnus* L	Labiatae
masterwort	*Peucedanum ostruthium* (L.) W.D.J. Koch	Apiaccac
mastic	*Pistacia lentiscus* L.	Anacardiaceae
mistletoe	*Viscum album* L	Loranthaceae
mugwort	*Artemisia vulgaris* L.	Asteraceae
	Myroxylon balsamum (L.) Harms var balsamum	Fabaceae
myrrh	*Commiphora abyssinica* Engl.	Burseraceae
myrrh	*Commiphora myrrha* Nees	Burseraceae
myrrh	*Commiphora schimperi* Berg	Burseraceae
myrrh, common	*Commiphora mukul* (Hooks ex Stocks)	Burseraceae
myrtle	*Myrtus communis* L.	Myrtaceae

O

opoponax	*Commiphora erythraea* (var glabrescens)	Burseraceae
opoponax	*Commiphora kataf* Engl.	
opoponax	*Opoponax chironicum* Koch	

P

patchouli	*Pogostemon cablin* (Blanco) Benth.	Lamiaceae
patchouli	*Pogostemon heyneanus* Benth	Lamiaceae
pine, extinct (the source of amber)	Pinus succinifera Schub.	Pinaceae
pine, mugo	*Pinus mugo* Turra	Pinaceae
pine, Scotch	*Pinus sylvestris* L	Pinaceae
pine, Scotch	*Pinus sylvestris* L.	Pinaceae
pine, Swiss stone	*Pinus cembra* L.	Pinaceae

Q

quince	*Cydonia oblonga* P. Mill.	Rosaceae

R

rhododendron, aromatic	*Rhododendron anthopogon* D.Don	Ericaceae
ring lichen	*Evernia prunastri* (L.) Ach.	Parmeliaceae
rose, cabbage	*Rosa centifolia* L.	Rosaceae
rose, damask	*Rosa damascena* P. Mill.	Rosaceae

rose, French	*Rosa gallica* L.	Rosaceae
rosemary	*Rosmarinus officinalis* L.	Lamiaceae

S

saffron	*Crocus sativus* L.	Iridaceae
sage, common	*Artemisia tridentata ssp. tridentata* Nutt.	Compositae
sage, garden	*Salvia officinalis* L.	Lamiaceae
sage, incense	*Salvia repens*	Lamiaceae
sage, oracle (pipiltzintzintli)	*Salvia divinorum*	Lamiaceae
sage, Russian	*Perovskia abrotanoides* Karel	Labiateae
sage, white	*Salvia apiana*	Lamiaceae
sandalwood	*Santalum album* L.	Santalaceae
sandalwood	*Santalum rurum*	Santalaceae
sandarac	*Tetraclinis articulata* (Vahl) Masters (syn. *Callitris quadrivalvis*)	Cupressaceae
spikenard	*Nardostachys jtamansi* (Wall) D.C.	Valerianaceae
spruce, Australian kauri	*Agathis australis* hort. ex Lindl	Araucariaceae
spruce, Norway	*Picea abies* (L.) Karst.	Pinaceae
storax	*Liquidambar orientalis* Mill.	Hamamelidaceae
storax	*Liquidambar styraciflua* L.	Hamamelidaceae
sweetclover, yellow	*Melilotus officinalis* (L.) Lam.	Fabaceae

T

thuja	*Thuja occidentalis* L.	Cupressaceae
thyme	*Thymus vulgaris* L.	Lamiaceae

V

vanilla	*Vanilla planifolia* Andr.	Orchidaceae
verbena	*Verbena officinalis* L.	Verbenaceae
vetiver	*Vetiveria zizanioides* (L.) Nash ex Small	Poaceae (Gramineae)

Y

yerba santa	*Eridictyon californicum* Bewnth.	Hydrophyllaceae

PHOTO CREDITS

Thomas Bäumel, page 171
Eugen Diederichs Verlag, page 123
Nigel Hepper, page 138
Walter Hess, pages 118, 119, 121
Helga Hirschberg, pages184, 185, 186
Hans-Jörg Magg, pages 8, 9, 17, 18, 19
National Museum of Modern Art, Tokyo, page 201
Ulla Mayer-Raichle, pages 4, 11, 15, 30–31, 46–47,
    60–61, 80–81, 108–109, 128–129, 131, 142–143,
    156–157, 164–165, 178–179, 190–191, 208–209
Doris Schaeffer, page 99
Anselm Spring, page 24

All other photos and artwork are from the private collections of Susanne Fischer-Rizzi and Peter Ebenhoch.

A WORD OF THANKS

to all who had a hand in writing this book

For support in my extensive search of the subject matter and for sometimes difficult-to-establish botanical terminology, my thanks goes to: Dr. Klaus Brenner, Andreas Neugebauer, Dr. Uwe Renzer, and Frau Rieger from the Association of Bavarian Botanists. For valuable support during my travel through mountains of books, I thank Karl Hollerbach, Karin Sand, Maria Gmeinder, Uwe Brenz, and Dr. Andrea Liebers. My son Silvano was involved in the search for resins and plants and contributed many photos to this book. Andrea Pabel, Cornelia Schütt, Chifumi Tezuka, Rosette Tsu, Pastor Renftle, Hans Mengert, and Inka Götzelmann gave me much important information for relevant chapters, and Dieter Simonet helped me sort it all out.

I would like to thank all who made their personal photos available or were present when photos were being taken: Helga Hirschberg, Chifumi Tezuka, Monika Ostermaier, Hans-Jörg Magg, Sabeth Ebenhoch, Liss and Anna-Lea Stengel, Petra and Pia Dröber, Thomas Bäumel, Daniel Fürst, and Doris Schaeffer. Ulla Mayer-Raichle enriched this book with her idyllic photographs. For their loving support in the background, I thank Lydia Kautt, Dr. Rita Pohle, and Simocho and Georg Lauer.

Many thanks also to those who participated in incense burning during my seminars and who inspired me with questions, ideas, and suggestions.

I want to extend my heartfelt thanks to Ann-u and Tokita, who burned incense on the prairie. Your support inspired and carried me through long hours of writing this book.

INDEX

M

magic, 42, 56

"Magic Land of Happiness" (Punt),
66–67

manabau, 206

manaka, 205

Maneton mixture, 83

manna grass, 78

marjoram, 96

Mary Magdalene, 137, 140

mastic, 75, 80, 90–91, 95

mastika, 90

Mayans
    incense-burning substances of,
        161–166
    reasons for incense burning,
        159–161
    recipes, 167

Mecca balsam, 74, 138

Medea, 104

medicinal incense burning
    Egyptian, 68–69
    Greek, 103
    South American, 159

meditation, 14

Meditation in the Evening mixture, 180

Meditation in the Morning mixture,
    180

menstruation, 41–42

Mesopotamia, 51
    Garden of Eden in, 52
    incense-burning substances from,
        57–61
    recipes, 63
    spirituality of fragrances, 55–57

Mexicans, 159

"midsummer's belt," 44

Minoans
    incense-burning substances of,
        88–95
    legends of, 86–88
    recipes of, 97

Minotaur, 86

mistletoe, 47

mixtures, 18–19. *See also* recipes; *specific
    mixtures*
    competitions, 198
    for planets/astrological signs,
        106–107

The Morning of Happiness mixture, 211

Morocco, 130

mortar and pestle, 17

Moses, 135–136

Mother Earth, 148

mother of herbs, 44

"Mother of the People," 27

"Mother Resin," 62, 77

mountain balm, 154

mugwort, 44–45, 47, 92

Muhammad, prophet of Islam, 123

musk, 123–124, 126, 127, 140, 144, 188,
    198, 210

myrrh, 80, 129, 143
    Alexander the Great and, 101
    in Bible, 139–140
    common, 175–176, 179
    in Egypt, 66, 67, 73, 80
    Greece and, 100
    healing properties of, 122
    in Northern Europe, 42
    sensuousness of Earth and, 121–122
    sweet or opoponax, 73–74, 80
    trading, 114, 115

Myrrha, 101

myrtle
    in Greece, 108
    in Mesopotamia, 54–55, 58–59, 60

N

naba (Peruvian balsam), 162

Nagarmotha grass, 78

nana soken breathing, 200

Native Americans, 148
    cleansing ceremonies of, 151
    feathers, 149–150
    incense-burning substances of,
        151–154
    reasons for incense burning,
        148–149
    recipes, 155
    sacred pipe, 150
    spiritual companionship and,
        148–150
    vessels for incense burning, 149

nature, incense burning and, 24–25

nerikoh pellets, 201

New Year's ritual, 14, 40

night copal, 161

Night Leaves mixture, 208, 211

nightmares, 40, 44

North America, 147–148

Northern Europe, 35
    ancient forests, 37–38
    Celtic people, 37–38, 39, 41, 43
    Druids, 38
    recipes, 48–49
    Stone Age, 36–37

O

"Oil of the Kings," 137–138

oleoresin, 62, 90

Oman. *See* Sheba

opoponax (sweet myrrh), 73–74, 80

oracle dreams, 104

oracle sage (pipiltzintzintli), 163

"Oracles of Delphi," 96

Oraibi mixture, 155

Oriental amber tree (storax), 62–63

P

Pan (god of nature), 102

patchouli, 179, 180

peacock feathers, 187

pellets, incense, 127, 200–201

perception, 10

perfume, 8

Peruvian balsam (naba), 162

Peruvians, 159

"pestilence pills," 122

Phythagoreans, 102

pine tree
    needles, 26, 30
    resin, 25, 26, 27–28
    substances, in ancient incense, 26

pipiltzintzintli (oracle sage), 163

Pisces, 107

pistachio resin, 90

Pistacia vera, 91

planets, incense-burning mixtures for,
    106–107

plant ghosts, 41

Pleasure of the Heart mixture, 82

poisonous vapors, 42

Polyporus fomentarius, 39

power and clarity mixture (Be-Ah-
    Dzill), 155

prayer, 12

Primeval Father, 54

Prince Genji, 198

problem solving, 14

propolis, 44, 46–47

prunes, dried, 209

psychosomatic incense-burning medi-
    cine, 186–188

Punt ("Magic Land of Happiness"),
    66–67

Pythia mixture, 111

Pythia (seer of Delphi), 104

Q

Queen of Sheba, 116

quince, 92, 94

R

rakoku, 205

recipes
    Arabian, 130–132
    Archaic, natural, 33